THE

HUMAN
AURA

THE
HUMAN
AURA

HOW TO ACTIVATE
AND ENERGIZE YOUR AURA
AND CHAKRAS

KUTHUMI · DJWAL KUL

SUMMIT UNIVERSITY 🌀 PRESS®

THE HUMAN AURA by Kuthumi and Djwal Kul
dictated to Mark L. Prophet and Elizabeth Clare Prophet
Copyright © 1971, 1974, 1982, 1996 Summit Publications, Inc.
All rights reserved

Library of Congress Catalog Card Number: 81-52927
ISBN: 0-922729-25-5

SUMMIT UNIVERSITY ॐ PRESS
Summit University Press and ॐ are registered trademarks.

Printed in the United States of America
06 05   8 7 6 5

To Discoverers
of the Non-Physical
Matrix of Self

CONTENTS

BOOK TWO

Prayers, Affirmations, Decrees, and Meditations

ILLUSTRATIONS

*Examples of How the Aura Looks
When Muddied by the Human
Consciousness*

THE

HUMAN AURA

BOOK ONE

KUTHUMI

1 THE PERFECTING OF THE AURA

As we commence these auric studies, let it be understood that the combined manifestation of body, soul, and mind creates around the spinal column and the medulla oblongata those emanations called by some the human aura and by others the magnetic forcefield of the body of man.

Let it be understood by all who read that each individual in whom is the flame of life reveals himself as though he were to shout it from the housetops— all that he really is, all that he has done, and even the portent of that which he shall be—right in the forcefield of his being and in the magnetic emanations surrounding his physical form.

The reading in depth of the human aura is no ordinary science. Those who would undertake to do so should understand that by a simple change in thought the fountain of the human aura, which pours forth from its own orifice, can change its color, its emanation, its magnetic affinity—its complete identity. Yet at the same time it may retain beneath the surface the capacities to poison the atmosphere of the individual or the auric emanation within, by virtue of his failure to cleanse himself in heart.

"Blessed are the pure in heart: for they shall see God"[1] is more than a beatitude issuing from the mouth of the living Christ. It is a fiat of strength shining, promised to all who behold it.

We have pondered the great need of humanity for purification, and we advocate above all the purification of motive. But when individuals do not see clearly just what their own motives are, it becomes exceedingly difficult, by reason of their own internal blindness, for them to purify themselves. Therefore, the purification of the faculty of vision has been given top priority by the masters, because it has been our experience that when men learn to see as God sees, they perceive the need to correct their problems and in most cases do so without further delay.

In the matter of our Brotherhood, those unascended devotees who wear the golden robe of cosmic illumination, who in truth are illumined concerning the many subjects ordinarily hidden from the average seeker on the path, are expected to perform more advantageously in directing their lives according to the instructions issuing from their lips. A good example is the best teacher.

Now, what is the object of humanity's desire to read the human aura? Is it simply to satisfy some quality of human curiosity, or do they find satisfaction in perceiving the wrongs of others without correcting their own?

All who undertake this study of auric emanations and of the human forcefield as it pours forth into space should recognize the creative nature already existing in mankind. By the misuse of the creative nature, men have fabricated in countless lives undesirable and unwholesome conditions which plague their young, disturb their elders, and in no way contribute to the growth of the quality of human life as originally envisioned by Almighty God.

The hope of the world as the light of the world is to be considered. The world today emanates an aura not at all resembling the Christic aura of the universal Christ consciousness; and the bulk of the people remain in ignorance of the simplest cosmic truths because the powers of darkness that are in the world have accomplished the distortions of the Scriptures which they desired long, long ago.

Man's interpretation of his relationship to the Divine involves itself in pagan, anthropomorphic concepts. God is seen as being appeased by sacrifice.

Even so, men fail to understand the true meaning of sacrifice.

In the case of the Master Jesus, because of the perfection in his nature, which he clearly perceived, he did not require any propitiation for sin. Yet he is portrayed as one who is able to save to the uttermost those who believe in him.

Those who understand the meaning of God, Christ, and life from a real standpoint see that there is no difference between the divine nature in Jesus and the divine nature in themselves. They understand that there is no partiality in heaven. All can equate with the image of the beloved Son.

The ninety and nine must be forsaken,[2] for they already possess the strength within themselves to perceive this truth: And the one who is lost, caught in the brambles of confusion, blinded to his own reality and the inward radiance of the divine image, must now forsake the false doctrine of the blind leaders of his blindness. He must heed the voice of God and return to it.

Through our auric studies that we are releasing herewith, we anticipate that many shall find their way back to the Father's house. There they will perceive that they must present themselves a living sacrifice unto God. It was never the Father's intent to collect penance from humanity nor to exact a form of sacrifice as appeasement of his wrath. For the only wrath of God that is valid in the cosmic courts of heaven is that karmic recompense, that weight of sin which imputes to humanity the darkness they have created, acceded to, or acknowledged.

In reality man lives in a universe of light and purpose. To veil that purpose from man was never the intention of God. For he has clearly said, "That which has been hidden shall be revealed."[3] In this sense, then —the higher sense of releasing the divine knowing within man, who in reality is both the knower and the known—do we finally establish the reality of God within the consciousness of the individual, thus producing right there in man the perfection that he craves.

It is amazing how by ignorance men are thwarted in their attempts to understand life. Simply because they do not know, they do not find out. Therefore, as our beloved Master once said, "For whosoever hath, to him shall be given and he shall have more abundance: but whosoever hath not, from him shall be taken away even that he hath."[4]

He spoke of understanding. This most precious treasure we shall attempt to bequeath to you in our releases on the studies of the human aura. All who read should bear in mind that we cannot increase the knowledge of those who do not first invoke it from the throne of grace.

It is of utmost importance that the student understand that there is a process whereby every observation of his five senses is transmitted automatically to subconscious levels within himself, where, by inner hieroglyph, events he has witnessed or matters which he has studied are recorded. Thus the entire transmittal of data from the external world to the internal lies in the akashic records of his own being.

The process of recall, while quite involved from a technical standpoint, is almost instantaneous. Out of the storehouse of memory, man quite easily calls forth these treasures of being. Unfortunately, not all events are benign; not all recordings are examples of perfection.

The sorting and classification of these records is the responsibility of the body elemental and the recording angel of the individual lifestream. You will find mention of the recording angels in the words of Jesus when he spoke of the little ones, "For I say unto you that their angels do always behold the face of my Father which is in heaven."[5]

Each individual has such an angel representing the purity of the infinite God, assigned to his lifestream by divine decree from the very foundation of the world. This angel has the ability not only to read the life record of everyone upon the planet but also to commune directly with the heart of God, "to behold the face of my Father which is in heaven." Thus the intent of God to reveal himself unto the angel of his Presence, attached to each of his children, operates through the Holy Christ Self in perfect harmony with the divine plan.

How unfortunate are those who, while always perceiving the height and depth of man, are never able to become impersonal enough in their approach to endow "the least of these my brethren"[6] with the quality of the living Christ. Men find it not at all difficult to believe that the fullness of the Godhead bodily dwelleth in Jesus,[7] but they do find it difficult to believe that it also dwelleth in themselves.

Yet this God has done. He has in the bestowal of the Christ flame placed the fullness of himself in every son and daughter. When the divine nature is properly understood then, how easily humanity can bring forth the *antahkarana* and thus begin the process of correctly weaving their life manifestation.

Now, as man studies the science of perfecting the aura, he should also understand that through the misqualification of thought and feeling, many undesirable traits are brought into manifestation. Most dangerous of all is misqualification in the emotional body of man, in the feeling world, for thereby the heart is touched and in turn often sways the whole life record of the individual into a miasma of doubt and questioning.

I do not say that the sincere student does not have the right to question or even to doubt. But I do say that once the truth is clearly presented to him, if the door of his heart be open, he will never doubt and never question the truth of the living God. He may not leap over the hurdle, but he will clearly perceive that it can truly be, that he will be able, yea, that he *is* able to realize more of God than that which his present awareness allows. Let us free humanity by right knowledge from all that has bound them and blinded them to their own great inner power, to the treasure-house God has locked within their consciousness.

Now I want to make very certain that all understand that misqualification in the feeling world—such as anger, self-righteousness, fear, hatred, jealousy, condemnation, and resentment—gives a certain leverage to the power of amplification. This is similar to the transponder system on your large aircraft. When the transponder button is pushed by the pilot, it triggers a signal from the transponder which causes an enlarged blip to appear upon the electronic board of the airport traffic controller, thereby enabling the plane to be easily identified.

Thus do the emotions of mankind often falsely amplify misqualified thoughts and feelings to the point where a dominant position is assumed by these misqualified feelings. Although this takes place without the consent of the real being of man, nevertheless, darkness does, then, cover the earth. Yet Christ has said, "I AM the light of the world."[8]

I have given you many thoughts in this my first release on the studies of the human aura. The Brothers
of the Golden Robe will joyously respond to the
depth of his wisdom which we shall release in the
completed series. From the archives of the Brotherhood our love pours forth.

2 THE SUSCEPTIBILITY OF THE AURA

Continuing auric studies, we examine the influences of the world upon the human monad. Man is a creature of simple design, yet complex in the externalization of that design.

Little do men realize, when first they ponder the nature of themselves, the ramifications of the consciousness of each individual. The influences of the world, the thoughts of the world, the feelings of humanity are easily transmitted consciously or unconsciously from person to person. And in the transmittal of thoughts and feelings, neither sender nor receiver has any guarantee that the patterns of his intent will be preserved intact.

If the light that is in man that he transmits is undesirable,[1] those who are easily made the victim of his thoughts and feelings or those who are naturally affinitized with him may reproduce the effects of those thoughts and feelings in their own worlds. So many in the world today are victims of the thoughts of others—even thoughts from other eras, which endure because mankind have fed their attention and their energies into them.

In effect, it can be said that man has endowed either his evil or his good deeds with a semipermanent existence, and that the consciousness of good and evil partaken of by Adam and Eve, because it has been perpetuated by his free will, is living in man today. Yet, through a return to the Edenic consciousness of God, man is able to find the tree of life, which is in the midst thereof, and to eat of the fruit and live forever.[2]

There is much that we shall transmit in our studies, but first we must ask that the students approach them with the right attitude in order that we may create a climate of the practical use of right knowledge.

Through the ages that have passed from spiritual innocence to worldly contamination, men have seldom observed the recycling process by which there has been regurgitated upon the screen of life a flood of undesirable qualities. Both world and individual problems have been prolonged entirely because of the vibrational patine of blackened and tarry substance with which man has coated his very being and then refused to surrender.

It is time humanity began to examine themselves as individuals having a creative potential which they may use to influence the auras of others and which in turn makes them susceptible to influences from others, both good and bad. Thoughts of love, joy, and peace—divine thoughts created in the hearts of the saints and the angelic hosts—should never be avoided, but should be enhanced by the magnetic forcefield of the aura. Men can learn from one another, and their auric emanations can benefit from contact with those whose auras are filled with virtue.

Because it is just as easy for the aura to absorb vice as it is for it to absorb virtue, the individual must understand how this process of thought and feeling transmittal can help or hinder him in his daily occupation. Because people are so completely unaware of the effects of the mass consciousness, as well as the mental pressures from neighbors and friends, we continue to stress the importance of using the violet transmuting flame and the tube of light as effective deterrents to the penetration of the aura by undesirable qualities and to their effects upon the mind and being.*

Needless to say, I am determined to transmit in this series definite information that shall make it easier for the soul within man to hold dominion over his life pattern, thus improving the quality of the human aura. Unless this be done, great pain and

*See pages 20–23 and the "Chart of Your Divine Self" in glossary.

suffering will undoubtedly come to humanity, and that unnecessarily.

The Brothers of the Golden Robe, in their devotions and study of the holy wisdom of God, have recently considered that a clearer revelation of matters involving the human aura would make it possible for more individuals who are oriented around spiritual knowledge to be assisted and to assist others; hence this series.

Now, without question there are problems manifesting in the world wholly as a result of the individual's contact with the auric field or forcefield of embodied humanity. Therefore, defenses must be clearly shown. They must be understood at the level of the individual.

In addition to that, methods of projecting the consciousness or the forcefield out of the physical body and to others in one's immediate family or circle of friends must be understood and then effectively mastered as a means of sending hopeful light rays of cosmic service to those who, while in need of assistance, have no idea whatsoever that such possibilities exist.

Although people are brought under the benign or harmful power of various auric manifestations and forcefields, they do not understand how this is done; and many times they are unaware that it is being done. It is not a question of scientific marvel to them or one of strange phenomena—they simply do not know that it exists. But we do.

Working effectively with this knowledge from a wholly constructive standpoint, the angelic hosts and Brothers of the Golden Robe yearn to see the day manifest when humanity, one and all, will understand how they may use this beneficent force of the human aura in a correct and proper manner. For they will see that the aura is designed to be a reflector of Good to all whom they meet and to the world at large.

Those skilled in mortal hypnotism and seductive practices have a partial knowledge of the use of auric and forcefield projections; and they do achieve limited results that lend credence to their work in the minds of some whose goals are likewise limited. As our beloved Master Jesus once said, "The children of this world are in their generation wiser than the children of light."[3]

In conference with us, beloved Jesus has made very clear that in making that statement it was never his intention to see this condition prevail. Rather it was his promise to all who believed in the Christ, "Greater works shall ye do because I go unto my Father."[4] Thus it is the will of God that each generation should attempt to improve the quality of the abundant life upon the planetary body through every available means that is in keeping with the teaching and practice of the Christ.

It has been our intent in these first two releases to give certain vital bits of information on our subject. Later in the series we shall develop that understanding of our instruction which, if correctly applied, can change your life and the lives of countless numbers among mankind because they will be better able to appreciate and to follow the way of truth and the way of hope.

Do you know how many individuals there are in the world today who by reason of their ignorance on these very subjects become the victims of the manipulators? Well, beloved ones, there are many, I assure you. And I do not want the graduates from our class to ever again be among them. Let me, then, go back to the basic principles of ascended-master law by citing for all the need to use your tube of light and the violet transmuting flame as the greatest protection you can ever have against the forces of manipulation.

How very dominant, God-endowed, and beautiful are the fragments of divine knowledge that have been received by you thus far.[5] Do you truly meditate upon them? Do you make them a part of your life? Or do you find them to be entertaining flowers that somehow the mind takes a fancy to?

Beloved ones, I want to prepare you for a most tremendous piece of information which I will transmit to you in a forthcoming lesson. But I want to make certain that when you receive this concept which I will bring to you, you meditate upon it like a flower.

Therefore, prepare yourselves in your meditations for this concept, which I assure you will give you a very concrete idea beyond the mechanical as to just how you can accomplish the purification of your aura. Without this knowledge that I am about to reveal, a great deal more time could very well elapse before you would truly understand the real freedom you have and how to use it for the blessing of all life.

When you divinely apply the wisdom of the Great White Brotherhood to the correct manifestation of reality in your world, I am certain that the improvement in your aura and in the quality of your life will be very great indeed.

Remember that I want you to be a flower—a rose or a lotus—waiting in the swamplands of life to receive the precious drops of truth that heaven has prepared for you. If you will do this, I am certain that you will need no further proof of the reality of your being, of the unfolding kingdom that is within you, and of how you can take dominion over that kingdom, as God intended, in a way that is safe, sane, and correct.

When there are so many books being written today, so many words being released into the stream of mankind's consciousness which are almost a complete abortion of the divine intent, I must urge you to appreciate the opportunity we are releasing to you today.

I remain devoted to your heart's light.

DISCIPLE INVOKING THE VIOLET FLAME AND TUBE OF LIGHT. The soul stands in the violet flame invoking the violet fire. We need the violet-flame action of the Holy Spirit to purify our bodies and our souls. The violet flame is necessary as an insulation and as a purifier. The tube of light surrounding the violet flame is necessary because we are separating ourselves from the world consciousness programmed in the laws of mortality and limitation.

Here you see the crystal cord by which God's energy is descending to you every moment. That means you have limitless power, limitless wisdom, and limitless love at your command—if you will draw it forth from your I AM Presence in the name of your own beloved Christ Self through the science of the spoken Word.

—ECP

HEART, HEAD, AND HAND DECREES
by El Morya

Violet Fire

Heart

    Violet Fire, thou Love divine,
    Blaze within this heart of mine!
    Thou art Mercy forever true,
    Keep me always in tune with you.

                    (recite three times)

Head

    I AM Light, thou Christ in me,
    Set my mind forever free;
    Violet Fire, forever shine
    Deep within this mind of mine.

    God who gives my daily bread,
    With Violet Fire fill my head
    Till thy radiance heavenlike
    Makes my mind a mind of Light.

                    (recite three times)

Hand

    I AM the hand of God in action.
    Gaining Victory every day;
    My pure soul's great satisfaction
    Is to walk the Middle Way.

                    (recite three times)

Tube of Light

Beloved I AM Presence bright,
Round me seal your Tube of Light
From ascended master flame
Called forth now in God's own name.
Let it keep my temple free
From all discord sent to me.

I AM calling forth Violet Fire
To blaze and transmute all desire,
Keeping on in Freedom's name
Till I AM one with the Violet Flame.

(recite three times)

Forgiveness

I AM Forgiveness acting here,
Casting out all doubt and fear,
Setting men forever free
With wings of cosmic Victory.

I AM calling in full power
For Forgiveness every hour;
To all life in every place
I flood forth forgiving Grace.

(recite three times)

3 THE COLORATIONS OF THE AURA

The reality of your God-perfection, latent in all life, is continually releasing the current of its magnificence into your consciousness. Whenever an impediment blocks the flow of this magnificent God-energy, it is as though an object has opaqued the light of the sun.

As the sun has its corona, so there is always a spillover of the delightful radiance of the vital life forces in man, which are so easily subjected to his negative influences and misuse. This discolors the aura with negative vibrations and leads man to draw the conclusion that he is less than the perfection of God.

Just as men recall on a cloudy day that the radiance of the sun is behind the clouds and can be seen from an aircraft which penetrates the clouds, so man should also begin to develop and maintain the habit of constantly telling himself that the blazing, dazzling reality of the fullness of God is being released to him moment by moment as the master plan of eternal purpose. Thus he should develop the habit of counteracting all examples of shadow and misqualification by applying the principle of internal reality.

What is real? What is real is released to man as he practices the ritual of penetration—of penetrating the light of the Son of God by the very power of the light that is within him—and thereby more and more of the divine radiance can infuse the aura in its manifest pattern.

Therefore, today the delight of the law of God will be in the mouth of the man or woman who will speak the living Word,[1] invoking from the heart of God that magnificence which he already is, claiming in the Word, I AM, the fullness of the Godhead bodily in himself[2] as a joint-heir with the universal Christ consciousness.[3]

Now, in the matter of the effects of one's thoughts and feelings upon the human aura, we shall briefly touch upon the subject of coloration. As the intensity of the white and the violet light is increased in the aura, especially those shades that are pale and ethereal, one notes the enlarging of man's perceptions and an increase in spirituality.

As the pale yellow—almost golden—light floods through the mind, the very fingers of cosmic intelligence manifest as interconnecting light rays, enabling the mind of man to contact the universal mind of God. By amplifying in the aura the beauty of pastel pink—vibrating fire of the cup of universal love—man is able to spill over into the world the very thoughts of divine love.

As so many know, the color of violet, vibrating at the top of the spectrum, is transmutative and buoyant. Born to the purple, the man who so infuses his aura is cloaked in the invincibility of the King of Kings. This royal color is the cosmic fire of the Holy Spirit which, when blended with the azure blue of the will of God, manifests as divine love in action in that holy will.

The green light, eternally new with abundance, charges the aura of man with the power of universal healing and supply. To seal all in the will of God is to drink from the goblet of that holy will. In the electric blue of the ascended masters, it denotes both purity and power.

Now, not all of mankind see the aura, and for some it is perhaps a misstatement to say that they do. What happens in most cases is a sensing, by the inner being of the reader, of the auric emanations of others and the interpolation thereof by the mind through the organ of vision.

The impressions of the impinging aura carried over the nerve pathway as a result of the extension of the reader's consciousness into the domain of the magnetic emanation seem themselves to be seen, when in reality they are only felt. Vibrations of anger often register as crimson flashes, just as black is seen in the aura as the opaquing by negative thoughts and feelings of the otherwise natural release of the light of the Presence through the being of man.

Remember, beloved ones, that the tone of the divine aura is an extension of God, just as the mode of thinking and feeling is the extension of the human consciousness. The interference with the aura in its natural, pure state by the mortal consciousness and its misqualification of light create the negative colorations that are both seen and felt by the more sensitive among mankind.

The muddying of the pure colors of the aura occurs whenever there is a mingling of the emanations of imperfect thoughts and feelings with the pure colors released through the prism of the Christ. This marked change in color and vibration is obvious to the trained eye.*

In this connection, may I say that one can learn to discern the thoughts and feelings of mortal men and to perceive what is acting in their world. The difference between momentary passions, consciously

---

*See illustrations of muddied auras, pages 301–17.

willed, and sustained deep-seated emotional trends must be considered.

How easy it is to see through the process of auric discernment that which is not immaculate in someone's feelings, thoughts, or acts without understanding that only a temporary surface disturbance may have taken place. Much later, if that one is not careful to override such disturbances by retraining the mind and feelings and consciously governing the energy flow, an in-depth penetration may occur whereby auric contamination will reach subconscious levels and thus prolong the time span of man's indulgence in negative states.

Great care should be exercised by all who desire to amplify the immaculate God-concept of others to see that they do not, by their incomplete perceptions, actually intensify those negative conditions which those whom they would assist may not be harboring at all, but are only entertaining momentarily.

Then, too, there is the matter of the projection of mass forcefields of negatively qualified energy which can become a patine, or layer of substance, overlaid upon the natural vibration of individuals. Although totally foreign to their forcefield, this overlay of darkness, if seen at an inopportune moment, may be diagnosed by the careless or untrained observer as an outcropping of the bedrock of his identity.

Always remember, dear hearts, that those who

fall in the swamp may come up covered with mud; for the quicksands of life, by their very nature, always seek to drag man down. But man can and does escape these conditions, overcoming through the same glorious victory that brings forth the lotus in the swamplands of life.

I want you to understand, then, that by a simple act of invoking the light of the Christ consciousness, man can overcome the ugly chartreuse green of jealousy and resentment, the muddied yellow of selfish intellectualism, the crimson reds of passion, and even the almost violet black of attempts of self-righteous justification.

To see others clearly, beloved hearts, remember that man must first perceive in himself the beautiful crystal of cosmic purity. Then, casting the beam out of his own eye, he can see clearly to take the mote out of his brother's eye.[4] By the purification of your perceptions, you will be able to enjoy the entire process of beholding the Christ in self and others, as one by one the little disturbances of the aura are cleared up through the natural manifestation of the childlike beauty of cosmic innocence.

What is innocence but the inner sense? And the poem of victory that God writes through man is already there in matrix and in creative form, waiting to be delivered upon the pages of life. Human density may have interfered with the manifestation of the

Christ in man, but the light and love of the law will produce for him the greatest purification, making possible the penetration of the aura by the beautiful colors of the Christ consciousness.

I should like our students throughout the world to join with me in a determined effort to let the crystal-clear grace of the throne that is within you as the threefold flame (three-in-one, hence *throne*) ray out into your world such ecstatic, electrical cosmic energy that you will literally vaporize the darkened elements of your own aura and hence develop that magnificent seeing that will bring the joy of the angels and the light of God to all whom you meet.

Perhaps we shall become more technical, but I think in no way can we become more practical than we have in that which I have already spoken.

Will you follow the Christ of your being in this regeneration?

4 THE READING OF THE AURA

The trials of life that come to man are in reality his teachers, that is to say, they substitute for his teachers because he will not hear them. Yet it has been clearly recorded in the Scriptures and ancient writings that the time would come when man should see his teachers and that they should not be far removed from him.[1]

So many today are concerned with the facial expressions and appearances of the teachers without ever realizing the lines of character and soul reality that comprise the inner being of a man or woman. Let the true seekers be concerned, then, not so much with the outer beauty of appearances, but with the inner beauty that produces those manifestations in the human aura which bring the admiration of every ascended master because they are the fulfillment of the God-design.

If any of you have ever been judges in a contest of beauty, you will understand the difficulty in making a selection from among the manifold aspects of God's beauty. In the case of the ascended masters and Karmic Lords, it is sheer delight that motivates them to pronounce their seal of approval on all that is the God-intent in those who aspire to represent the Brotherhood and to glorify God in their body and in their spirit.[2]

What a marvelous forte of possibility exists for every man! I want our students to think of the richness of the natural, radiating, consecrating devotion that God has placed within man. The opportunity to express the perfection of the Holy Spirit, when rightly apprehended, enables man to fashion the wedding garment of his very Christed being.

Now, I know that through the years many of the students of the occult have stressed the ability of the advanced disciple to read the human aura, to interpret it, and, in effect, to see it. May I say at this time, and quite frankly so, that no psychic ability or even the ability to read the human aura denotes in the person who does so, that mastery by which the true adept overcomes outer conditions.

I do not say that adepts do not have this ability. I simply say that the possessing of this ability, in partial or even in total proficiency, is not necessarily an indication of the advanced spiritual development of the individual.

Also, it should be realized that those who profess to read the human aura may do so very poorly, in a confused manner, or in a very limited depth. In order to correctly interpret the reading of the human aura, one must be able to read the karmic record and to have some insight into the total being of a man.

I would far prefer that the students would consider the benefit that can come to them through beholding good in themselves and in others and through striving for the good, as my beloved cohort El Morya has said. For the fruit of striving may not always be apparent on the surface, even on the surface of the aura; but it stands behind the real life record of man's attainment. This is why God has said, "Judge not, that ye be not judged."³

Here at Shigatse⁴ we concentrate on the sending-forth of holy wisdom. We concentrate on harmony and on true loveliness. There are times, of course, when man must perceive that what is acting in his world is not of the Christ. It is then that he must be able to disentangle himself from his problems and to recognize that neither his problems nor the unwholesome conditions that surround him are the nature of God. Therefore, the Lord does not require him either to prolong his problems or to be weighted down by his environment.

Might I add that by nurturing the divine nature, man finds that the aura will quite naturally resemble the Presence in its radiant perfection. This is the pattern that appears in the heavens of God's consciousness and that can appear in the heaven of every man's consciousness, for it flows out from the seed pattern of perfection within man even as it manifests in the Presence above.

When Jesus said, "I and my Father are one,"[5] he referred to the balancing of the divine radiance of the God Presence and Causal Body within the outer manifestation, which through his reunion with reality had become one with God. Hence the color rays which had been focused through the "coat of many colors"[6] now became the nimbus, halo, or radiance of the Christ consciousness around him—the seamless garment that he wore as the Son of God.[7]

We have tried to make apparent in this discourse the fact that ordinary human beings are not endowed with this sense perception of the human aura, and this should always be borne in mind. Pilate heeded the dream of his wife, who warned him to have nothing to do "with that just man,"[8] more than the testimony of virtue manifest in the one who stood before him. He could find no fault with Christ Jesus,[9] but he did not bear witness to his perfection, else he would never have permitted the crucifixion of Christ, nor would he have turned him over to the Sanhedrin.

The commonsense approach to the realities of God is to be found in depth in the being of man. Man is a veritable treasure-house of beauty and perfection when he returns to the divine image—and I know of no better way to produce the miracle of the star of divine radiance in the human aura than to become one with God.

This seemingly impossible hurdle is the panacea man seeks, and he shall find it if he seeks diligently enough and does not fear to surrender his little self. For all human ills will be cured by virtue of his becoming the Divine in manifestation.

More harm has been done in the world by fraudulent readings of the human aura and false predictions based upon these readings than man is aware of. What a marvelous thing it will be when man turns his faculties of perception to the beholding of the reality of God in his very thought and standard!

Now I must, in defense of some arhats and advanced adepts upon the planet, affirm the accuracy of those who are able instantly to detect in depth the vibratory patterns manifesting in the world of others. It is incorrect to suppose that these will always speak out concerning their discernments. Naturally, gentleness and the will to see perfection supplant darkness will guide their motives and acts.

But I solemnly warn here that whenever you are in the presence of a true adept or even an unascended being who has mastered many elements of perfection in his life, you should understand that if there is darkness of motive within you, he may see it or he may choose to ignore it.

By the same token, I solemnly warn those who fancy themselves adepts but who in reality have not overcome more than an iota of their imperfections and who have achieved in the eyes of God but a small portion of that which they imagine, to take heed that they do not incorrectly discern, in their so-called readings of the lives of others, some quality that may not even exist; for thereby some have brought great karma down upon their heads.

All should exercise humility and care in placing their value upon the development in the soul of the higher consciousness of the God Presence, for this is "without money and without price."[10] It is the invincible attainment by which men become truly one with God.

5 THE INTENSIFICATION OF THE AURA

Man thinks of himself as solid. He lives within an envelope of flesh and blood that is penetrated by his consciousness. Consciousness must be regarded as man's connection with his Source, and its flexibility as man's greatest asset; yet when wrongly used, it is his greatest weakness. The consciousness of humanity today is so easily influenced by banal and barbaric doings that the magnificent cosmic purpose heaven has prepared in the creation of man is seldom recognized even minutely.

Man so easily becomes involved in the trivial manifestations of the footstool kingdom. And his indoctrinations, being what they are, make him believe that the divine purposes and the doings of the ascended masters would not be to his liking. The singing of devotional songs, the chanting of holy mantras, the engaging of the mind in spiritual conversation and prayer to the Almighty are regarded today by the sophisticates as a milksop endeavor which could not possibly produce any good for them, but is reserved only for the weak-minded.

May I challenge this concept *in toto* and say that the greatest strength, the noblest ideal and truest valor, is to be found in the aspirant who ultimately achieves first his adeptship in his fulfillment of the divine plan, and then his eventual mastership in the ascension. Men erroneously think that only Jesus and a few other notable figures from the biblical centrum have ascended. How they would change their minds if they could see the cloud of witnesses above them in the heavens![1]

It is time that men understood the effects of their consciousness and their thoughts upon the human aura. I would go so far as to say that even their opinions have a strong influence upon them for good or for ill.

I suspect that many have decided that I do not intend to discuss the negative aspects of the human aura. Perhaps they are right—we shall see. I am interested in stressing how that grandiose aura of the Christed one, surging with light, radiates out a divine quality in its very emanation that carries healing, nobility, honor, and cosmic strength to all who come in contact therewith.

This aura of which I speak is not and never can be the product either of man's environment or of his social involvements. It is produced by divine doings, by entering into the cosmic consciousness of God through involvement with universal purpose, and especially by contact with our Brotherhood.

There is still too much vanity, however, in the whole business of God-seeking. There are times when we would gladly chasten men because of our great love for them, if doing so would stimulate a greater involvement in the only and true purpose behind the manifestation of their lives.

Remember, the light shines in the darkness; and whereas the darkness comprehends it not,[2] those who do begin to open their understanding because this is their desire will find an absolute intensification of the light taking place within themselves. Hence a great deal more spirituality is involved in the God flame within the heart of each individual than he at first realizes.

In this very flame man has a catalyst posited right within himself, a spark plug that can motivate him to make such attunement with his Presence whereby the magnificent influences of our Brotherhood can shine through his aura and he can become the outpost of heaven upon earth.

Whoever said, and who dares to say, that any one

person has the exclusive possession of this quality when it is the divine plan for all to radiate the one light? Just as man and all things were made by one Spirit, so the one Spirit expects all to enter in at the door. The door of the Christ consciousness literally trembles with anticipation of the moment when the individual will joyously enter into the sheepfold of his own reality.[3]

Probably some of you may wonder just what I am driving at and why, when I have offered to you studies on the human aura, I seem to be going around Robin Hood's barn. I can understand that, and I feel that now is the time for me to tell you that by this method I am seeking to develop a special quality in all of our students. That quality, which is of the Christ, will enable you to develop the kind of an aura that I will call *self-proving*, because it can be consciously intensified to do the most good.

In effect, man's aura is literally a broadcasting station for God's energy and his cosmic rays. Energies of light and the very thoughts of God himself and of the ascended masters combine with the benign thoughts that emerge from the very life plan of the individual and are then beamed or broadcast in all directions into the world of form.

Those who are sensitive and can attune with these waves may perceive their nature and their origin, while those who do not understand cosmic law may become beneficiaries of these wondrous energies without ever knowing their source. It makes little difference. We are concerned with overcoming the preponderance of human darkness that is abroad in the world today by literally flooding forth more light through the auras of many souls who shall dedicate their lives as outposts of cosmic regeneration to the planet.

Christ said, "I AM the light of the world: he that followeth me shall not walk in darkness."[4] When we speak of the light of the world, we speak of the light of the aura, and we are talking about a tangible manifestation.

It is difficult for me to restrain myself when I hear the thoughts of individuals who carelessly read my words and then say, "What a nebulous concept he brings forth!" Contrary to their opinions, my concepts are incisive and they are given with a very definite purpose in mind and directly in accord with the one law of God.

I say this because I am talking about permanent manifestations of universal grace, and withal I am trying to impress upon your minds the great fact that the law of God—the law of his love—is very much involved with the human aura. What is the human aura if it is not an extension into the world of form, into the universal web of the sum total of what the individual really is?

Well, then, if a man manifests a whimsical attitude, working his own or another's will without discrimination—sometimes good, sometimes bad or indifferent—can this be compared with the one who is literally harnessed to the divine dynamo and whose aura can be seen by those who truly see, as beginning to vibrate with the universal purpose?

Not only do I know that these states of consciousness cannot be compared, but I know that one day in the changing consciousness of humanity the former will cease to be altogether. For God will win; of this I am certain. And those who follow the way of darkness because of the consuming of the thread of their own identity will ultimately be extinguished altogether by the very fires of creation.[5] For God is the Creator, the Preserver, and the Destroyer, and we have seen him in these and many guises.

In heaven's name, from whence cometh energy? What is it that beats your heart? A wish obviously not your own, or it would not so suddenly terminate. Instead, the will of God, the desire of God, beats your heart. Men's lives would not be paltry, then, if they also let him determine their consciousness and their thoughts.

Now that we have created a certain measure of understanding in many of our students about the factors that influence the human aura, we shall begin to show in greater detail the processes involved in broadcasting the qualities of the Christ so that great good can flow from your being out into the world in these troubled times and create in the brilliance of the sunshine a new awareness that fulfills the destiny of the children of men under the cosmic teachers for this age.

Extending my love to each of you, I hold the chalice of holy wisdom to be of special value in creating a new future out of which shall be born a greater summoning of understanding and its use. For knowledge must be correctly used and appropriated by transcendent magnificence rather than consumed on a few short years of sense pleasures without purpose.

The Brotherhood beckons to the many. The many can respond. If only the few do, I am certain we shall take delight in opening the curtain for them upon a new era of possibility. Let the weaving of regeneration begin anew the spinning of the tapestry of heaven's deepening involvement in the raising of humanity into the folds of the Brotherhood, into the delight of revealed purpose.

I remain firmly established in that purpose.

6 THE STRENGTHENING OF THE AURA

The thrust for a purpose envisioned by Master El Morya should be brought to bear not only upon the activities of the Brotherhood mutually coordinated on earth and in heaven, but also upon the life of each and every student.

One of the first exercises I wish therefore to give to the students for the strengthening of the aura involves a threefold action. The student begins by visualizing the threefold flame expanding from within the secret chamber of his heart.[1] He then seals himself and his consciousness in a globe of white fire, and when he is set he proceeds to recite the following words with utter humility and devotion:

> I AM Light, glowing Light,
> Radiating Light, intensified Light.

God consumes my darkness,
Transmuting it into Light.

This day I AM a focus of the Central Sun.
Flowing through me is a crystal river,
A living fountain of Light
That can never be qualified
By human thought and feeling.

I AM an outpost of the Divine.
Such darkness as has used me is swallowed up
By the mighty river of Light which I AM.

I AM, I AM, I AM Light;
I live, I live, I live in Light.
I AM Light's fullest dimension;
I AM Light's purest intention.

I AM Light, Light, Light
Flooding the world everywhere I move,
Blessing, strengthening, and conveying
The purpose of the kingdom of heaven.

As you visualize the cosmic white-fire radiance
around yourself, do not be concerned with the errors
in your thought that through the years may have
intruded themselves upon your consciousness. Do
not allow yourself to concentrate upon any negative
quality or condition. Do not let your attention rest
upon your supposed imperfections.

Instead, see what the light can do for you. See how even your physical form can change, how a strengthening of the bonds of your health can occur in body, mind, and spirit. Try this exercise, simple though it may seem, and know that many ascended beings will be performing it with you.

So many times adults fear to be thought childlike.[2] They would rather appear to be worldly-wise and sophisticated—if they only knew that they are running from deep-seated fears and insecurities which they have buried beneath the clamor of social doings. Surely with all they know about the physical universe, their environment, and the patterns of the mind, they must be able to reveal how great they really are!

But, dear hearts, what a shock some men and women are in for when they shall come face to face with the blazing truth of reality and realize that so much of what they have learned must be unlearned and that what they have thought to be their own greatness must be sacrificed upon the altar of the true greatness of the Christ Self. Then, perhaps, they will compare that which they do not yet know with that which they do know, and they will see how very lacking in luster they are in the eyes of the cosmic hierarchy.

It is not needful to impress the masters with any quality you may have. Heaven already knows exactly what you are above and below. Heaven already knows that you were made in God's image and likeness.

If you return to that image in a simple, sweet, and childlike manner, I can promise you that heaven will not allow you an overabundance of time in which to function in the domain of the child, but it will elevate you into the consciousness of a mature son or daughter of God.

While you maintain the attitude of the child, you will be able to do something for yourself that will be both valuable and valid. You will be able to loose the ties that bind you to your egocentricities, until at last the little bird of the soul shall flit into the heavens and behold the glory of the eternal sun.

We in our Brotherhood of the Golden Robe are devoted to the freeing of those who are yet enmeshed in the vain aspects of the human consciousness. That they may develop spiritually, free at last to express the purposes of life as God intends them to do, is our prayer.

Many think it would be "so nice" if God would speak the word and, suddenly, as with the rushing of a mighty wind, all could speak the heavenly language.[3] Men forget the karmic patterns that others have carelessly woven and even the patterns that they themselves have woven. They forget that these are the self-made prison walls that keep them from discovering the delights of heaven and from becoming gods among men. They do not understand that this planet is a schoolroom and that in these latter days many have permitted their consciousness to grow dark even while knowledge seems increased across the land.

The knowledge that is important is the knowledge whereby man becomes first the master of his own consciousness and then the master of his world. Whereas in a relative sense one man may attain greater mastery than another in the manipulation of energy within a finite circle, this in no way guarantees that the big frog in the little pond will be able to navigate in the circle of the infinite.

We are concerned with the measure of a man's advancement according to the divine precepts of the Brotherhood, which have been established under the guidance of the eternal Father from the beginning. We are interested not in generation, but in regeneration.

Now, I am well aware that for some of our readers it is even a new idea that their thoughts can impinge upon others or that the thoughts of others can influence their own moods and manner of life. Nevertheless, it is so. The wise will therefore seek scientific methods of dealing with the problems of auric influences and thought penetration.

If everyone knew how to use the tube of light and the violet consuming flame and believed in this method of self-transformation, I am certain that the world would be a different place. The dissemination of such practical knowledge is invaluable when it is applied by those who receive it. Hence I urge those disciples who have been calling for more light to be alert to properly use that which we shall release as they practice the aforementioned exercise.

So many misalignments in the human aura, so many nodules of dark and shadowed substance continually spew out their pollutants into the mainstream of man's energy, sapping his strength and weakening the entire manifestation of his life, that there is a great need for the flushing-out of darkness by a bubbling action of the light. Naturally, I am concerned that we first clear up these centers of shadow—the shadow of misqualification that is within man—before we energize the consciousness of our students.

This problem sometimes presents a moot point. For those who pray often, who decree much, who love much, who involve themselves with the whole repertoire of the mantras of our Brotherhood seldom realize that as they gain in the power aspect of God, or even the love aspect of God, they also need the holy wisdom that shall direct their proper use of their forte of energy.

To misuse energy, to send out enormous power into the world like billowing storm clouds, is not the fulfillment of the divine intent. Energy should be directed as the perfect day coming from heaven into the lives of all it contacts. Let radiant blue skies and golden drops of sunlight pour through the foliage of man's consciousness, increasing the green, the beauty, and the color of the day of perfection in all men's thoughts.

May I chasten some by pointing out that sometimes knowingly and sometimes unknowingly you are using the energy of God to further your own moods and feelings in the world of form. Try God's way, the way of perfection.[4]

For just as the Christ consciousness is the mediator between God and man, so man can become a joint mediator with Christ. And inasmuch as he does what he wills with the energy God gives him, he controls, in a relative sense in the world of form, a portion of the divine energy for the entire planet. When he realizes this, the whole foundation of his life can be altered if he wills it so. This thought is injected as a direct quote from a conversation I had with beloved Morya, and I trust that the students will take it to heart.

What a wonderful opportunity lies before you as a gift from God as you correctly use his energy. Why, you can literally mold yourself and the whole world in the divine image! The potential for goodness lying within man is wondrous indeed. And as he learns how to properly extend and guard his auric emanations, he will realize more and more of that potential.

We shall do our part to make known the wondrous kingdom of heaven to as many as we possibly can. Will you help us to reach out in God's name, as his hands and feet, to lovingly become more and more the manifestations of the grace of God?

The auric cloud glows, the auric cloud grows. The beauty of the kingdom of heaven solidifies in man as he gains a greater understanding of his own real nature.

I remain serenely in the light of purpose.

7 THE EXPANSION OF THE AURA

Coalescing around the spinal column are little portions of magnetic energy which I choose to call pieces of human destiny. As a man thinks, so is he.[1] As a man feels, so is he. As a man is, so goes his relationship with God, with purpose, and with the whole domain of life.

The fabric of a man's being is composed of minutiae. The fabric of a man's being is composed of thought, and thought is indeed made up of the same substance as that faith once delivered unto the saints.[2]

Now, as we recognize the need to let the sense of struggle cease, we want the students to develop in their consciousness the living tides of reality that flex the muscles of true spiritual being, enabling it to take dominion over the earth.

Just as Christ walked upon the waters, so humanity must learn the way of the possessor of light. It has been said that the way of the transgressor is hard,[3] but those who possess the divine potential and exercise it in the divine way are in contact with the cloud of witnesses that from spiritual realms extend the energies of the purpose of God to the earth.

There is a time in the lives of most children when heaven seems very near. Their journeys through the portals of life and death reveal the celestial truth of soul-knowing often forgotten with the passing of the years. Contact with heaven through the reestablishment of the threads of light between the heart and being of man and the living Father is beautiful and necessary if the world is to mature into an age of renewed innocence and tenderness expressed by mankind toward one another.

Grace is a very special quality of God that charges the aura with a buoyant and joyous expression of heaven's beauty and wonder continuously expressed here below and continuously expressed above. There is neither boredom nor unhappiness in the celestial state, but only a joyous sense of ongoingness that knows no defeat of sordid thought nor shame in its reflections.

The miracle of eternity is caught in the web of time as man momentarily understands the power of his influence at the courts of heaven—as he realizes through oneness with his Christed being that he is the maker of his own destiny.

How much help is given and how much help can be evoked from the Universal is a subject in its own right. Yet I feel the need to assert on behalf of the students everywhere their friendship with those who dwell in the ascended master consciousness, in the Christ consciousness—a friendship maintained through the liaison of the angelic hosts and God-free beings and even the tiny elementals who are involved in the very outworkings of physical manifestation.

The words of the Psalmist "For he shall give his angels charge over thee...lest thou dash thy foot against a stone"[4] are intended for every son of God. Yet the temptation to command that these stones be made bread, for the purpose of assuaging mortal hunger, is very great. Nevertheless, every son of God must be prepared to overcome this temptation as the Master did when he rebuked the lie of the carnal mind with the words "It is written, Man shall not live by bread alone, but by every word that proceedeth out of the mouth of God."[5]

Just as the world has its conspiracies practiced against the sons and daughters of God by those conspirators of Satan whose lives are literally snuffed out without their ever knowing the end from the beginning, so heaven has its own conspiracy of light. And its emissaries are conspiring to evolve the wondrous

God-designs which the Father hath prepared for
them that love him.[6]

Now as the celestial bower is momentarily low-
ered into view, the shape of things to come is revealed

When God does do his perfect work as planned
To right the wrongs of men by soul demand
And newly bring to view the hopes the ages sought
But never understood—
   the love and sacrifice he bought
To gather sheep and consecrate all lives
To higher goals and drives
   they little understood.
He vowed the plan to sweep from man
That hoary dust of ages overlaid,
To make men unafraid.
By love he showed to them
   that they should understand
The power of the pen
   that's mightier than the sword
And teaches all that I AM casting out all fear
From those who call upon me, far and near.
My light beams like a star of hope,
Dimension's newest opening
   upon the words I spoke;
For there is hope for all
Beneath the sun and star, or even moon.
For all things neath thy feet

Reveal the way complete
Is ever found within my Word,
The precious bread I broke;
For thou art mine and I AM thine—
Our living souls awoke.
Oh, see the magnet purpose,
   glorious connecting chain,
Eternal joy revealed as love does ever reign!

Devoted ones, the pathway to the stars is found in the thread of light anchored within the heart whence the individual auric pattern expands naturally. Man has so often been concerned with the concepts and the many manifestations of the human aura—how to protect it, how to direct it, how to increase it, how to see it, how to interpret it—that he has seldom taken into account these simple words Jesus long ago revealed, "Let your light so shine before men."

This light of which he spake is the light that can be magnetized through the human aura, for it is the human emanation which heaven would make divine. Therefore, "let your light so shine before men, that they may see your good works and glorify your Father which is in heaven."[7]

In our studies of the human aura, which are given to those who journey to our retreats as well as to you who are fortunate to receive our instruction, we seek to promote the same understanding that Jesus imparted to his disciples—sometimes through parable, sometimes through objective analysis of themselves and their contemporaries, sometimes through direct teachings on the law which he read to them from the archives of the Brotherhood.

His entire effort was to demonstrate what man can do and what man can be when he unites with the God flame. And I say to you today that it is to be, it is *be-ness,* it is to understand that you are a ray of intense light that cometh from the Central Sun into the world of form. This is the key to creative mastery.

You must understand that you can draw forth renewed magnificence and devotion to the cause of your own immaculate freedom, and that this freedom can be a crystal river flowing out from the throne of God through your aura—which you have consecrated as a vessel of the Holy Spirit—and into the world of men.

You must understand that wherever you go, your opportunity to let your light—your aura—shine goes with you, and that because you *are,* because you have being and are being, you can take the sling of enlightened fortune and fling into the world, with almost delirious abandon, your cup of joy that runneth over in simply being a manifestation of God.

You must increase your understanding of the magnificence of flow—the flow of the little electrons in their pure, fiery state that seem to dance with total abandon and then again to march like little soldiers in precision formation—now disbanding as they assume what at first may seem to be erratic shapes, now regrouping in their intricate geometric patterns.

Purposefully man pours out into the universe the healing balm that is his Real Self in action. Its flow is guided by the very soul of the living God, by an innate and beautiful concept of perfection steadily emanating to him and through him.

Does man do this? Can man do it of himself? Jesus said, "I can of mine own self do nothing; but the Father that dwelleth in me, he doeth the works."[8]

Understand that the inner fires banked within yourself by the fire of the Holy Spirit can be expanded by your own desire to be God's will in action. Understand that these fires will act as a divine magnet to increase the flow of perfection into your aura and thence into the world. Understand that you must therefore wax enthusiastic about daily expanding your light through your meditations upon the Holy Spirit.

Because it is our belief that men would do better if they knew better, we have written this series even as we long ago dedicated our service to the enlightenment of the race. It is our desire to teach men that the human aura need never be a muddied sea, but can ever be an eternal *seeing* into the streams of immortal perfection whence cometh each man's being.

One of the facts men should understand is that along with the pollution of their consciousness with impure thoughts and feelings and the emanations of the mass mind, which seem to take possession of the very fires of being and entrap them within imperfect matrices, is their desire for self-perpetuation.

Hence, often the little, pitiful, dark-shadowed creatures of human thought and feeling will clothe themselves with a sticky overlay of qualities and conditions calculated to preserve the loves of the little self—thereby gaining acceptance in the consciousness bent on its own preservation. This is done in order to obscure the light of truth and to impugn it by reason of its very simplicity and perfection.

Do not be deceived. The light is yours to behold. The light is yours to be. Claim it. Identify with it. And regardless of whether or not men may mock simplicity, be determined in your childlike efforts to mature in God.

One day the Divine Manchild will come to you, and the aura of the living Christ will be yours to behold and to be. To follow him in the regeneration is to follow him in the sun tides of the light that he was, that he is, that he ever shall be. You cannot cast yourself upon the rock and not be broken. But this is preferable to having the rock fall upon you and grind you to powder.[9]

There are more things in heaven than men on

earth have dreamed of,[10] yet wondrous threads and penetrations have occurred and many have come home.

We await the redemption of the world and we need in our Brotherhood those who, while having fallen in error, can simply trust and place their hand in ours as in the hand of God. For then the shuttle of the highest cosmic workers can move to and fro, from above to below, to carry greater instruction to the race of men, to the fountain of the individual life, where the shield of the aura is esteemed for the wonder God has made it.

Next let us talk about the shield of the aura. God be with you each one.

8 THE SHIELD OF THE AURA

Some men upon the planet are little aware of the need for protection to the consciousness, nor are they aware of the possibility of others creating a barrage of negative energy calculated to disturb the equilibrium of their life-streams. Let us set the record straight.

There are many who are at various stages of mastering the control of negative energy and manipulating their fellowmen by a wide range of tactics and techniques. There are also spiritual devotees of varying degrees of advancement who are in the process of mastering the godly control of energy and who understand somewhat the Brotherhood's systems of protection and the countermeasures they can take in defense of their own life plan.

A God-endeavor indeed! Upon this earth, heaven

needs many who can work the handiwork of God. If a planet is to fulfill its destiny, it must have those who can work in the light of God that never fails, unhampered by the forces of antichrist that would, if they could, tear down every noble endeavor of the sons and daughters of God.

From time to time these are and will be viciously assaulted through psychic means whereby the garments of their individual auras are sometimes penetrated and even rent, unless they are spiritually fortified. Yet that blessed aura, when it is properly intensified and solidified with light, becomes the shield of God against the intrusion of all negative energy, automatically and wondrously repelling those arrows that fly from the dark domain,[1] seeking to penetrate the peace of God that abides within, hence destroying peace.

Let me remind all of the natural envelope of invulnerability that serves as the protection of every man against those arrows of outrageous fortune[2] that fly so loosely in the very atmosphere of the planet betwixt men. However, through extraordinary measures the forces of darkness are often able to engage men in some form of argument whereby through inharmony they momentarily forfeit their protection. This is the game they play to catch men with their guard down. Then again, they launch such an attack of viciousness as to cause them, through fear, to open up their worlds to discordant energies, which results in the rending of their garments.

Earlier in the series I gave an exercise for the strengthening of the aura through the development of the consciousness of invulnerability. Now I would make plain that in addition to spiritual fortitude one must also have spiritual reserves—what could almost be called reserve batteries of cosmic energy.

The storing-up of God's light within the aura through communion with the Lord of hosts and through invocation and prayer, plus the sustaining of the consciousness in close contact with the angels, with the tiny builders of form acting under divine direction, and with all who are friends of light, creates an alliance with the forces of heaven. Through contact with each devotee's aura, these veritable powers of light can then precipitate the necessary spiritual fortifications that will give him a more than ordinary protection in moments of need.

Let the student understand that his protection is threefold. First of all, he enjoys, by the grace of God, the natural immunity of the soul, which he must not forfeit through anger or psychic entrapment. Then there is the assistance of the angelic hosts and cosmic beings with whom he has allied himself and his forcefield through invocation and prayer.

And last, but certainly not least, there is the opportunity to request of his own Presence the continuation of godly defense through an intensification of the tube of light that will also establish in his aura the needed protective strata of energy which create a protective concept that cannot be penetrated.

Bear in mind that sometimes the best defense of man's being is a necessary offense. And when you find that it becomes necessary to momentarily engage your energies in this way, try to think of what the Master would do, and do not allow your feelings to become negative or troubled by your contact with human discord of any kind.

If you will consciously clothe yourself with the impenetrable radiance of the Christ, asking yourself what the Master would do under these circumstances, you will know when to take the stand "Get thee behind me, Satan!"³ and when to employ the tactic of gently holding your peace before the Pilate of some man's judgment.⁴

Remember always the goal-fitting that is required of those who would remain on the path. You did not begin upon the path in order to become involved in strife. You began in order to find your way back home and to once again hold those beautiful thoughts of celestial fortitude and cosmic intelligence that would create in you the spirit of the abundant life.

Birthless, deathless, timeless, eternal, there springs from within yourself the crystal fountain of light ever flowing, cascading in its own knowingness of the joys of God that create a chalice from which can be drunk the very water of life.[5] Freely you have received and freely you must give,[6] for the heart of each man can gather quantities without measure of this infinite love in its superabundant onrushing.

There is an erroneous thought in man that I must decry. It is the idea that man can get too much of spirituality. Oh, how fragile is the real thought of truth about this subject, and how easily it is shattered by human density and the misappropriation of energy.

Man can never secure too much of God if he will only keep pace with him—with his light, with his consciousness, with his love. It is up to each one to do so, for no one can run the eternal race[7] for you. You must pass through the portals alone; you must be strengthened by your own effort.

And you must also face the dragons of defeat and darkness that you once allowed free rein in your own arena of thought and feeling. Slay these you must by the sword of spiritual discrimination, thus building an aura of use to the Masters of the Great White Brotherhood.

Of what use is an electrode? Like the hard tip of a penetrating arrow flying through the air, an electrode becomes a point of release of giant energies that leap forth to conquer. And there are many things that need to be conquered. Above all, there are within oneself conditions of thought and sensitivities of feeling that require man's dominion.

The man of whom I speak is the heavenly man—the man who abideth forever, one with God as a majority of good. His heart must not be troubled. And the injunction of the Master "Let not your heart be troubled"[8] must be heeded. For the aura is a beautiful electrode that can become of great use to heaven, and it must be consciously strengthened if man is to truly realize his potential.

Won't you understand with me the need to be the shield of God, to remain unmoved regardless of what conditions or difficulties you may face? For it is the power of heaven that liveth in you to strengthen the emanation of light from your being, both from the within to the without and from the without to the within.

You can receive, both from without and from within, of the strengthening light that maketh man truly aware that he can be, in his aura and in his very being of beings, a shield of God—impenetrable, indomitable, and victorious.

I remain firm in the love of the purpose of your being.

9 THE PROTECTION OF THE AURA

Beware of those who by intellectual argument or religious dogma seek to destroy your beautiful faith in the gossamer-veiled protection of the angels!

By his unbelief, man has failed to realize the magnificent protection that the human aura can receive from the angelic hosts. By his lack of recognition and his lack of attunement, he has allowed himself to pass through many harrowing experiences that could have been avoided by a simple cry for assistance to these beings whom God ordained from the foundation of the world to be his swift messengers of love, wisdom, and power.

Have you thought upon the love, wisdom, and power that the angels convey? May I suggest that you do it today. For over the track of your thoughts and the extension thereof into spiritual realms, over the swift and well-traveled pathways of the air, these infinite creatures of God's heart, serving so gloriously in his name and power, fly on pinions of light to do his bidding and to respond to your call.

What a pity it is that some men lack the sweet simplicity of heart and mind that would allow them to speak unto the angels! By their sophistication, their worldly-wise spirit, their hardness of heart, and their refusal to be trapped by the "plots" of heaven, they literally cut themselves off from so much joy and beauty; and their lives are barren because of it.

Will you, then, begin today the process of initiating or intensifying your contact with the angelic hosts as a means of fortifying your aura with what amounts to the very substance of the outer corona of the flame of God's own reality directed and glowing within the auric fires of the angelic hosts?

How they love to receive the invitation of mortal men who desire to align themselves with the purposes of God! And do you know, these powerful beings cannot fail in their mission when they are invited by an embodied flame of light, a son of God, to come and render assistance!

Once mankind understand this fact—that the angelic hosts will respond to their calls—once they understand that these emissaries of heaven are bound by cosmic law to respond to their pleas and to send assistance where it is needed, they will also realize that even Christ availed himself of the ministrations of the angels throughout his life. Standing before Pontius Pilate, he said, "Thinkest thou that I cannot now pray to my Father, and he shall presently give me more than twelve legions of angels?"[1]

The angelic hosts are the armies of God, the power, the service, the perfection, and the strength of God, flowing from the realm of immortality into immediate manifestation in the mortal domain, establishing the needed contact between God and man.

Consider for a moment how the Master employed the angelic hosts, not only in Gethsemane but also in his healing ministry, how he remained in constant attunement with them, acknowledging their presence in a spirit of oneness and brotherhood, esteeming them as the messengers of his Father. By startling contrast, the spurning of the angelic hosts by an ignorant humanity has caused many to fall under the negative influences of the dark powers that hover in the atmosphere, seeking to destroy mankind's peace, power, and purity.

I cannot allow this series to terminate without sounding the trumpet of cosmic joy on behalf of the angelic hosts. Many of us who are now classified as saints by some of the Christian churches[2] invoked the angels when we, as spiritual devotees, offered ourselves unto Christ in the service of humanity, knowing full well that of ourselves we could do nothing.

Therefore, we looked to the assistance of the angelic hosts as God's appointed messengers. We did not expect God himself to come down into the everyday situations we encountered that required some special ministration from heaven, but we knew that he would send legions in his name, with the seal of his authority and power, to do his bidding.

How tragic it is that some men, through the puffiness of human pride, will speak only to God directly, thereby ignoring those whom God has sent, including the ascended masters and the sons and daughters of God upon the planet to whom is given a special ordination of conveying the message of truth unto humanity. It is so unnecessary for a distraught humanity engaged in numerous wars and commotions betwixt themselves to also launch an offensive against those who in truth defend every man's Christhood in the name of God.

To go forth with his power and in his name is a calling of considerable magnitude. May our protection abide with the Brothers of the Golden Robe serving at unascended levels, who in wisdom's gentle name would teach men the truth of the ages and thereby receive within their auras that celestial song that is the glory of God in the highest and the peace of God on earth to all men of good will.[3] The message of the angels that rang out over the plains of Bethlehem at the birth of Christ has since been heard by the few in every century who have communed with the angel ministrants; yet the light of the angels is for all.

How could it be that we would so carelessly forget, as mankind have done, the service and the devotion of the angels directed from an octave of power and beauty interpenetrating your own? Will you, then, consider in the coming days and throughout your whole life the blessed angels—not only the mighty archangels, but also the cherubim and seraphim?

For there are many who will reach up to the great archangels, such as the beloved Michael, Chamuel, and Uriel, without ever realizing that even they in their great God-estate have their helpers who, in the performance of their novitiate and in their own aspirations to rise in the hierarchy of angels, will do almost any divine kindness on behalf of the children of God on earth when called upon by them to do so.

All should understand, then, the need to make the request. For heaven does not enter the world of men unbidden, and the tiniest angel in all of heaven welcomes the love and invitation of men to be of service.

The information I have given you can help you to consummate in your life the building and charging of an aura with a radiance so beautiful that as it sweeps through your consciousness, it will sweep out the ignorance of the human ego and replace it with the light of the Christ.

Wherever you move, God moves, and his angels accompany him. Let your auras be charged with such purity and determination to do the will of God and to be an outpost of heaven, that if your shadow should but fall upon another whom God has made, healing, joy, beauty, purity, and an extension of divine awareness would come to him.

You belong to God. Your aura, the garment of God given to you, was designed to intensify his love. Do not tear it. Do not carelessly force it open. But as a swaddling garment of love and light, keep it tightly wrapped around you.

For one day, like the ugly duckling that turned into a swan, the aura will become the wedding garment of the Lord—steely white light reinforced by the divine radiance that no man can touch—that literally transforms the outer man into the perfection of the Presence, preserved forever intact, expanding its light and glowing as it grows with the fires of home and divine love.

DECREE TO ARCHANGEL MICHAEL

In the name of the beloved mighty victorious Presence of God, I AM in me, my very own beloved Holy Christ Self, Holy Christ Selves of all mankind, beloved Archangel Michael, the entire Spirit of the Great White Brotherhood and the World Mother, elemental life—fire, air, water, and earth! I decree:

1. Lord Michael, Lord Michael,
       I call unto thee—
    Wield thy sword of blue flame
    And now cut me free!

Refrain: Blaze God-power, protection
             Now into my world,
          Thy banner of Faith
             Above me unfurl!
          Transcendent blue lightning
             Now flash through my soul,
          I AM by God's mercy
             Made radiant and whole!

2. Lord Michael, Lord Michael,
       I love thee, I do—
    With all thy great Faith
       My being imbue!

3. Lord Michael, Lord Michael
       And legions of blue—
    Come seal me, now keep me
       Faithful and true!

(continued)

"I AM" Affirmation: (recited three times)

I AM with thy blue flame
      Now full-charged and blest,
I AM now in Michael's
      Blue-flame armor dressed!

And in full faith I consciously accept this manifest, manifest, manifest! (three times) right here and now with full power, eternally sustained, all-powerfully active, ever expanding, and world enfolding until all are wholly ascended in the Light and free!

Beloved I AM! Beloved I AM! Beloved I AM!

TRAVELING PROTECTION

Lord Michael before, Lord Michael behind,
Lord Michael to the right, Lord Michael to the left,
Lord Michael above, Lord Michael below,
Lord Michael, Lord Michael wherever I go!

I AM his love protecting here!
I AM his love protecting here!
I AM his love protecting here! (give entire decree three times)

Note: You can recite these decrees to invoke the protection of Archangel Michael, Prince of the Archangels. The abbreviated "Traveling Protection" decree can be used at any time but especially while traveling. Give this decree in full voice when you are driving your car and softly on public forms of transportation. Visualize Archangel Michael and his legions sealing you, your loved ones and all other vehicles on land and sea and in the air in an invincible wall of blue flame.

10 THE PURIFICATION OF THE AURA

Remember that your aura is your light. Remember that Christ said: "Ye are the light of the world. A city that is set on an hill cannot be hid. Neither do men light a candle and put it under a bushel, but on a candlestick; and it giveth light unto all that are in the house."[1] Remember that he left this timeless advice as a means of inculcating into the consciousness of the race the inner formula for the proper employment of the human aura.

How many men have misunderstood what the aura is and what it can do! The aura is the sum total of the emanation of individual life in its pure and impure state. Often gently concealing from public view the darker side of human nature, the aura puts forth its most beautiful pearly-white appearance before men as if mindful of the words of God that have come down from antiquity "Though your sins be as scarlet, they shall be as white as snow."[2]

Occasionally the aura will momentarily turn itself inside out, and the more ugly appearance of a man's nature will come to the fore and be seen by those who are sensitive enough to perceive the human aura. This shouting from the housetops of a man's errors[3] ought not always to be deplored; for when the gold is tried in the fire of purpose, the dross often comes to the surface to be skimmed off.

Therefore, when from time to time some negative influence appears in yourself or in someone else, consider it not as a permanent blight, but as a thorn which you can break off and remove from the appearance world. The fact that the within has thrust itself to the surface is an application of the principle of redemption. And when properly understood, this purging can mean the strengthening of your aura and your life.

As a part of the blotting-out process in the stream of time and space, dear hearts, God, in his greater wisdom, often uses exposure to public view or to your own private view as a means of helping you to get rid of an undesirable situation.

Have you ever thought of that? What a pity if you have not. Suppressing evil or driving it deep within, tucking it away as though you would thereby get rid of it, does not really do the trick. For all things ought to go to God for judgment—willingly, gladly, and freely.

Men ought not to remain burdened by the inward sense of guilt or nonfulfillment that the suppression of truth often brings. For the cleansing of the human aura of these undesirable conditions need not be a lengthy process. Just the humble, childlike acknowledgement that you have made an error and the sincere attempt to correct it will do much to purify your aura.

God does not angrily impute to man that which he has already done unto himself through the misuse of free will, for man metes out his own punishment by denying himself access to the grace of God through his infringement of the law. Therefore, the gentle drops of mercy and of God's kindness to man are offered as the cleansing agent of his own self-condemnation. They are like a heavenly rain, refreshing and cool, that is not denied to any.

Fill your consciousness, then, with God-delight, and observe how the purification of the aura brings joy unto the angels. Have you never read the words of the Master "Joy shall be in heaven over one sinner that repenteth, more than over ninety and nine just persons, which need no repentance"?[4]

Oh, what a wonderful world will manifest for humanity when the power of God literally rolls through the heart and being of man untrammeled, flooding the planet with light! Yes, a great deal of instruction will still be needed, for there are so many things that we would reveal, not even dreamed of by the masses. And there is so much ongoingness in the Spirit of the Lord that my enthusiasm knows no bounds.

Yet mankind should understand that until they have prepared themselves for the great wedding feast to which they have been bidden,[5] they cannot fully know the meaning of the ongoingness of life. For the dark dye of human sorrow and degradation creates such a pull upon the consciousness that it is difficult for man to recognize the bridegroom in his God Self.

Alas, man, although heavenly by nature, has through the misuse of free will decreased the natural, God-given vibratory rate of his atoms to such a low point that even the body temple must be broken again and again in order to arrest the cycles of the sense of sin. This breaking of the clay vessel affords him the opportunity to catch glimpses of reality, which he would never do—unless he had first attained self-mastery—if his life were to continue indefinitely in one physical body.[6]

How deep and how lovely are the mercies of God! How carefully he has provided for the gift of free will to man so that through the making of right choices man can find his way to the throne of grace and there receive the affirmation of his own God-given dominion, "Thou art my Son; this day have I begotten thee."[7]

I am also reminded of the many devoted souls who through the ages have suffered the condemnation of their fellowmen as the result of the misunderstanding of their devotion to purpose. Like Joan of Arc and others who revealed a fiery determination for heaven to manifest upon earth, these great spirits have received little welcome from their peers and little understanding of their mission.

Let us hope together for the world that through the spreading-abroad of the balm of Gilead and the mercy of God as an unguent of healing, mankind will become unflinching in their devotion to cosmic purpose, even as we intensify our love through the student body. Tearing down any altars you may have erected in the past to the false gods of human pride and ambition and surrendering your momentums of failure to apprehend your reason for being, you will turn now with your whole heart to the development of the most magnificent focus of light right within your own aura.

Oh, I know something about the angstrom units, about the vibratory rate of the aura, about its impingement upon the retina of the eye and the interpolation of auras. I know about the subtle shadings that indicate gradations of tone in the thoughts and feelings of the individual which vacillate as a spunky wind or a frisky colt that has never been ridden.

But how much better it is when, rather than label

these as typical of the life pattern of another, men see at last the original image of divine perfection which God himself has placed within the human aura. For in most people some light can be perceived as a point of beginning, as a vortex around which greater light can be magnetized.

How much better it truly is when men hold the immaculate concept for one and all and concern themselves not with the probing of the aura, but with the amplification of all that is good and true about the real man. I do not say that advanced disciples should not use methods of discrimination to discern what is acting in the world of another at a given moment or that the soul does not use these methods to give warning and assistance to other lifestreams.

Nevertheless, those who are able to discern the face of God in the face of man can retain the perfect image and assist the cosmic plan even while correctly assessing the present development of a lifestream. To hold faith in the purposes of God for another until that one is able to hold it for himself is to ally one's energies with the omnipotence of truth, which intensifies both auras in the richness of cosmic grace even as it intensifies the aura of the whole planet.

I want to bring to every student the realization that just as there is the flame of God in the individual aura, so there is the flame of God in the aura of the planetary body. Every act of faith you perform adds to the conflagration of the sacred fire upon the planet, just as every act of desecration tears down the great cosmic fortifications so gently and carefully builded by angelic hands who join with men and masters in service to life.

Let all understand the building of the cosmic temple within the microcosm and the Macrocosm. The cosmic temple of the aura is an enduring edifice of the sacred fire. The cosmic temple of the world is made up of many auras dedicated to the indwelling Spirit of the Lord. Illumined thoughts and illumined feelings will enable individual man and humanity, striving together as one body, to cast into the discard pile those thoughts and feelings and actions not worthy to become a part of the superstructure of the temple of being.

Oh, be selective! Oh, be perfective in all your doings! For someone is assigned to watch and wait with you until the moment comes when you can watch and wait with others.

Just as the buddy system is used between soldiers in battle and between law-enforcement officers keeping the peace in your great cities, so there are cosmic beings, guardian angels, and lovely nature spirits of God's heart who watch over thee to keep thy way in peace and security, unmoved by mortal doings. For immortality shall swallow up mortality as death is swallowed up in victory,[8] and light shall prevail upon the planet.

The strengthening of the aura is a step in the right direction. Let none hesitate a moment to take it.

Devotedly and firmly I remain wedded to the precepts of the Brotherhood.

THOU MERCY FLAME

Mercy is the grace of love,
Forgiveness from above,
Beauteous star-fire might,
Falling rain of light.

Mighty God-caress,
Freedom from distress
Touching mind and heart
With love's divinest part,

Frees the soul from blindness,
Ope's the mind to purest kindness.
Glorious light, enfold all now
In heaven's greenest bough!

Joy of nature's band,
God's extended hand,
Living flame most holy
Answers now the lowly.

No difference does he make—
All his children who will take
His offered cup of love
Perceive his comfort dove.

No darkness in his motive,
But only light and life.
Behold the flaming votive:
We share one common light!

                                    Kuthumi

11 THE STAR OF THE AURA

The garment of God is the most transcendent man can ever wear. It represents the highest echelon of life, the development not only of the love nature of God and of the wisdom of God, but also of the element of power. This so many seek without willing first to make the necessary preparation in the refinements of love and holy wisdom in manifestation within the soul.

How easy it is for individuals to accept primitive as well as intellectual ideas that rationalize the thrust of ego upon ego, without ever analyzing the attitude and the aura of the masses, who are saturated with the concept of oneness as the blending of human personalities. The oneness men should seek to understand and manifest is that of the individuality of God reflected in man. Oneness in Spirit is ever consecration in the Gloria in Excelsis Deo—the Glory to God in the Highest.

Through the linking-together of the great and the trivial in human consciousness, mankind defeat evermore the manifestation of true spiritual transcendence. The ongoingness of the nature of God as it manifests in man is a study in individual development. As one star differs from another star in glory,[1] so by the process of linking together the mediocrity of man and the sublimity of God, the latter is compromised beyond recognition.

But only in the human consciousness does the ridiculous detract from the sublime. By the splitting of divine images and by the subtle process of image distortion resulting in the redistribution of the soul's energies according to astral patterns which nullify the original spiritual design, man begins to feel that the magnificence of cosmic ideas is in reality too far from him and the gulf between the human and the Divine too great. Thus his consciousness remains in the doldrums of mortal experience.

Wise is the chela who guards against this invasion of the mind and heart, who recognizes those negative subtleties that seek to stealthily enter the aura and turn it from its natural brightness to darkening shadows of gray and somber hue.

The strengthening of the bonds of the aura with light and virtue will enable the soul to leap as a young deer across huge chasms of erroneous ideas separating man from God when once the esteem of the immaculate concept is given preeminence in his consciousness. To involve oneself in the distractions of the world and to love the things of the world,[2] being consumed by them, deprive one of the magnificent occupation of seeking to become one with God, a cosmic occupation of permanent reality.

There may be a time to plant, to water, to love, and to die;[3] but we are concerned with the abundant life, which is nowhere more abundant than it is in the magnetic shower of Cosmic Christ power that pours forth to the individual from the heart of his own God-identity when he fixes his attention upon the Presence and understands that herein is his real, eternal, immortal, and permanent life.

As long as he, like a potted plant, sits in the limited circle of his own individuality, he remains tethered to its ranges. But once he allows the power and the pressure of the divine radiance to descend from the heart of his God Presence, he becomes at last the recipient of immortal life in all of its abundance and unlimited outreach.

The illusion of the self must remain an illusion until the self is surrendered. Therefore, men ready and willing to be delivered from the bondage of a self-centered existence into the infinite capacities of the God Self must surrender unconditionally to the Divine Ego.

Then there is not even a sense of loss, but only of gain, which the soul perceives as cosmic worth as he increases his ability to develop in the aura the consciousness of the absolute penetration of the Absolute.

Physically, the very atoms of man become drenched with a shower of cosmic wave intensity—the drinking of the elixir of life, the magic potion by which a man is transformed. In a moment, in the twinkling of an eye, the trump of true being sounds.[4] This is God, and no other will do.

The carnal mind cannot remain in command of the affairs of such a one. A Christ is born, a nova upon the horizon, one willing to follow in the footsteps of cosmic regeneration. Thus the purity and power of the Presence strike a new note, and old things truly pass away as all things become new.[5]

The domain of destiny is all around us. As man evolves, so cosmic beings evolve—wheels within wheels, leading to the great hub of life and to the reality of spiritual contact as the *antahkarana* is spun, perceived, and absorbed.

How beautiful is contact with hierarchy, with the hand of those brothers of light whose garments are robes of light, whose consciousness, reflecting the anticipation of spiritual progress, is joyously attuned to those God-delights that remove from the mind of man the sense of the comparable or the incomparable.

The world of comparison diminishes; the world

of God appears. The aura is drenched with it—no sacrifice too great, no morsel too small to be ignored, no grasp too significant not to find its own integral pattern of usefulness.

And so the domain of the human aura is lost in a sea of light, in the greater aura of God. The windows of heaven open upon the world of the individual, and the showers of light energy resound as an angelic choir singing of the fire of worlds without end.

The anvil of the present is the seat of malleability. All things less than the perfection of the mind of God mold themselves according to progressive reality, plasticity, the domain of sweetness, the chalice of new hope to generations yet unborn. The historical stream, muddied no longer, appears as the crystal flowing river from which the waters of life may be drunk freely.[6] The monad makes its biggest splash as it emerges from the chrysalis of becoming to the truth of living being as God intended.

Sensing the human aura as a star, man gains his victory as he sees the universe flooded with stars of varying intensity. By comparison his own auric light glows more brightly, for the fires of competition fan the flame of aspiration.

But all at once he staggers with the realization that he is in competition with no one, for the incomparable mystery of his own exquisite being is revealed at last. Questioning and doubts as to the purpose of life no longer engage his mind, for all answers are born in the ritual of becoming. The fascination of truth envelops him, and he weans himself from the old and familiar concepts that have stifled the glow of perpetual hope within his soul.

He is concerned now that others shall also share in this great energy source of reality flowing forth from on high. Naught can transpire with his consent that God does not will, for the will of God and the will of man are become one.

When each man consents to this victory, the struggle lessens and then is no more, for faith in the fatherhood of God reconciles men through Christ to the fountainhead of their eternal purpose. The glow of a new hope, infusing all, lends direction to the expansion of the auric light. The forcefield is magnified, and in the magnification thereof the star of the man who has become one with God shines on the planes of pure being as the angels rejoice.

A new life is born—one for whom the expectancy of life will continue forever. For in the endlessness of cycles, the aura, as a glowing white-fire ball, a summer radiance of the fruit of purpose, continues to magnify itself in all that it does. God is glorified in the auric stream.

We shall soon conclude our dissertation on the human aura. The richest blessings of our Brotherhood be upon all.

MEDITATION ON SELF

I AM no blight of fantasy—
    Clear-seeing vision
      of the Holy Spirit,
      Being!
Exalt my will,
      desireless Desire,
    Fanning
      flame-inspired fire,
      glow!
I will be the wonder
      of Thyself,
    To know
      as only budding rose
      presumes to be.
I see new hope
      in bright tomorrow
      here today—
    No sorrow lingers,
      I AM free!
O glorious Destiny,
      thy Star appears,
    The soul casts out
      all fears
And yearns to drink
      the nectar of new hope:
    All firmness wakes
      within the soul—
I AM becoming
      one with Thee.

12 THE CRYSTAL FLOWING STREAM OF THE AURA

The aura is a crystal flowing stream that issues from the heart of God. No negation is here: only an indomitable fountain continually pouring forth a steadfast stream of magnificent, gloriously qualified substance—the substance of life itself.

As a little child presents his first freshly picked bouquet of flowers to his mother, so the innocence of the child-mind tunes in with this crystal flowing stream of God's consciousness infusing the natural aura of God in man with the life that beats his heart.

O children of the day, the night should not be given preeminence! Your energy should become qualified by the eternal flow of hope that, if you will it, can enlarge its own opening into the fountain of your mind and heart—into the fountain of God's own mind and heart. Your mind must become the mind of Christ; the desire of your heart must become the desire of the Holy Spirit, flowing assistance to those awaiting the loving hand of perfection in their lives.

May I tell you that when you come in contact with the dark and sullen auras of those who have misqualified the bulk of their energy throughout their lives, you ought to recognize that in reality these are not happy individuals. They may laugh, they may dance, they may sing and make merry, they may wail and utter lamentations—they may run the gamut of human emotion. But they shall not prevail, for the law inexorably returns to each one exactly that which he sends out.

The way of perfection is the natural way of the aura. But, almost as a mania, individuals seldom fail to misqualify the energies of their lives, bringing their very nerves into a taut state. They become like a tightened spring of energy wound in erratic layers, and they refuse the stabilizing influences of the Christ mind and the divine heart. Having no other energy, they are compelled to use this which they have locked in the coil of their mental and emotional incongruities.

Thus through psychic imbalance, the spring is sprung and the impure substance of the aura pours forth in a putrid stream. All of the delicate refinements of the soul and the natural culture and grace of the Holy Spirit are spilled upon the ground, and the kingdom of heaven is denied the opportunity to function through the individual auric pattern.

To say that they suffer is an understatement, for through their own denial of the hope of Christ they are punished *by* their sins, not *for* them. The light of God that never fails continues to flow into their hearts, but it remains unperceived and unused. For instead of flowing into vessels of virtue—those pure forms and noble ideas that retain the light of God in man—it is automatically channeled into the old and crusty matrices formed in earlier years through ego involvement and contact with the forces of antichrist that permeate society.

These patterns sully the descending light as dark clouds that filter the sunlight of being and preclude the spiritual advancement of the soul. Yet in moments of naked truth, men and women admit their inner need, and their hearts and minds cry out for the preservation of the immortal soul within them.

They fear the response of heaven. And, failing to recognize the all-pervading love of the Spirit, they watch helplessly as the soul, little by little, loses hold upon the steadily outpouring energies of life, for each misqualification brands them with the fruit of retribution.

While for a time it seems that those who dwell in

error escape the wrongs they have inflicted upon others, let me remind you that life will make her adjustments and none shall escape the responsibility for their actions. As he whose voice was of one crying in the wilderness said, "[his] fan is in his hand, and he will thoroughly purge his floor, and will gather the wheat into his garner; but the chaff he will burn with fire unquenchable."[1]

We are not concerned with matters of crime and punishment, but with the joy and courage that are born in the soul through the crucible of experience— the courage to be the manifestation of God, the courage to walk in the Master's footsteps, to feel the surge of his hope wherever you are, and to know that even though you walk in the valley of the shadow, you will not fear,[2] because his light is surging through you.

Beware the sin of complacency and of passing judgment upon the lives of others. Before allowing your thoughts and feelings to crystallize around a given concept, ask yourself this question: Is the evidence indeed conclusive, and do you possess absolute knowledge concerning the motive of the heart and karmic circumstances surrounding other lives? If so, are you able to weigh these factors better than heaven itself? Wisely did the Master speak when he said, "Judge not, that ye be not judged."[3]

Therefore, point by point, let the Holy Spirit remold the vessels of thought and feeling that hinder your flight. And let the fruit of the crystal flowing stream, the fountainhead of life, be perceived for the diadem that it is—a crowning radiance that bursts around your head. Then the emanation of the Spirit Most Holy shall take dominion over all outer circumstances and, like the branches of a willow, trail upon the ground of consciousness by the still waters of the soul.

The Lord comes down to the meek and lowly;
His peace none can deny.
His light that glows most brightly
Is a fire in the sky.

The children hear him coming,
His footsteps very near;
They 'wait his every mandate,
His word "Be of good cheer."[4]

They feel a joy in knowing
That deep within their hearts
There is a glimmer showing,
Enabling all to start

Release from all earth's bondage,
Each weight and every care—
Open sesame to being,
Helping all to know and share.

The Lord is in his heaven,
So childlike is his love.

The Christ, the heavenly leaven,
Raises each one like a dove.

His face in radiant light waves
Is pulsing ever new;
Freedom from past error
He brings now to the few.

But many are the sheep,
His voice each one may hear.
This is his very message,
Wiping 'way each tear.

Oh, see him in the burdened,
The hearts o'erturned with grief,
The lips that mutter murmurs,
The tongues that never cease.

For social clamors babble,
Their judgments utter bold—
A child of light untrammeled,
A soul made of pure gold.

Each moment like a rainbow,
The presence ever near
Caresses in the darkness,
Bids all, "Be of good cheer."

Oh, take then life's great banner,
I AM God Presence true,

And hold me for the battle,
A victor ever new.

For life's own goalposts show me
The way I ought to go.
My hand is thine forever,
Enfold me with thy glow.

May all be reminded each day as they utter the words of Jesus "Our Father which art in heaven"* or any prayer, any call to God, that the aura is the Father's light and that his Son has said to all, "Let your light so shine before men, that they may see your good works and glorify your Father which is in heaven."[5]

May the sweet concepts of the living Christ, recalling a lost youth and the era of holy innocence, remind you of life's noble opportunities to be the grace and sweetness that you expect others to be. Then, regardless of what men do unto you, you will know that what you do unto them is a part of the age to be, of a mastery to become, of an adeptship now aborning.

Through night and day, through time and space, through life and death, you shall remain undismayed as the outpost of delight that melts away the darkness now gathering o'er the land. Thus shall the world's tears be wiped away as the mantle of God

*See page 99.

covers the earth. Everywhere through the night, let the shafts of light right where you are pierce the gloom of the world by the "good cheer" of the Master.

We, the brothers of our retreat, together with each Master, each angel, and each adherent of the sacred fire of the living God from their place in cosmos, beam our love to you wherever you are. We shall never forsake those who do not forsake the light of their own God Presence.

Eternal devotion,

K.H.

I AM LORD'S PRAYER
by Jesus the Christ

Our Father who art in heaven,
Hallowed be thy name, I AM.
I AM thy Kingdom come
I AM thy Will being done
I AM on earth even as I AM in heaven
I AM giving this day daily bread to all
I AM forgiving all Life this day even as
I AM also all Life forgiving me
I AM leading all men away from temptation
I AM delivering all men from every evil condition
I AM the Kingdom
I AM the Power and
I AM the Glory of God in eternal, immortal
    manifestation—
All this I AM.

Note: This prayer is mentioned by Kuthumi on page 97.

THE
HUMAN
AURA

BOOK TWO

DJWAL KUL

To Knowers
of the Great God Self
beyond the self

1 THE PULSATION OF LIFE BECOMING LIFE

I address myself to those of you who have pursued the auric studies set forth by my colleague and friend the Ascended Master Kuthumi. And to all who have not had the privilege of reading his words and following the cadences of his thought as the ever-widening circle of the aura of this blessed Brother of the Golden Robe encompasses the world in the love-wisdom of his heart, may I recommend that you do so. For our studies here will be laid upon the foundation that Kuthumi has laid.

To those who have not known me or my work with the hierarchy, which was registered concurrently with that of Morya and Kuthumi upon many disciples of the masters both in the East and the West during the last century and a half, may I introduce myself as the Tibetan Master and as one who has chosen to expand the love fires of the heart to woo mankind to the center of Christ awareness where the balance of the threefold flame perceives and is perceived by the fullness of that mind which was in Christ Jesus.[1]

The motto of the brothers who keep the flame of life with me on behalf of earth's evolutions is summarized in the words of the writer of the Book of Proverbs "Keep thy heart with all diligence; for out of it are the issues of life."[2] Some of our disciples who have followed with us the long trek in pursuit of the star of his appearing, the great I AM Presence of the Bethlehem babe, will recall that it was I who accompanied the Masters El Morya and Kuthumi to the place where Jesus was born.[3]

We came to pay homage to the heart of God made manifest as the heart of the Son of God. We came to adore the light of the Christos. We came with the wise dominion of the masters of the Far East to form a circle of protection around mother and child and to impart to Joseph an aura of protection for the flight into Egypt.

We come again in this series on a similar mission. We come to pay homage to the Christ aborning in the heart of children of God everywhere. We come to expand the circle of protection. We come to teach mankind to keep the fires of the heart with all diligence and to conserve the crystal-flowing waters of life that issue forth from the luminous fount of love, wisdom, and power. We come to show forth a trinity of the mastery of the aura.

And so brother Kuthumi has nobly stated his case for the expansion of soul consciousness through the aura. He has shown how, by replacing the personality patterns and perversions with soul consciousness— which you call, and that rightly so, solar awareness— you can increase the forcefield of the aura and use it to intensify the light of God on earth and to make of the aura the wedding garment of the Lord.

The work of Kuthumi given forth as an exercise in the expansion of the soul and its faculties reaching out to contact the Spirit of God is intended to awaken mankind from the sleep of the ages to a new perception of life, a perception of God, through the faculties of the soul. It is a work that all devotees of the sacred fire may use to diligently begin the process of the personal cleansing that is so necessary to the realization of the consciousness of God.

As you meditate, then, with beloved Kuthumi, recognize that he has a momentum of auric light which he extends from his forcefield to your own for the specific purpose of bringing about the quickening and the cleansing of your soul consciousness. As we proceed in these studies to expand and expound upon his work, we pursue the action of the Christ consciousness that develops from the mastery of soul awareness.

We begin, then, with our meditation on the heart as the seat of the authority of the Christ mind, as the altar of the love fires of being. And we intend, as it is our assignment from the Darjeeling Council, to present to mankind the noble example, the precepts of the law, and the action of the sacred fire that will clearly mark the way of the expansion of the aura through the mastery of the Christ consciousness, not only in the heart but in all of the chakras of being.

When we have concluded these studies and the souls of our chelas have become prototypes of the Christed One, then the Master El Morya will set forth his course on Advanced Studies of the Human Aura presently being given to certain initiates of the white fire attending classes in their finer bodies at the etheric Retreat of God's Will in Darjeeling, India. As my own humble effort is toward the plane of the Christ, so that of the Lord of the First Ray will be toward the development of God consciousness, not only for the Aquarian age but for all ages to come.

O you who would become and put on the garment of God, you who would practice his presence, take this our threefold offering of gold, frankincense, and myrrh, and pledge yourself anew to the Covenant of the Magi* as we come again—Melchior, Caspar,

*See pages 115–16.

and Balthazar—to salute the birth of the Christ and to inaugurate a light that will surely envelop worlds within and worlds to come. For this is the age of the coming of the sons and daughters of God!

In the heart there is a pulsation of life becoming life that is the established rhythm of the cosmos reflected from the heart of God to the heart of the Great Central Sun, through the heart of the Elohim, thence to all lifewaves evolving in time and space. The heart is the focal point for the flow of life individualized as the I AM Presence, the Divine Monad of individuality, and the Christ Self that is the personification of the reality of being for every soul.

The heart is the connecting point for all being, for all self-consciousness. Through the heart all mankind are one. And through the heart, the Christ of the One, the only begotten Son of the Father-Mother God, becomes the Christ of all lifewaves unfolding God's life throughout the cosmos.

Through obedience to the first and great commandment of the Lord, "Thou shalt love the Lord thy God with all thy heart and with all thy soul and with all thy mind,"[4] the heart of man is wed to the heart of God and the alchemy of a life lived on earth even as it is lived in heaven is begun.

The act of loving produces the action of the cosmic flow; and it is the flow of energy from the heart of man to the heart of God that rejuvenates the being

INDIVIDUALIZATION OF THE GOD FLAME FROM OUT THE PRESENCE OF THE I AM THAT I AM IN THE GREAT CENTRAL SUN. "In the heart there is a pulsation of life becoming life that is the established rhythm of the cosmos reflected from the heart of God to the heart of the Great Central Sun, through the heart of the Elohim, thence to all lifewaves evolving in time and space. The heart is the focal point for the flow of life individualized as the I AM Presence, the Divine Monad of individuality, the Christ Self that is the personification of the reality of being for every soul.

"The heart is the connecting point for all being, for all self-consciousness. Through the heart all mankind are one. And through the heart, the Christ of the One, the only begotten Son of the Father-Mother God, becomes the Christ of all lifewaves unfolding God's life throughout the cosmos."　　　　　　　　　　　　—DJWAL KUL

of man, that strengthens the citadel of consciousness, that expands the auric forcefield, and that ultimately magnetizes the soul of man to the Spirit of God in the ritual of the ascension in the light.

It was love as he lived and breathed the essence of the Holy Spirit that paved the way for mastery in the life of Jesus, a way that became a spiral of ascending currents of love over which the soul fulfilled its immortal destiny, being received in a cloud of love,[5] the forcefield of his very own I AM Presence.

Through the threefold flame within the hidden chamber of the heart, the threefold nature of God is realized in man and in woman. How clear is the word of the Lord throughout the ages! Two thousand years ago and throughout an eternity before and after, the law remains. To love God with all thy heart is to attain his Christ consciousness. To love God with all thy soul is to attain his soul consciousness. To love God with all thy mind is to attain his God consciousness.

So we build upon the rock, and no other foundation can be laid than that which is laid in Christ Jesus.[6] Understand, then, that obedience to the laws of God as these have been set forth by the great prophets and teachers of all time in the sacred scriptures of the world will lead you to the place where you can move forward in the cycles of self-mastery that are even now unfolding as the signs of the Aquarian age.

And the second great commandment that is like unto the first, "Thou shalt love thy neighbour as thyself,"[7] is the means whereby you realize that the love that God has placed within your heart, your soul, and your mind is also in every part of life. Therefore to love God in the heart, the soul, and the mind of friend and foe alike is to come into unity—into the union of the Spirit Most Holy that pervades all consciousness and being, worlds without end.

When you can love the self as the threefold action of God's consciousness, you will have fulfilled the first and great commandment. And when you can love every part of life as this great God Self individualized, you will understand why Jesus said that on these two commandments hang all the law and the prophets.

For the law is the Alpha spiral of Father. And the word of the prophets is the *mater*-ialization of the Mother flame through the power of the spoken Word that completes the Omega spiral of God Self-awareness and enables man and woman to return to the point of origin in the Divine Whole.

O children of the sun, children of the sun, let the fires of Helios and Vesta be released now through your heart! Do not hold back this great conflagration of the sacred fire burning within you as the desire of God to love and to love and to love. Do not hold back the flood tides of love! Let your consciousness, your heart, be washed by the waters of the word of love.

Now let the sacred fires from God's heart inscribe within the auricle and ventricle of the heart the name of God "I AM THAT I AM"[8] for the receiving and the giving of the flow of love.

And now, ye who would be priests and priestesses of the sacred fire, this commandment is for you: "If ye will not hear and if ye will not lay it to heart to give glory unto my name, saith the Lord of hosts, I will even send a curse upon you and I will curse your blessings: yea, I have cursed them already, because ye do not lay it to heart."[9] In the words of Malachi is the key to the dominion of the heart and the heart's energies.

The consecration of life, and of the blood as the essence of life, with the name of God is like the consecration of the Eucharist. The consecration by the name of God is the process whereby the body and the blood of Jesus became the body and the blood of the Lord. When you participate in the ritual of Holy Communion, you assimilate that substance of the bread and the wine which have become, through transubstantiation, the body and the blood of the Christ.

Now then, in our meditation upon the heart you see how the altar of the heart, situated in the center of the tabernacle of being, becomes the place where

God's substance and his energy, consecrated by the priest who is each one's own Christ Self, takes on and is imbued with the aura and the frequencies of the Holy Spirit.

Precious ones, we begin at the beginning. "If ye will not lay it to heart to give glory unto my name," no amount of study or endless pursuit of the chronicles and rituals of the chosen people will lead you to the awareness of the I AM THAT I AM. Jesus illustrated this law in this wise: "Whosoever shall deny me before men, him will I also deny before my Father which is in heaven."[10]

The curse that returns upon those who turn away from the angel of the Lord who comes to impress the name of God "I AM THAT I AM" upon the heart is the curse of death and decay, disease and disintegration. This is the personal-impersonal action of the law of love which returns to mankind that which mankind have sent forth.

Understand and meditate upon this simple yet profound precept: Unless the energies of Matter be consecrated in all ways by the flame of the Spirit, their cycles will pass as the grass withereth and the flower fadeth.[11] From dust to dust[12] proceed the cycles of materialization until these are imbued with the cycles of Spirit.

And when it comes to pass that man within his heart determines to give glory unto the name of the

Lord, the being that is corruptible in Matter becomes incorruptible in Spirit and the cycles of Spirit and Matter merge in the expressions of the sons and daughters of God who walk the earth as Christed ones prepared to be received in the heart of God.

Won't you meditate upon this teaching in all humility as you offer the "Introit to the Holy Christ Self"* in preparation for my next release on the heart.

Ever enfolding you in the trinity of love, I am Djwal Kul.

*See pages 117–18.

THE COVENANT OF THE MAGI

Father, into thy hands I commend my being. Take me and use me—my efforts, my thoughts, my resources, all that I AM—in thy service to the world of men and to thy noble cosmic purposes, yet unknown to my mind.

Teach me to be kind in the way of the Law that awakens men and guides them to the shores of Reality, to the confluence of the River of Life, to the Edenic source, that I may understand that the leaves of the Tree of Life, given to me each day, are for the healing of the nations; that as I garner them into the treasury of being and offer the fruit of my loving adoration to thee and to thy purposes supreme, I shall indeed hold covenant with thee as my guide, my guardian, my friend.

For thou art the directing connector who shall establish my lifestream with those heavenly contacts, limited only by the flow of the hours, who will assist me to perform in the world of men the most meaningful aspect of my individual life plan as conceived by thee and executed in thy name by the Karmic Board of spiritual overseers who, under thy holy direction, do administer thy laws.

So be it, O eternal Father, and may the covenant of thy beloved Son, the living Christ, the Only Begotten of the Light, teach me to be aware that he liveth today within the tri-unity of my being as the Great Mediator between my individualized Divine Presence and my human self; that he raiseth me into Christ consciousness

(continued)

and thy divine realization in order that as the eternal Son becomes one with the Father, so I may ultimately become one with thee in that dynamic moment when out of union is born my perfect freedom to move, to think, to create, to design, to fulfill, to inhabit, to inherit, to dwell and to be wholly within the fullness of thy Light.

Father, into thy hands I commend my being.

Note: This prayer to our Eternal Father is mentioned by Djwal Kul on pages 106–7.

INTROIT TO THE HOLY CHRIST SELF

In the name of the beloved mighty victorious Presence of God, I AM in me, and my very own beloved Holy Christ Self, I am calling to the heart of the Saviour Jesus Christ and the servant-sons of God and legions of Light who are with him in heaven: By and through the magnetic power of the sacred fire vested in the threefold flame of love, wisdom, and power burning within the secret chamber of my heart, I decree:

1. Holy Christ Self above me,
   Thou balance of my soul,
   Let thy blessed radiance
   Descend and make me whole.

Refrain: Thy flame within me ever blazes,
   Thy peace about me ever raises,
   Thy love protects and holds me,
   Thy dazzling light enfolds me.
   I AM thy threefold radiance,
   I AM thy living presence
   Expanding, expanding, expanding now.

2. Holy Christ Flame within me,
   Come, expand thy triune light;
   Flood my being with the essence
   Of the pink, blue, gold, and white.

(continued)

3. Holy lifeline to my Presence,
   Friend and brother ever dear,
   Let me keep thy holy vigil,
   Be thyself in action here.

And in full faith I consciously accept this manifest, manifest, manifest! (three times) right here and now with full power, eternally sustained, all-powerfully active, ever expanding, and world enfolding until all are wholly ascended in the Light and free!

Beloved I AM! Beloved I AM! Beloved I AM!

Note: This meditation is mentioned by Djwal Kul on page 114.

2 THE NAME OF GOD IS THE KEY

Heart friends of the ages, I come to you in the company of the hidden man of the heart,[1] your own Christ Self. I come as a teacher; and yet I bow before your own mentor of the Spirit, the mediator who is Christ the Lord. For as I instruct the outer consciousness according to the precepts of the inner law, it is the Christ, the light of the manifestation that you call your self, who releases inspiration, intuition, and intelligence from the seat of authority that is the heart chakra.

Concentric rings of illumination expand from the heart center as a golden pink glow-ray, and the aura of man expands from the center of the heart proportionately as levels of awareness in the four lower bodies are purified to become receptacles of God's light.

Those who walk after the flesh[2] allow the concerns of the flesh, the outer senses, and the world of material things to fill the four lower bodies with the memory of experiences, impressions, data, facts and figures of all kinds. They allow emotions and sympathetic attractions within the mass consciousness, not to mention the effluvia that collects in the physical body itself, to cave in on the heart chakra, to stifle the flow of energy through it, and to prevent the natural flow of the spiral of the Christos[3] through the vehicles that are provided solely for the experience and the expansion of soul consciousness.

Those who walk after the Spirit are those who exert the will to press the light of the heart outward into manifestation in a spiral of glory for the fulfillment of the law of the Christ in the four lower bodies. Walking after the Spirit, these do not fear to replace the anxieties of the flesh that have taken hold in the four lower bodies with the verities of the eternal Spirit.

To these, that which some have considered the pain of surrender or the so-called sacrifices of the spiritual path are neither painful nor sacrificial, but the entering in to the joy of the Lord, the joy of communion in the flame and of congruency with the law.

Once you have accepted the gift of the angel who comes with the flaming sword to write upon the heart forevermore the name of God "I AM THAT I AM," this gift can never be taken from you, except it be by your own betrayal of that name and that flame. Like the law that is written in the inward parts of man,[4] in the core of every cell and atom of life, so the name of God written in the heart reverses the process of the law of sin and death and frees you for the law of the Spirit of life which was in Christ Jesus[5] and in every other Christed one who has walked the earth by the grace of God.

Thus the righteousness of the law is fulfilled in those who walk not after the flesh, but after the Spirit as the spiral that proceeds from the threefold flame within the hidden chamber of the heart, qualifying the energies of the physical, emotional, mental, and etheric bodies with the frequencies of the Holy Spirit.

Once the name of God is written in the heart in fire, once the entire being and consciousness of man moves daily, hourly to live that law, to expand that fire, to glorify the name of God, then the light of the heart fills the being and consciousness of man until he becomes a blazing sun of righteousness.

Now understand, then, the sacred writing "To be carnally minded is death, but to be spiritually minded is life and peace."[6] It is a question of alchemy; it is a question of attention.

The alchemy of your attention is part of the gift of consciousness whereby through the faculties of concentration—even the seven chakras of the being of man—you focalize energy for a purpose. Whether that purpose is life or death must forever be the determination of your free will. Therefore, to be carnally minded is death, but to be spiritually minded is life and peace.

"Choose you this day whom ye will serve!"[7] thunders the voice of God. And the initiate standing before the mount of God-attainment must make the decision whether to the right or to the left of the Y. And the Y is you.

Which you will you become? You can be life or you can be death. You can fulfill the spirals of life through the outward flow of the spirals of the heart. You can fulfill the spirals of death by allowing all that is carnal to destroy the last vestiges of spirituality, until the flame within the hidden chamber of the heart is extinguished in the process that is known as the death of the soul.

I call to your attention, O chelas of the sacred fire, as we begin to impel the soul higher and higher in the walk with God, that to take this teaching and to employ it for the glorying in the Lord is to rise into the dominion of the Spirit and to be, with Christ, alive forevermore.[8] But to retain the intellect as the perversion of God consciousness, to enthrone the ego in place of the Christ, and to allow the human will and the human personality to replace the destiny of the soul and its individuality is to enter the negative spiral that cycles through the long night of carnality, which terminates in self-annihilation.

The carnal mind is enmity against God because it is not subject to the law of God.[9] Because the carnal mind exalts the human ego in place of the Divine Ego, it is impossible for it to merge with the positive spirals of the Christ consciousness. Those who remain in the consciousness of the flesh, which consciousness is governed by the carnal mind, therefore cannot please God, because while they remain in that consciousness, they cannot conform with his laws.

You who would come with me into a greater awareness of God, you who would have the gift of greater power, greater wisdom, and greater love, must understand that the filaments of mortal identity must be replaced with the filaments of immortal Selfhood.

In order for you to be successful in this course, then, I recommend that you go before the altar of God, before the threefold flame within, that you kneel before that altar within the tabernacle of your own hidden chamber of the heart and make your commitment to Almighty God to defend truth, honor, and righteousness in his name.

You cannot remain neutral. For to fail to render a decision, to fail to make a choice, is in itself a decision. It is a choice, although a not-choice. To be the not-self is still recorded in the Book of Life as a choice.

Once you have made the commitment to defend the light as the energy of the Christ, to expand the flame of God and to glorify his name, you will stand forth as the sun in its zenith and you will know a power and a flow, an expansion of your aura, and an increase in the fires of the heart, the likes of which you have not seen in many incarnations.

Therefore, in this release on the heart, I cannot fail to make known to you that the simple yet compelling act of unswerving devotion, of absolute conviction to be and to follow the Christ and to take both an active and a passive stand for Christ, is the sure way to transcend the former state of limitation and to live in the light of heaven and earth forevermore. Truly you have not begun to develop the aura, to expand the consciousness, until you have made this commitment and until the name of God is written in your heart.

Those who choose the left arm of the Y, to live for the carnal mind and the lusts of the flesh and the pride of the intellect, openly profess their amorality. And their code is the code of pleasure and their cult is the cult of death.

They pay allegiance to Satan while denying his identity, not realizing that they are the dupes of the archdeceivers of mankind who pretend that death is life and that life is death. By thus distorting reality, they fool those who pride themselves in making fools of the children of God. Indeed, "there is a way that seemeth right unto a man, but the end thereof are the ways of death."[10]

And so the prophet Malachi foretold the judgment and the death of the wicked: "For, behold, the day cometh that shall burn as an oven; and all the proud, yea, and all that do wickedly shall be stubble: and the day that cometh shall burn them up, saith the Lord of hosts, that it shall leave them neither root nor branch."[11] This is the end of those who misuse the energies of the heart and the light of the Christ.

Before imparting unto you, then, the secrets of the heart, before unlocking the crystal fires of the heart in those who take their vow before the living God, I must make clear that since the day when God bestowed free will upon man and woman, there have been those who have gone to the right and there have been those who have gone to the left. And the name of God is the key to their allegiance. For unto those who fear the name "I AM THAT I AM" shall the Sun of Righteousness arise with healing in his wings![12]

The rising of the Son of Righteousness is the rising of the Christ consciousness. And it is the Christed ones who shall tread down the wicked, and the spirals of the wicked shall be as ashes under the soles of the feet of the Christed ones until the prophecy is fulfilled "And I will put enmity between thee and the Woman and between thy seed and her seed; it shall bruise thy head, and thou shalt bruise his heel."[13]

You live in the end of an age when the judgment of God draweth nigh. All over the world, mankind are making choices. Little do they know that the choices they are making in little things and in great things will soon be tallied, and they will be weighed in the balances to see whether the majority of the soul is on the side of the light and the law or on the side of darkness and chaos.

To all who would continue in these intermediate studies of the human aura, I say, beware! For if you have failed to choose God and his Christ, it would be well for you to refrain from entering the path that leads to the holy of holies. For those who enter there without the wedding garment that marks the surrender of the soul to the Cosmic Virgin will be consumed by the fires of God.[14]

Choose you this day whom ye will serve. And having chosen aright, come with me as we proceed to release, one by one, certain techniques for the expansion, the control, and the empowering of the aura essential for Christed man and Christed woman to enter the golden age of Aquarius.

I await the sounding of your commitment upon

the sounding board of life. And when it is written in the book of record by the recording angels, I will come to you and make my presence known to you as the Tibetan Master come again to deliver the word of God to the age.

I am committed to your God-reality.

3 THE INTERLACED TRIANGLES

Let us enter into the consciousness of the heart. "Draw nigh to me, and I will draw nigh to you"[1] are the words of the Lord spoken within the soul of the Apostle James as the key to the union of God and man through the blessed mediator, the Christ Self. This union has been depicted in the symbol of the six-pointed star—the interlaced triangles that reveal the energies of man ascending and the energies of God descending.

The point at which these energies meet is in the center of the threefold flame of life, sealed within the hidden chamber of the heart. Let it be realized that the threefold flame itself is the flaming consciousness of the Christ, the only begotten of the Father, that is anchored within every individualization of the Father-Mother God, every son and daughter of the flame.

As you know, all energy has frequency, or vibratory rate, but you must understand that the frequencies of man's energies are not the same as the frequencies of God's energy. For the Lord God has said, "My thoughts are not your thoughts; neither are your ways my ways."[2]

In order for God and man to be one on earth even as the soul of man is one with the Spirit of God in heaven, the Christ comes forth to mediate the frequencies of Matter and of Spirit. The perfect blending of the energies of God and man are realized, then, through the Christ Self of the individual or through masters ascended or unascended who have attained the harmony of the Christ mind.

When Paul said, "Let this mind be in you which was also in Christ Jesus,"[3] he spoke of the Christ Self and he directed the disciples of the Lord to let the Christ Self be within their hearts the mediator of perfection. The mind of which Paul spoke has been referred to as the higher mental body. The terms "higher mental body" and "Christ Self" are synonymous, and they refer to the force or presence of the Christos—even to the Logos who becomes the Word incarnate to every son and daughter who recognizes his joint-heirship with the Christ.[4]

To fulfill, then, the first half of the equation "Draw nigh to me, and I will draw nigh to you," mankind must raise the energies of consciousness to the level of the heart chakra through meditation on love, through the application of wisdom, and through the garnering of God's energy as the will to be. As you center your attention more and more upon the heart through the visualizations, precious indeed, imparted to you by our brother Lanello,[5] you magnetize the energies of the four lower bodies day by day to the heart center, thus according the Christ the preeminence and the dominion of your soul awareness.

The magnet that you create within the heart chakra is the ascending triangle. And the more you meditate upon this triangle superimposed upon the heart chakra, the more it becomes the reality of the dimensions of the Sacred Trinity, embodied in the threefold flame sealed in the hidden chamber of the heart.*

As surely as the call compels the answer, so the presence of this forcefield, of this triangle, combined with the letters of living flame "I AM THAT I AM," will draw the descending triangle of God's consciousness into the heart chakra. And this merging of Creator and creation through the intercession of the Christ Self is the foundation of our exercise whereby the aura of man becomes the aura of God.

In God's holy name, O mankind, I say, awake from the sleep of the ages! In God's holy name, I say, do you not understand that you can become only that which you already are?

*See pages 138–145.

If you would expand your aura as the forcefield of consciousness, you must possess the matrix within the heart chakra for that expansion. The matrix is the six-pointed star centered in the heart chakra superimposed with the name of God "I AM THAT I AM." Now the second half of the equation is fulfilled as the Lord God himself declares, "I will draw nigh to you."

Down through the ages, many have said: "Why do I need Jesus or Buddha or Confucius or the Virgin Mary to get to God? I will go straight to God. I will bypass all others." And thus in their ignorance, mankind have displaced the Christed ones. Understand, then, that the law of intercession by the Christ is scientific and mathematical. It is based on the inner geometry of the interlaced triangles and on the science of the frequencies of material and spiritual energies.

In those periods of history when mankind have ignored the fact that the Christ light has ignited the flame within the hidden chamber of the heart as the gift of life and consciousness to *every* soul,[6] darkness has covered the land. When mankind have seen through a glass darkly and have not beheld the Lord face to face as the Christ within themselves,[7] the Divine Presence has sent intermediaries—avatars, teachers, and prophets—who have exemplified the Christ light personified as the Christ Self of each and every one.

Until mankind come to know the Christ as the inner self, they may, according to cosmic law, appeal to the saints and holy ones both on earth and in heaven who, as Christed beings, intercede for them that they might merge their energies with the beloved I AM Presence.

By and by, as the merging is reinforced by faith, by hope, by works of charity, one by one the children of God come to know the Christ Self within as their own individualized mediator, their own Christ consciousness. And as this truth is realized, their auras become the aura of God; and the halo of the saints, as the crown of glory, rests upon them as the grace of the Holy Spirit.

The aura of man marks the circumference of his awareness of God. It is a forcefield in Matter which God has created as an extension of himself—of his own God Self-awareness. The size of the aura is directly related to the individual's mastery of the frequencies of God's energies within the chakras—the key chakras being the seven most commonly referred to by Buddhists and Hindus as the wheels of life and death.*

As the Christ becomes the light of the world of each chakra, so the energies of God and man meet in that chakra. And in this alchemical union—the balance of the triangles of Alpha and Omega and the converging of the energies of God and man—there is precipitated the law of perfection as the flame of living truth.

---

*See pages 136–38.

The aura of man is like a giant balloon, and this balloon is filled with neither oxygen nor helium, but with the flow of energy that is released from the seven chakras. The greater the energy that is released, the greater the size of the balloon. The greater the size of the balloon, the more God can release his consciousness into the planes of Mater. For the balloon is the coordinate in time and space of the great causal body of the Father-Mother God.

Each of the chakras has a special function, and we shall consider these functions step by step. Each of the wheellike vortices that comprise the chakras has, according to the teachings of the masters of the Himalayas, a certain frequency that is marked by a number of petals, so-called. These petals determine the flow of the energies of God to man, and they govern certain aspects of God's consciousness, commonly called virtues, which may be amplified within the chakras.

The chakras that are presently operative in the being of man are anchored in the lower etheric body, and their positions conform to the organs in the physical body that receive the flow of vitality from the higher bodies necessary to its functioning. These chakras are located at the base of the spine, midway between the base of the spine and the navel, over the navel, over the heart, at the throat, on the brow, and at the crown.

The placement of these chakras to correspond with nerve centers in the physical body was adjusted during the epoch of the Fall of Man. There remains, however, in the higher etheric body the line of the seven chakras as forcefields for the seven rays. And these are for the distribution in the four lower bodies of the frequencies of the seven Elohim, known as the seven Spirits of God.

At this point in our dissertation, we are concerned with the interaction and the flow of the energies of the heart chakra as these are divided into the twelve petals, frequencies or aspects, of the Christ consciousness. In order for mankind to attain the Christ consciousness, it is necessary for them to balance the threefold flame within the hidden chamber of the heart so that that flame might be realized by the power of the four (four times the three plumes of the threefold flame equals twelve)—marking the four sides of the temple of being.

Students of cosmic law therefore pursue the externalization of the twelve sacred virtues in order to attain the mastery of the heart chakra, for they know that the heart as the seat of Christ-authority is the key to mastery in all planes—in all chakras.

As you meditate upon the fires of the heart, I ask you to chant the name of God "I AM THAT I AM." Then call in the name of the Christ for the following God-qualities to be focused in the geometry of the twelve according to the distribution of frequencies in this lotus of twelve petals: God-power, God-love, and God-mastery; God-control, God-obedience, and God-wisdom; God-harmony, God-gratitude, and God-justice; God-reality, God-vision, and God-victory. You may also alternate your chant of the sacred name with the AUM, or OM.*

These chants, combined with the fervent application to your God Presence to focus these frequencies within the heart, will bring balance to both your inner and your outer being and restore the equilibrium of the Christ flame that is so often lost in the wild and the welter that marks your "modern" civilization.

So now, my beloved in Christ,
My gift of love, a cup of light,
A cup of illumination rare,
I bring to you as holy prayer.
It is *my* prayer that you become
The fullness of his glory.
It is *God's* prayer
That his energy we share.
So, my beloved,
Let it be *your* prayer
That Almighty God will be there
As virtue flowing, as light all-knowing
In the center and the circumference
Of the sacred center,
Sacred fire of the heart.

I am in the Buddha the turning of the wheel of the law.

*See pages 146–48.

CROWN CHAKRA
Sahasrāra

THIRD-EYE CHAKRA
Ājñā

THROAT CHAKRA
Vishuddha

HEART CHAKRA
Anāhata

HIDDEN CHAMBER
OF THE HEART
Ānanda-Kanda

SOLAR-PLEXUS CHAKRA
Maṇipūra

SEAT-OF-THE-SOUL CHAKRA
Svādhishṭhāna

BASE-OF-THE-SPINE CHAKRA
Mūlādhāra

THE SEVEN CENTERS OF GOD-AWARENESS. The seven centers in your being are for the release of God's energy. God's awareness of himself as love is anchored in your heart chakra. God's awareness of himself as power is anchored in your throat chakra, in the authority of the Word. God's awareness of himself as vision is anchored in your third-eye chakra. God's awareness of himself as wisdom is anchored in your crown chakra. God's awareness of himself as peace is in the solar-plexus chakra. God's awareness of himself as freedom is in the seat-of-the-soul chakra. And God's awareness of himself as purity is in the base-of-the-spine chakra.

These seven centers are seven planes of consciousness. We experience God differently in different frequencies. We experience God as love in the heart and as our communication of love. We experience him as law and authority in the spoken Word and in its power. We experience him as vision, as seeing, as precipitation, as science and truth in the third eye. This experiencing of God enables us to become God, to know God, to be filled with God, and finally to put on totally the consciousness of God in the ritual of the ascension.

We cannot inherit immortality as mortals. The mortal must put off its mortality to become immortality. The mortal itself cannot be immortalized. It must be replaced. This is why Paul said that this corruptible must *put on* incorruption, that this mortal must *put on* immortality. And yet Paul said that flesh and blood cannot inherit the kingdom of God.

(continued)

What, then, is worthy to inherit God? Only God is worthy of God. Unless we sense ourselves in and as God, we will not consider ourselves to be worthy of God. It is not our four lower bodies that can contain infinity. They are finite cups holding a portion of infinity while we move in time and space. But the centers of God-awareness are coordinates of infinity actually anchored in our body consciousness. Therefore, that which inherits immortal life is the immortal flow of God that we make our own through the chakras. —ECP

THE HEART CHAKRA. The most important chakra is the twelve-petaled heart chakra. From the heart chakra, the energy of life is distributed to the other six major chakras and to the five minor chakras (of the secret rays), thence to all the cells and nerve centers in the four lower bodies. The heart is where the pink fires of love burn brightly. Your heart is a focus of the Great Central Sun. God made it so. When you keep the heart in the vibration of Christ's love in compassion for all life, you discover all life as one. For out of the heart are the issues of all life that lead to the One Source. —ECP

"The magnet that you create within the heart chakra is the ascending triangle. And the more you meditate upon this triangle superimposed upon the heart chakra, the more it becomes the reality of the dimensions of the Sacred Trinity, embodied in the threefold flame sealed in the hidden chamber of the heart.

"As surely as the call compels the answer, so the

(continued)

pink

presence of this forcefield, of this triangle, combined with the letters of living flame 'I AM THAT I AM' will draw the descending triangle of God's consciousness into the heart chakra. And the merging of Creator and creation through the intercession of the Christ Self is the foundation of our exercise whereby the aura of man becomes the aura of God."   —DJWAL KUL

THE HIDDEN CHAMBER OF THE HEART. Your threefold flame of life is sealed in the eight-petaled chakra called the hidden, or secret, chamber of your heart. The threefold flame, or "divine spark," makes your heart a replica of the heart of God. It is literally a spark of sacred fire from God's own heart. The threefold flame is your soul's point of contact with the Supreme Source of all life. It is your potential to become the fullness of all that your Real Self is.

The threefold flame has three "plumes" that embody the three primary attributes of God. The blue plume (on your left) embodies God's power. The yellow plume (in the center) embodies God's wisdom, and the pink plume (on your right) embodies God's love. By accessing the power, wisdom, and love of the Godhead anchored in your threefold flame, you can fulfill your reason for being.

The white-fire core out of which the flame springs forth is the wholeness of the Father-Mother God, the Alpha and Omega, which manifest the beginning and the ending of all cycles of your being.

peach

THE THREEFOLD FLAME. "Your heart is indeed one of the choicest gifts of God. Within it there is a central chamber surrounded by a forcefield of such light and protection that we call it a 'cosmic interval.' It is a chamber separated from Matter and no probing could ever discover it. It occupies simultaneously not only the third and fourth dimensions but also other dimensions unknown to man.

"This central chamber, called the altar of the heart, is thus the connecting point of the mighty silver cord of light that descends from your God Presence to sustain the beating of your physical heart, giving you life, purpose, and cosmic integration.

"I urge all men to treasure this point of contact that they have with Life by giving conscious recognition to it. You do not need to understand by sophisticated language or scientific postulation the how, why, and wherefore of this activity.

"Be content to know that God is there and that within you there is a point of contact with the Divine, a spark of fire from the Creator's own heart called the threefold flame of life. There it burns as the triune essence of Love, Wisdom, and Power.

"Each acknowledgment paid daily to the flame within your heart will amplify the power and illumination of Love within your being. Each such attention will produce a new sense of dimension for you, if not outwardly apparent then subconsciously manifest within the folds of your inner thoughts.   (continued)

"Neglect not, then, your heart as the altar of God. Neglect it not as the sun of your manifest being. Draw from God the power of Love and amplify it within your heart. Then send it out into the world at large as the bulwark of that which shall overcome the darkness of the planet, saying:

I AM the Light of the Heart
Shining in the darkness of being
And changing all into the golden treasury
Of the Mind of Christ.

I AM projecting my love
Out into the world
To erase all errors
And to break down all barriers.

I AM the power of infinite Love,
Amplifying Itself
Until it is victorious,
World without end!

"With this gift of infinite freedom from God's own heart I make you a never-ending promise to assist you to find your immortal freedom as you determine never to give up and never to turn back. Remember that as long as you face the Light, the shadows are always behind. And the Light is there, too, to transmute them all.

"Keep your gaze toward 'the City' and be not over-come of evil but overcome evil with Good."

—SAINT GERMAIN

BALANCE THE THREEFOLD FLAME IN ME!

In the name of the beloved mighty victorious Presence of God, I AM in me, and my very own beloved Holy Christ Self, I am calling to the heart of the Saviour Jesus Christ and the servant-sons of God and legions of Light who are with him in heaven and to the World Mother to balance, blaze, and expand the threefold flame burning within the secret chamber of my heart until I AM manifesting all of thee and naught of the human remains.

Take complete dominion and control over my four lower bodies and raise me and all life by the power of the three-times-three into the glorious resurrection and ascension in the light! In the name of the Father, the Mother, the Son, and the Holy Spirit, I decree!

> Balance the threefold flame in me! (three times)
>   Beloved I AM!
> Balance the threefold flame in me! (three times)
>   Take thy command!
> Balance the threefold flame in me! (three times)
>   Magnify it each hour!
> Balance the threefold flame in me! (three times)
>   Love, wisdom, and power!

And in full faith.... (see page 148).

Note: Repeat stanza four times, using the verbs *blaze, expand,* and *intensify* in place of *balance* the second, third, and fourth times.

DJWAL KUL, COME!

In the name of the beloved mighty victorious Presence of God, I AM in me, my very own beloved Holy Christ Self and Holy Christ Selves of all mankind, I am calling to the heart of the Saviour Jesus Christ and the servant-sons of God and legions of Light who are with him in heaven—beloved Djwal Kul and the World Mother:

> Djwal Kul, come!
> In the center of the One,
> Anchor now thy radiant sun,
> Magnet of the threefold flame,
> Expand God's aura in God's name!
>
> Djwal Kul, come!
> Threefold fountain, fill my heart;
> Let thy angel now impart
> The name of God—I AM THAT I AM,
> I AM THAT I AM, I AM THAT I AM,
>   I AM THAT I AM!
>
> Djwal Kul, come!
> Flame of gold, pink, blue, and white,
> Seal thy victory star of light;
> Renew my vows to God's own name;
> Come, O Christ, in me now reign!
>
> Djwal Kul, come!
> Expand the fire of the Sun;
> Alpha 'n Omega, make us one,

Seal my energies in Christ,
Raise my energies in light!

Djwal Kul, come!
Align my consciousness with thee,
Make us one, O make me free!
Seal my heart and hand in thine,
In God's mind I AM divine!

Djwal Kul, come!
Blaze the action of the Whole,
With light of victory fill my soul;
Return me to the Flaming One,
I AM begotten of the Son!

Coda: I AM God-power, I AM God-love,
I AM THAT I AM, I AM THAT I AM,
I AM THAT I AM!
I AM God-mastery and God-control,
I AM THAT I AM—
AUM (chant)
I AM THAT I AM—
AUM (chant)

I AM God-obedience now,
To thy law I vow,
I AM THAT I AM, I AM THAT I AM,
I AM THAT I AM!

God-wisdom flame I AM,
God-wisdom flame I AM,
God-wisdom flame I AM!

(continued)

AUM—God-har-mo-ny (chant)
AUM—God-har-mo-ny (chant)
AUM—God-har-mo-ny! (chant)

God-gratitude, God-gratitude, God-gratitude!
I AM God-justice in full view,
I AM God-justice in full view,
I AM God-justice in full view!

God-re-al-i-ty! (chant)
I AM God-vision, God-victory won,
I AM God-vision, God-victory won,
I AM God-vision, God-victory won!

And in full faith I consciously accept this manifest, manifest, manifest! (three times) right here and now with full power, eternally sustained, all-powerfully active, ever expanding, and world enfolding until all are wholly ascended in the Light and free!

Beloved I AM! Beloved I AM! Beloved I AM!

Note: This meditation is to be used with the instruction given by Djwal Kul in chapter 3.

4 THE CHALLENGE OF THE MIND

If you are in earnest in your determination to expand the aura, it is time that you challenge the carnal mind even as Jesus challenged the Pharisees who derided the Christ, saying: "Ye are they which justify yourselves before men; but God knoweth your hearts: for that which is highly esteemed among men is abomination in the sight of God."[1]

The carnal mind deviously employs the human intellect, the human emotions, and the human will to justify itself before mankind; and thereby it gains the esteem of the world. And thereby there is formed the personality that is popular with the people.

The carnal mind is the manipulator of the mass energies of the mass consciousness. Since the carnal mind is in control of the world, the flesh, and the devil, Jesus said to the children of light, "Make to yourselves friends of the mammon of unrighteousness, that when ye fail they may receive you into everlasting habitations."[2] Thus the Lord showed the initiates of the sacred fire that there was a time to challenge the carnal mind and a time to be wise in the ways of the world.

I come to distinguish these precepts of the law of the Father and of the grace of the Son, that you might understand your place in society. For the fire which you bear is not of this world, yet the frame that you wear is of the "earth, earthy."[3]

When to agree with the adversary and when to disagree with the adversary, then, is a matter that must be settled once and for all. For to antagonize the carnal mind is most dangerous to our cause. To poke the sleeping serpent with a stick is to invite trouble.

You must understand that in many among mankind, the innocence of the soul predominates over the pride and the ambition of the ego; for in many, the ego has not been awakened as a deleterious force. The carnal mind has not been aroused, and therefore it has not overtaken the Christ Child cradled within the heart.

These are the sheep of the Good Shepherd that are grazing upon the hillsides of the world waiting for the voice of the Son of God. Meek and mild are they, and without guile. They do not respond to the temptations of the tempter; for they are moved and impelled by the energies of the Holy Spirit, the momentum of the soul to move Godward.

Although their consciousness of God and Christ is the simple message of salvation in the Lord, yet they remain firm in their conviction of the promised one. The level of their awareness does not compel the search for the understanding of the complexities of the law.

We do not challenge their belief. We remand their souls to the cloudlike forcefields of the Holy Spirit, which seal them in the love of God until that age when they shall find themselves in another fold of the Creator's consciousness, prepared to receive the strong meat of the Word.[4]

Take care, O chelas of the masters, as you walk among the flocks of the Good Shepherd, that you do not arouse the carnal mind that remains dormant in these blessed ones—whether by direct confrontation, by challenging their seemingly simplistic view of life, or by superimposing upon their hearts and minds grids and forcefields of God's consciousness that will prematurely rend the veils of innocence, causing them much grief, unnecessary guilt, and even despondency.

With these, the precepts and the parables of the Christ will form a common meeting ground of heavenly love abiding on earth, sealing the bonds of brotherhood and allowing for the free expression of the faith of the Galilean Master. For freedom of religion is a tenet of the law and of the Lord that allows for agreement in disagreement, whereby the children of God agree to disagree in love, in respect, and in honor for the many rays of the Son consciousness that lead to the one path of the ineffable light.

To impose the teachings of the ascended masters upon those who are unprepared to receive them because the Christ is yet a babe and the carnal mind doth sleep can truly be an imposition whereby carnal energies are stirred and the child is overpowered by the strong meat when the milk of the Word would suffice. Take care, then, that you do not preempt the cycles of the Creator when dealing with the sheep of the many folds of God's heart.

And realize that an encounter with anyone is always an exercise in the psychology of the Christ as well as in the psychology of the carnal mind. It is always an opportunity to balance these two factors of identity so as to produce the greatest soul advancement and the greatest blessing to all.

When you encounter those such as the covetous Pharisees, the hypocrites, and the children of this world, you find that the carnal mind is not only awakened, but that it has total command of the consciousness. And it is absolutely necessary to deal with that mind and its energies at its own level.

In this instance, it is mandatory that in the devotee the fire of the heart remain sealed in an ovoid, and that in all relationships with the earth-minded, the devotee allow that aspect of himself which equates with the form and the form consciousness of the "earth, earthy" to predominate. Thus the carnal-minded may entertain the spirits of the flaming ones without reacting or overreacting to the light that is encased within the form, and thus you can make your way in this world and make a mark for the Lord free of the encumbrances of the carnal mind.

It is not necessary to make those whose consciousness is dominated by the carnal mind uncomfortable in your presence by spouting platitudes and displaying holy virtue or condemning amorality. This is but to arouse the antagonism of the world; and to put it bluntly, it is no way to win friends and influence people for the light.

When there are so many souls receptive to the teaching and the inner fires of the heart, why bring upon the masters, our emissaries, and our organization a holocaust of controversy from those who are already committed to the way of the lesser self?

And so to agree with thine adversary quickly while thou art in the way with him[5] can also be a means of learning the mastery of time and space in the cycles of Mater. And you may learn the lesson of faithfulness in the responsibilities of the world whereby, working among the mammon of unrighteousness which is built in to the very structure of civilization itself, you may by and by learn the mastery of the coils of the Spirit and therefore have committed to your trust the true riches because you have been faithful in the "unrighteous mammon."

There comes a time in the life of every disciple when the injunction "Resist the devil, and he will flee from you!"[6] must be obeyed. In that moment there is no substitute for the fierce rebuke of the Christ "Get thee behind me, Satan!"[7]

While the evolving soul consciousness is to be forgiven seventy times seven,[8] the serpentine mind that would override the innocence of the soul must be firmly put in its place and kept there. Above all, take care that you do not destroy "these little ones"[9] while you are destroying the carnal mind.

Now then, if you are still perplexed concerning what may seem to be a double standard of the presentation of the law and the promulgation of the prophecies of the prophets, I will let you ponder my words and juggle for a bit the ball-like precepts, variegated in hue, with which the fingers of the mind must become familiar if you are to advance in the higher studies of the human aura.

For you see, as you rise in the dimensions of the Christ consciousness, you will begin to realize that every teaching of the law and every parable of the

Christ gains new meaning as you approach closer and closer to the center of the heart.

Let us take, then, as an example of this spiritual phenomenon the statement of the Lord "The law and the prophets were until John [meaning John the Baptist]; since that time the kingdom of God is preached, and every man presseth into it."[10] Do you see that this is exactly what I am talking about?

In a certain dimension of consciousness for a cycle of two thousand years, the law and the prophets as these are expressed in the Old Testament predominated as the rod of understanding—the lexicon of learning. But with the coming of John the Baptist, who prepared the way for the Christ, suddenly the kingdom of God—"behold, the kingdom of God is within you"[11]—is preached, and every man, not the privileged few, presses into this kingdom that is within.

I would also speak of the kingdom of God that is within you in reference to the heart chakra. For the kingdom of God that must come into manifestation in the planes of Mater begins with (1) the three-fold flame within the hidden chamber of the heart, (2) the twelve petals, or frequencies, of God's consciousness that blossom from the stem of the heart chakra, (3) the interlaced triangles that make up the six-pointed star, and (4) the name of God "I AM THAT I AM" written in the heart.

Specifically the soul's awakening to the consciousness of the kingdom begins in the hidden
chamber of the heart. I would speak of this chamber
as the house of the Lord of which David spoke when
he said, "Surely goodness and mercy shall follow me
all the days of my life: and I will dwell in the house
of the Lord for ever."[12]

David knew his Lord as the hidden man of the
heart dwelling in the hidden chamber of the heart.
When David said, "The Lord is my shepherd; I shall
not want,"[13] he spoke of his guru, his own Christ
Self, upon whose law he meditated day and night.

Throughout all time, the sons and daughters of
God who have come into the initiations of hierarchy
have been received in sacred audience in the hidden
chamber of the heart by the hidden man of the heart.
To Hindus and Buddhists, this hidden chamber is
the secondary heart chakra, an eight-petaled lotus
that is identified within the twelve-petaled heart
chakra.

It is the place where the chela contacts the guru.
It is the place where the laws of cosmos are written
in the inward parts of man, the laws handed down
through the world's religions—the precepts of the
Vedas and Upanishads, the Avesta, the Tao Te
Ching, the Dhammapada and Eightfold Path of
the Buddha, the Torah and the Ten Commandments,
the Sermon on the Mount, and the Koran.

For the law is inscribed upon the inner walls of the hidden chamber of the heart. Here the psalmist delighted in the law of the Lord.[14] Here he visualized, like his counterpart in the East, the sea of nectar, the island of gems, fragrant flowers, trees symbolizing the branches of spiritual teaching bearing the fruit of the Spirit. Here the Eastern devotee visualizes the platform and the throne constructed of fiery jewels.

Here on the throne ensconced in lotus flame is the guru, the Christ Self, who receives the soul of the initiate. Here the psalmist also walked. Here he became like the tree of life planted by the rivers of water bringing forth the fruit, the flow of the energies of the heart chakra, in season and in cycle.[15]

This chamber is the sanctuary of meditation, the place to which the souls of the lightbearers withdraw. And here in this chamber we shall pursue the Master Presence, that each disciple of the Christ might come to know him as he is.[16]

Thus God knoweth your hearts. And the pure in heart see God[17] within the chamber of the heart, whereas those who dwell in outer darkness, esteemed among men, are an abomination in his sight.

We shall continue our discourse to those who would become just stewards of the heart.

I am your initiator in the flame.

5 THE HIDDEN CHAMBER OF THE HEART

To enter into the garden of the heart is to enter a chamber that exists in the mind of God which can come into being as the kingdom of God within you through meditation and through visualization. The Psalms were written as praises to the Lord whom David knew as he entered this chamber. And so I bid you enter also.

This chamber is the place where the planes of Mater are consecrated by the fires of the heart to the very point of perfection. Thus the Eastern devotee sees the earth transformed into jewellike crystals. Emeralds, diamonds, rubies compose the island in the midst of the nectar sea; and the essence of the Spirit Most Holy is the fragrance from flowering trees. You should also use your imagination to create this royal scene befitting your own Christ Self and your ascended-master guru.

That you might attain the Christ consciousness of the seven rays, I give to you the exercise of visualizing each of the seven chohans (lords) of the rays.[1] And thus we will proceed step by step to expand the aura according to the masterful consciousness of these ascended-master gurus. The eight petals of the secondary heart chamber symbolize the mastery of the seven rays through the flame of the Christ (called the threefold flame) and the integration of that mastery in the eighth ray.

In all precipitation it is well to be specific. Therefore, draw a specific outline in your mind of this bejeweled island suspended in a glistening sea. Then see yourself walking from the shores of the sea through the tropical trees and vegetation to the center and highest promontory of the island.

Tropical birds and flowers of delicate and brilliant colors make the scene more vivid. And by and by you hear the songs of the birds as they sing the song celestial and key the soul to the frequencies of that plane where the ascending triangle of Mater meets the descending triangle of Spirit.

When you come to the center of your island in the sun, visualize specifically the platform and the throne that are consecrated for the image and the sacred presence of the master. You may wish to examine historical works showing the most beautiful thrones that have been built for the kings and queens of this world.

Select a design that is richly carved, gold leafed, and inlaid with precious and semiprecious stones, and visualize upon it a velvet cushion. There will be a cushion for each of the colors of the seven rays upon which the chohans will sit on the seven days of the week and receive you in the name of the Christ.

As you contemplate the blue-skyey dome and this place prepared to receive the Lord, give the following invocation for the integration of your soul with the consciousness of the Christ and its perfect outpicturing in the hidden chamber of the heart:

> Almighty God, Maker of heaven and earth,
> How bountiful are thy blessings!
> How beautiful are thy flowings,
> Immortal soul-knowings!
> I acknowledge thee,
> O thou Creator of me!
> I acknowledge thy law
> And the stars in the firmament
> As the presence of the Christ
> Who inhabits the cosmos,
> As the boundaries of thy habitation
> Here in the planes of *Mater*ialization
> That reach like the rising and the falling
> Of the waves of the sea calling
> For the planes of the Spirit,
> The reaches of infinity.

O Lord my God,
Come and talk and walk with me
In this my paradise garden,
My island in the sea!
Come, O Lord, in the cool of the day.
Come! For I have prepared the way,
And my offering is the sacrifice of the lesser self
Upon the altar of the heart.
My offering is the twelve virtues—
Oh, let the Christ now impart!
I kneel before the altar,
I kneel before thy throne.
My soul does long for unity,
The wisdom to atone.

O come, thou Divine Master,
The chohan of my life!
Come, O Lord,
In the form of El Morya,
Of Paul the Venetian and of Lanto.
Come, O Lord of heaven,
To consecrate my earth and my heaven.
Come with the truth,
With the freedom,
With the potential and the leaven.
Come, Serapis Bey, Hilarion!
Come, Nada and Saint Germain!
For I am not alone in the garden,

But all one with thee in thy name.
I AM THAT I AM, I AM THAT I AM,
   I AM THAT I AM—
Threefold action of threefold flame of threefold law.
So the name of God
Releases now the holy awe.

I come before thy presence, Lord.
I see thee in thy essence, Lord.
I am thy omnipresence, Lord.
O holy one of God,
Come now be the Christ of me
As the fulfilling of the law
Of the Personal Personality.
For in that flame and by thy name,
Ascended-master gurus do proclaim
That in the person of the Son of God,
The Christ, the Christed Self of all,
Becomes the mentor and the guide
And ultimately the flame
Of purest son and daughter pressed inside
The hidden chamber of the heart.

Teach me, O chohan of my life,
How to be thyself,
How to walk the earth
As heart and head and hand
Responding to thy will at thy command.
Teach me, O chohan of my love,

How to feel the flow,
How to give thy succor
To all hearts below.
Teach me now, O chohan of the law,
To fulfill the promise of the seven rays
And to be forevermore
Prism'd awareness of thy grace.

O just stewards of the heart, understand how your aura can be enflamed with the presence of your Lord. And give this meditation as you renew your visualization of the chohans of the seven rays on the days of the week consecrated to those rays[2] by the impartations of Helios and Vesta, Father-Mother Presence of Life in the heart of this solar system where you make your home.

Thus on Monday receive blessed Paul the Venetian and be tutored in the intuition and the mandates of love as he imparts creative fires and creativity of soul desire seated in the throne of the heart.

On Tuesday let your Christ Self lead you to the altar where you kneel before Lord Morya El, where you commune in silent meditation with the will of the flame and imbibe the Personal Personality of the one who has consecrated his mind as the diamond shining mind of God. And as you look upon his face, you see the twinkle of mirth that is needed upon earth. You hear the strains of "Panis Angelicus," and you know that your soul is fed the holy bread of angels. You drink the communion cup, and you vow obedience to the will of God.

On Wednesday as you contemplate the action of the emerald ray with joy and anticipation, you await the coming of Hilarion, who occupies the throne as the master philosopher, the master scientist. And from his forehead to your own, as the two of you are alone in Christ, there is a transfer of the divine gnosis; and the geometry of Mater integrating spirals of Spirit becomes clear.

On Thursday, the queen of the chohans, the Lady Master Nada, who practices law before the bar of heaven, comes to portray the law of justice and the noble way of ministration and service. In her aura is the music of those blessed words "Inasmuch as ye have done it unto one of the least of these my brethren, ye have done it unto me."[3] And in the presence of the lady chohan, you perceive the wonder of the feminine ray in the mastery of the seven rays. All is clear: You live to serve forevermore—forevermore in the service of the Lord.

On Friday you hail Serapis Bey, Lord of Ascension's Flame. Marching to the sound of victory, of trumpets sounding the sound of your natal day, of the soul's rebirth—being born anew first in Mater and then in the glorious array of the ascension flame —you are born into Spirit for eternity.

On Saturday, which is the sabbath of the seventh ray, you greet the Master of the Aquarian age: "Saint Germain, friend of old, I am honored at thy presence here! So may I know the cosmic honor flame that is entwined with strands of gold and violet as elementals weave a garland of praise to the Knight Commander of my heart." And you tarry before the alchemist of the Spirit who has come to teach you the science of the amethyst ray and the ritual of grace that will be the law for the next two thousand years.

On Sunday you rise to greet the dawn of illumination through Lord Lanto, who holds in his hands the book of the law of life for your soul—for the soul of a planet and a universe. His wisdom is a scroll that never ends; 'tis a scroll whereby you make amends. And in the profound understanding of the Lord of the Second Ray, lo, your sins are washed away!

Through the week with the seven chohans of the rays is a way of life for Brothers of the Golden Robe, for Sisters of the Wisdom Flame, who come to receive the instruction that is given in the etheric retreat of the Tibetan Master. For many centuries now, I have sponsored the tutoring of souls who have desired to enter in to a direct relationship with one or more masters of the hierarchy of the Great White Brotherhood.

We begin our course with meditations for self-purification. And for those who have for several lifetimes practiced the way of silence, I come to break the silence with a shout of acclamation, with that joyful noise that is the true fiat of the Word!

And thus the decrees[4] of the devotees ring forth not as a murmuring or as a mumbling, but with the determined shout of warriors bold, of sons and daughters of God rejoicing in the fold! And the fold is a new level of awareness where the chela meets the master face to face and the energies of meditation become the fullness of the expression of the Christ mind, the Christ heart, and the Christ soul.

You who would become the Christ, you who would kneel at his feet, be prepared then to roar as lions over the hillsides of the world—not as the devil seeking whom he may devour,[5] but as king and queen, as lion and lioness going forth to claim dominion in the kingdom of God that is within.

If you would attain and retain the consciousness of the chohans, you must then be willing to exercise the throat chakra whereby you take the energies garnered in the chamber of the heart, the fruits of the Spirit and the fragrance of the Spirit, and allow these gifts of the chohans to mesh in Mater through the peaceful thrust and the all-commanding power of the fiats of the Word.

Speak boldly, plainly—slow or swiftly as you will. Speak in rhythm. Speak in love. Speak in fervor and with zeal. But come before the presence of the chohans prepared to voice the soundless sound and to direct atoms and molecules of being by the authority and the grace of the law.

Hence, as you develop the heart chakra and become a just steward of the heart, you must learn to release the resources of the Spirit through the spoken Word and to give decrees in time and space that are for the transmutation of that place into the dominion and the domain of the kingdom of God.

I am leading you gently yet firmly by the hand to that Promised Land where ascended masters yet walk and talk with unascended man. Come with me! Hold my hand!

6 THE SPECTRUM OF GOD'S CONSCIOUSNESS

As you advance in the knowledge of the law and make progress on the path of self-mastery, you come into the awareness of the love of the Father-Mother God that is fulfilled in the law which is proclaimed by the Son.

To love the law of God is to be aflame with the awareness of that law as it moves from the Impersonal Impersonality of the Godhead to identification with the Impersonal Personality of the sons and daughters of God. For these, while retaining the impersonal aspects of the Creator, do modify, by the flame of the Christ, those energies of the law which become in Matter as in Spirit the manifest personality of the Divine One.

And so we acknowledge the preceptors of mankind as beings who remain impersonal by the very fact of the remoteness of the Spirit to the things of this world. Yet they come forth as divine personalities, ascended-master teachers, as the shining ones who personify some facet of the jeweled splendor of his will, his mind, and his compassion.

Those who seek to depersonalize all aspects of being, who count themselves sophisticated in their rejection of the "personality" of our messengers, both ascended and unascended, must realize that God is both the formed and the unformed. He is the Spirit that cannot be contained in form and yet who dwells immortally in form as the intelligent, free-flowing sacred fire that burns upon the altar of the heart of every son and daughter of God.

I speak to you who take pride in refraining from idolatry and the "superstitions" of the idolatrous generation: Take care that in your categorical rejection of the personality of God in the saints and ascended beings of all ages, you do not raise up in its place the human personality of the lower self.

How often the intelligentsia, so-called, counting themselves to be above such childishness, have rejected the sacredness of the personality of God as it manifests above in the heavenly hosts and below in devotees, pilgrims, and disciples the world around. The elite who follow the cult of the serpent are the ones who worship the Moloch of human greed. Operating as they do outside the body of God, they

THE FOUR ASPECTS OF THE GODHEAD. "From the least to the greatest minds of earth, all need the benefit of lasting attunement with the universal consciousness of God . . . .

"Using the tremendous outgoing energy of being, men have diligently imagined and imaged forth the nature of God, while only the few have apprehended the truth that God is consciousness, and as consciousness he is life, intelligence, will, and love manifest in a rich variety of dimensions and attributes.

"Now I tell you, God is a benign Impersonal Personality, a Personal Impersonality, a Personal Personality, and an Impersonal Impersonality comprising the manifold consciousness of being. He gives and gives of his creative Self to the creatures he has made in the hope that they will apprehend his purposes and emulate his consciousness to the fullness with which he has endowed them."

—SAINT GERMAIN

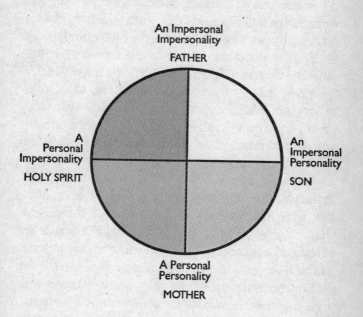

are the electrodes of a mass entity that makes up the pseudo-personality of the Antichrist.

As you seek to master the science of expanding the forcefield of self-awareness that we call the human aura and that by practice can become the divine aura, let us set at naught the arguments of the ages concerning whether God as a Spirit is personal or impersonal.

Again it is a question of frequencies, a question of levels of identification. Man identifies with God through the centers called the chakras. Depending on where his consciousness is at the moment, he may see God as the Impersonal Impersonality—as the flaming Presence of the I AM THAT I AM, the Father Principle, the Supreme Lawgiver—or he may identify with the Impersonal Personality of the Logos that is the Word made flesh,[1] the Christ incarnate in sons and daughters of the One who embody aspects of the seven rays of the Only Begotten of God.

On the other hand, he may become enamored with the most Personal Personality of the Godhead, which bespeaks the Mother image and the Mother flame, the dearest and most tender, the gentlest and most flowing aspect of God. Then, too, he may see God as the Holy Spirit, as cloven tongues of fiery Love[2] piercing the night and balancing the day star[3] right within the very heart and soul of man as the most Personal Impersonality of the Comforter.

Over the centuries of mankind's Godward evolution, the followers of various religions have centered on one or more of these levels of identification with God. The Impersonal Impersonality of the God of Israel was seen in the religion of the patriarchs, the commandments of the law, and the descent of the kings and prophets as father figures to both the Arabs and the Jews.

The religion of the Christ has centered in the concept of the incarnation of the Word, and John the Baptist and Jesus illustrated the true nature of this Impersonal Personality of the Logos by their example and their ultimate sacrifice.

Whereas the religion of the Mother has appeared in and as the greatest cultures the world has ever known—for her flame precipitates science and invention, art and music, philosophy and mathematics— devotees of the World Mother address her according to the traditions of their lands—as Mary or one of the many feminine saints, as Kali or Durga, Vesta or Venus, Isis or Athena.

Finally, those who have attuned to the delicate Presence that moves in the rushing mighty wind of the Holy Spirit[4] are those who in all ages have known no other religion but love—love as action, love as contemplation, love as the consuming fire,[5] love as "I AM my brother's keeper."[6] These are the mystics and the priests of the sacred fire, Zoroastrians and the spiritual lineage of Melchizedek,[7] members of holy orders and communities of the Spirit. Theirs is the practical realization of the most Personal Impersonality of the Godhead.

There are many paths, but all lead to the one Source of life. All are necessary to the balanced manifestation of God in man. And seeing that mankind in their state of limitation could not resolve the four aspects into one, the Lord God did create these religions to satisfy the diversity of temperaments that make up the many faces of humanity.

From East to West, the body of God on earth has realized the spectrum of God's consciousness, facet by facet, nation by nation. And who can say, observing the whole, who is right and who is wrong? It is not a question of rightness or wrongness, but one of wholeness and of the measure of a man.

These archetypes of God show forth at once his universality and his ever-present personality. Therefore, to know him as he is, mankind must realize that the four lower bodies are given for the realization of the God of very gods,[8] who allows a portion of the Infinite Self to be seen, to be heard, and even to be recognized—yes, dear ones, in finite form.

Not that we aver that man could ever contain the allness of God. But then, cannot God contain within himself the allness of man? And as man is contained therein, so can he not now become a portion of the Infinite Self?

To deny this truth is to limit the ability of God to express himself in his most cherished creation—male and female made after the Self Image of the Divine Us.[9] And therefore it is written that one day the soul that has overcome will merge with the Presence of the I AM to realize the allness of that Self.

And so then, as you begin to press the aura of God upon the aura of the world by your determination to be holy vessels of that Holy Spirit, know that that Spirit, through you, in you, can influence all of life. By defining the lines of force as these compel Spirit's energies to flow in Mater, you can deliver to the age the mandate of God's awareness of himself as the omnipotent Father-Mother, as the omniscient Logos, and as the omnipresent Spirit.

Have you had success in your meditation with the chohans of the rays? Have you entered into oneness with the Christ Self through the communion of the heart? Have those majestic impersonal personalities of ascended Christed ones endeared you to the very Person of God himself?

Dare you think of such a concept of the Person of God? Dare you think of meeting that Person, whether here on earth or in the flaming yod, sun center that all one day shall enter?

Do you understand that it is the nature of Antichrist, of that force which opposes the pure personalities of Christed ones, to deny the reality, yea, the necessity of the personification of the God flame?

And thus the Antichrist has convinced the worldly-wise of the nonexistence of both the personality of God and the personality of the devil. And thereby Antichrist continues in many quarters unchallenged in his work of tearing down the personality of Good while reinforcing the personality of evil, all the while placing upon it the mask of anonymity.

In a world where the lines of definition that mark the individuality of those who strive for the goal of perfection through the individualization of the Christ flame of the seven rays grow less and less, it is essential to proclaim the personality of the Christ as the identifying mark of all who are born of the Father-Mother God.

In a world where the mass consciousness is leveling mankind to a common denominator of the human personality, where the herd instinct and animal passions govern the monotonous manifestations of egos who are becoming automatons—whether to a totalitarian state, a godless economy, a religion of rote formulae, or a runaway science—in a world where the definition of man and woman made in the image and likeness of God is becoming blurred as though seen through the mists of maya, it is imperative that all who are alert and awake as watchmen on the wall of life challenge the Antichrist.

This should be done daily with the following fiat:

"In the name of Jesus the Christ, I challenge the carnal mind, the Antichrist, and all satanic power in every man, woman, and child upon this planet!"

David gave the formula for beholding the Christ and holding the immaculate concept on behalf of the sons and daughters of God when he said, "Mark the perfect man, and behold the upright: for the end of that man is peace."[10] The identifying mark of all who are born of God is the point of light, of sacred fire, that expands from the secret chamber of the heart through the rings of self-awareness that comprise the aura. This point of light pulsates in the forcefield of the aura as a unique identity recognizable to God and man both in heaven and on earth.

Those who seek to deny this personality or to circumvent it as they steal the energies of the Spirit in the sin against the Holy Ghost[11] have the mark of the beast.[12] These are the idolaters in every age who reject the Christ, replace it with the lesser self, and proclaim that self as God.

We have initiated the cycle of your meditation with the chohans in order that you might put on and become the personality of the Christ as it is realized through the seven rays. And thus it is the work of each of the seven chohans to show you what your options are as you amplify the seven rays through the seven days of the week. These options are to be the most exact and exacting replica of the flame as

Father, Mother, Son, and Holy Spirit define the personality of the Christ in each devotee of the light.

By practicing this exercise, then, you will come to know the likeness of the Christ as it ought to manifest in your life in small ways and in big ways, in minutest detail and on a larger scale, as you expand here below the very specifications of the length and breadth and height and depth of the City Foursquare,[13] which is composed of the four elements (planes) of God's being within your body temples fair.

And thus while the heathen rage and the people imagine a vain thing,[14] while the dragon sends forth the flood to devour the Manchild who is the personality of God that is realized through the Woman,[15] while forces and forcefields and interplanetary rays are being sent forth from the evil one to erase, if it were possible, the very energies of the elect,[16] I stand forth with the teaching that will enable you to exert the power of the very living Presence of God as that Presence in you becomes personal wisdom and personal love individualized for all.

The communications of the chohans given to your soul upon the island suspended in the glistening sea are specifically for the individual needs of devotees on the Path. Therefore I say, raise up your voice! Raise up your energies of the heart to the level of the sixteen-petaled chakra of the spoken Word!

And let the mastery of that chakra be in the

communication of the ideations of God that have become the formulae of the Logos. Let the silence be broken as atoms and molecules coalesce through the fiats of the light to form within your own temple four-square the sacred squaring of the hallowed Trinity!

You see, precious ones, the twelve petals of the heart that were for the balancing of the Trinity in each of the four lower bodies are transformed in the throat chakra into the sixteen aspects of virtues flowing in the breath of the Holy Spirit. And behold, now there are four petals in each of the four lower bodies!

This tells you that the threefold flame in etheric, mental, emotional, and physical quadrants has become the fourfold action of the law. The triangle has become the square; and Spirit's flame is now ensconced in Matter through the original decree of Alpha, "Let there be light!" and the response of Omega, "And there was light!"[17] And lo, the womb of creation, the Cosmic Egg, was the materialization of the God flame!

Learn, then, that by the action of your word, all that you garner in the hidden chamber of the heart—the wisdom and the love of the guru and the will of the law—is sent forth as the *sword* of the sacred Word to coalesce in Matter both the personality and the patterns of the Infinite One. How the demons attack the descent of the Word into form! What a

THE THROAT CHAKRA. The power center in man and woman. The sixteen petals, or frequencies, correspond to the thoughtform of the pyramid (four petals on each side), which represents the power of precipitation—the Word becoming flesh, Spirit becoming tangible in Matter.

The throat chakra is the center of the blue flame and the inner blueprint of the will of God. It is the key to the shortening of the days for the elect that Jesus Christ said would occur (Mark 13:20). The shortening of the 'days', or cycles of karma, occurs through the correct use of the spoken Word.

When we speak the name of God "I AM" and follow it with affirmations of light, we begin the transmutation process. Anything and everything that proceeds from the throat chakra coalesces in form, for good or for ill, by the action of the power of the spoken Word. Its scientific use is the Truth that shall make you free when you apply it diligently every day.　　　　—ECP

blue

blessing when the Word *is* made flesh!

Take care, then, that you refrain from misusing this sacred chakra that is the mouth of God. For is it not written that "every idle word that men shall speak, they shall give account thereof in the day of judgment; for by thy words thou shalt be justified and by thy words thou shalt be condemned"?[18]

When you speak the word in righteousness and love, the energy of the heart flows with God-control to bless other parts of life. When you speak unrighteousness and allow the demons to mouth their unutterable mutterings through you because you have confused the image of the Holy One with that of the unholy one, then you distort the pattern of the City Foursquare. You unbalance the energies of life, and the grid of the new dimensions that we seek to align with your aura is broken and there is a shattering of crystal patterns as the crystal-fire mist is dissipated in time and space.

Those who maintain the steady flow of the compassionate word, the gentle word, speaking the firmness of the law as it relates to the evolving soul consciousness, are those who overcome the accuser of the brethren by the blood of the Lamb (the essence of fire flowing from the heart chakra) and by the word of their testimony[19] (the release of that fire in the flowing water of the Word).

As you then go forth to speak the word of truth,

know that by the confirming of the Word with signs following[20] you build the kingdom of God on earth while laying up for yourselves treasure in heaven.[21] And the spiral of the aura expands with each affirmation of the law, each decree—each fiat of the Word.

As the pink is the glow of love that expands from the heart, so the blue is the ray of God's will that amplifies each expression of the law, each word of praise, and is the authority for healing and science in this octave. And if in the depths of darkest night the tempter would tempt you to doubt the power of the spoken Word as it is released through the omnipotent personality of the Godhead, remember then the one who appeared to John the Beloved in the midst of the seven candlesticks:

"One like unto the Son of man, clothed with a garment down to the foot and girt about the paps with a golden girdle. His head and his hairs were white like wool, as white as snow; and his eyes were as a flame of fire, and his feet like unto fine brass, as if they burned in a furnace, and his voice as the sound of many waters. And he had in his right hand seven stars: *and out of his mouth went a sharp twoedged sword* [sacred word]: and his countenance was as the sun shineth in his strength."[22]

And know, then, that the Lord God himself is able to appear to the exalted consciousness of man and to proclaim to him directly by the power of the spoken Word: "Fear not; I AM the first and the last: I AM he that liveth and was dead; and, behold, I AM alive for evermore, Amen, and have the keys of hell and of death."[23]

This, my beloved, is the Impersonal Impersonality, the Impersonal Personality, the Personal Personality, and the Personal Impersonality which you can and shall become right within your forcefield, right within your aura, through the mastery of the power of the spoken Word.

I am forever in the center of the flame.

7 THE LAW OF CONGRUENCY

Understand that there are surrounding the body of man concentric force-fields as envelopes within envelopes. These are energy molds that determine the quotient of light that can be contained within the human aura. Just as the causal body consists of spheres of light surrounding the I AM Presence, each sphere noted by a certain frequency depicted as a ring of color, so around the body of man, lines of flux indicate layers of frequencies that can be magnetized as you expand your awareness of God.

Beginning at the point in the center of the heart, concentric rings of fire can be expanded in the aura of the initiate who pursues the Presence of the Flaming One. As the I AM Presence releases the light of God in man, these energies expand outward from the heart in ever-expanding rings like those that form when a pebble is thrown into a pond.

The soul that descends into the planes of Matter has, then, the potential to be a point of contact for solar hierarchies. For inherent within the soul's own energy field are the electronic matrices that enable it to become a center for the distribution of the light that is needed to nourish and sustain a planet and its evolutions.

Now, as you read my words, sitting in meditation perhaps before the statue of the Buddha, the image of the Christ, or the Chart of Your Divine Self, visualize these concentric rings of light emanating from the center of your heart[1] and realize that each successive attainment in cosmic consciousness anchors the light of the Cosmic Christ as a permanent layer of light within your aura.

The layers of the aura that are filled with light mark the levels of initiation—of the neophyte, the postulant, the acolyte, the disciple, the adept, and so on in the hierarchical scale. When each layer is filled with light and the soul moves in its expanding self-awareness to the point where it magnetizes more light than the capacity of the layers, the aura is translated from the human to the divine. And it is not long before the soul is elevated in its expression from the planes of Matter to the planes of Spirit—for the world can no longer contain it.

As you increase the intensity of the aura through meditation and application of the sacred fire by giving mantras of the Spirit such as the "Transfiguring Affirmations of Jesus the Christ,"* which he taught to his disciples, you not only increase the dimensions of your aura in time and space, but you find that your aura becomes a means of communicating with new dimensions of the Spirit even while it transports your soul into higher frequencies of Matter.

Whereas your communication with beings and energies in the planes of Spirit may occur in periods of meditation and invocation, soul travel occurs most often while your body temple is at rest during the hours of sleep. For, you see, the aura that you build as a reflection of your awareness of God in many planes surrounds not only the physical form, but also the etheric, mental, and emotional vehicles.

The aura, then, serves as the forcefield of light that has been called the seamless garment. This garment adorns the etheric body as that body becomes the vehicle of the soul in its journeying in other octaves of Matter.

To develop the aura, then, is to prepare the place of consciousness where, by the law of congruency, you can receive here and now in the planes of Mater those ascended masters and Christed ones whose light bodies will mesh with your own because your

*See page 197.

aura has taken on and become the frequency of the Holy Spirit that is individualized by various members of the Great White Brotherhood. To be sure, it is the dimensions of life with which you identify whereby the attainment of your cosmic consciousness is measured.

The action of the law of congruency is indeed wondrous to behold! As the magnet of the heart in its rising action is the equilateral triangle that compels the descent of the triangle of Spirit, so that very six-pointed star will magnetize to your heart an identical momentum of light that is held in the heart of one or more ascended beings.

By your free will you can qualify the interlaced triangles of the heart with any of the frequencies of the seven rays or of the Holy Ghost that is the unifying Spirit of the Great White Brotherhood. When, for instance, you dedicate the fires of your heart to the Divine Mother and diligently give the salutations to Mary,[2] your heart becomes an orifice of the Mother's love, your aura contains the very patterns that flow from the Virgin Queen to your own over the arc of your adoration.

At a certain point in your devotions and in the evolution of your solar awareness of the Divine Mother, the magnet of the aura and the heart reaches, as it were, a critical mass—that is, an energy momentum sufficient to magnetize the very living Presence of the

Divine Mother herself. And by the law of congruency, your aura then becomes the aura of the Virgin Mary.

Then as you recite the Hail Mary,* you are giving the salutation to the flame of the Divine Mother that now burns within your own heart. And as you have called to become her hands and her feet, her body and her mind, so the call has compelled the answer and the answer has come not as a miracle— not as an exception to natural law, but in fulfillment of that law.

Thus as you increase the intensity and the light frequency of the heart, which in turn feeds energy to all of the chakras in Matter and expands the rings of the aura, you come to the place where, through the merging of the aura of the ascended masters with your own, you can proclaim the joy of God's geometry; "Behold, I and my Father are one, I and my Mother are one!" And lo, the star above has become the star below!

Wherever you are in consciousness at this moment, know, O chela of the light, that you are one with every other soul, whether in Matter or in Spirit, who is at this moment experiencing that level, that frequency, of God's being. If you are meditating upon Jesus the Christ and his great life example, then you are one with all others who have an identical appreciation for his ministry. And if by your meditation

*See page 198.

upon Jesus you become that Christ, then you are also one with every other soul who has ever become the Christ—past, present, and future.

No matter where you are or what you are doing, you cannot escape the inevitable law of congruency. If you allow yourself to become angered, willful, rebellious, or entangled in the threads of maya, then so long as you sustain that vibration by your free will, you are one with and you reinforce the consciousness of all others who are similarly preoccupied with the mists of mortality. And the soul's apparatus to be a distributing center for light is used to proliferate the energy veil, and the light that is in thee is darkness.[3]

When you consider the state of your mind and your feelings at any hour of the day or night, consider whether or not you would desire to have your aura amplify that state a million times, and consider whether you would have that state reinforced by other millions of auras that reflect your own and project the images of their consciousness upon the screen of the cosmos.

Consider that your aura is a mirror of forces both within the microcosm of your individual world and within the entire macrocosm. Consider that you, in your determination to focus a particular virtue of the Godhead, a certain aspect of the Holy Spirit, by the very intensity of your determination can magnetize the determination of God to be that virtue, that aspect.

Therefore by maximizing the sacred fire within your heart through invocation, you can increase the concentric rings of influence that make up your aura. You can make your vote for light and for right count across the entire planetary body as your aura becomes a sounding board for the honor flame of ascended masters and cosmic beings whose light emanations are drawn by the very purity of your love and your determination to be a component of the divine consciousness.

Consider the enormous power of influence that you wield when you align yourself with cosmic forces and cosmic principles. And this is another key in understanding the simple statement "One with God is a majority."

Consider also how your indulgences in the petulance and the pettiness of the ego reinforce the myopic existence of mankind who pursue an endless round of ego-centered activities and use their auras to amplify the ego personality of the synthetic image instead of the Christed personality of the Real Image.

When a man or a woman comes to the place where he realizes the enormous responsibility of influencing life for good or for evil, he begins to understand the statement written in the law "I have said, Ye are gods."[4] Surely the power that a man can wield through the correct or the incorrect use of the aura can make of him instantaneously a god or a devil.

The more you learn of the science of the aura, the more you will come to realize that there is no in-between. For every erg of energy and every microbe of thought, every wave of feeling, by the law of congruency and the oneness of all life in all planes, resounds throughout the creation either to increase or to decrease the light momentum of the aura of the cosmos.

Because of mankind's gross misuse of the power of the human aura in past ages, this power was taken from him by divine decree. The scientific and mathematical formulae for the development of the powers of the aura were withdrawn from the masses, and mankind's sensory and extrasensory perceptions became dulled according to their misuses of the powers of the aura.

Finally, as abuses led to density and density to further abuses, even the knowledge of the existence of the aura was withdrawn. No longer having empirical proof of the existence of the aura, mankind, excepting the few, ceased to experiment with the science of auric emanations and control; and the soul's conquest of other dimensions of Matter that can be accomplished only through this science came to a halt.

In recent years, through Kirlian photography and

experiments with plants, scientists have postulated the theory of the L-field as the blueprint of life and a forcefield of energy that can be observed and photographed with either scientific instruments or this specialized photography which uses neither camera nor lens. Suddenly now, after thousands of years of blindness and of the blind following the blind, mankind have awakened to new planes of Matter that exist and can be verified just beyond concrete Matter.

What a vast area of exploration and discovery experiments in parapsychology have opened, and mankind are once again pushing back the frontiers of knowledge! Hierarchy would provide extraordinary insight into the delvings of scientists, and especially those who are in fields of research that probe beyond the present bounds of finite existence.

Man is on the brink of discovering the Higher Self. His head peeping above the clouds, he beholds himself alone against the backdrop of infinity. Beyond mortality man must have the courage to proceed alone—in the understanding that he is here and now *all one* with life.

In the stillness of the dawn man meets the Infinite. As the last stars are put to bed and the morning light quickens his solar awareness, man gazes into the infinite blue. And he is aware that by the power of an inner sight, a faculty of the soul, he is contacting dimensions beyond the contemporary world and beyond the knowledge of that world as man has counted knowledge for thousands of years.

What is this infinite blue that the soul of man can inhabit by simply expanding the faculties of soul? Is it not the aura of God in the Macrocosm? As you contemplate the self all one with the Higher Self moving through the being of God, won't you give this my prayer for the oneness of all life?

O Infinite One,
Thou God of all above, below,
It is thyself that I would know.
Come unto me, come into me,
O God of love!
Let me dwell with thee, in thee.

My soul longs to climb the ladder of thy law.
As children play on the playground
  in their jungle gym,
So I would move along the parallel bars
  of thy congruency,
Of thy formlessness and form.
I would exercise my soul
Along the grids and forcefields
Of the antahkarana of life.
O God, let me feel
The rods and cones
That compose thy being.
For thou knowest, O God,

That I would heal
All those who have made themselves
Exceptions to thy law of congruency.

O God, how I love thy geometry
In time and space!
How I love thy design, thy creativity,
Thy bountiful grace!
O God, let me come home,
Let me tarry in the threefold essence
Of thy throne.

Ah yes, I would work thy works on earth
According to thy law—
Sacred wonder, sacred awe.
But for a moment, Lord,
Let me tarry in thy Word,
Let me come and kneel before thy throne.
Oh, let me sit at thy feet,
Divine Master, in thy retreat,
That I might renew the sacred essence
And the memory I once knew
Of our togetherness in the foreverness
Of the infinity I would view.

O God, as thou art
The point of light within
The hidden chamber of my heart,
Let me enter there,

Let my soul be washed by flowing flame,
Let me be renewed to serve mankind again.
I am thy servant, Lord!
I am thyself in form, O Lord!
O Formless One, make us one,
That I might be the fullness of thyself
In and out of immortality.

Thy law is love, thy Word is truth.
Now let my soul be living proof
As thou art here and everywhere,
So I affirm I AM here and I AM there.
This, then, is the humble prayer
Of one who would become
The fullness of thy blazing Son.
I AM the oneness that I AM!

In the fullness of his love, I bid you welcome to
my aura. Will you welcome me to your aura?

TRANSFIGURING AFFIRMATIONS
OF JESUS THE CHRIST

I AM THAT I AM

I AM the Open Door which no man can shut

I AM the Light which lighteth every man
  that cometh into the world

I AM the Way

I AM the Truth

I AM the Life

I AM the Resurrection

I AM the Ascension in the Light

I AM the fulfillment of all my needs and requirements
  of the hour

I AM abundant supply poured out upon all Life

I AM perfect Sight and Hearing

I AM the manifest Perfection of Being

I AM the illimitable Light of God made manifest
  everywhere

I AM the Light of the Holy of Holies

I AM a son of God

I AM the Light in the holy mountain of God

Note: These affirmations are mentioned by Djwal Kul on page 187.

HAIL MARY

Hail, Mary, full of grace!
The Lord is with thee.
Blessed art thou among women and
  blessed is the fruit of thy womb, Jesus.
Holy Mary, Mother of God,
  pray for us, sons and daughters of God,
  now and at the hour of our victory
  over sin, disease and death.

Note: This prayer is mentioned by Djwal Kul on page 189.

8 THE SACRED FIRE BREATH

As the inbreathing and the outbreathing of God is for the integration of cosmic cycles, for the sending-forth of worlds within worlds, and for the return of those worlds back to the heart of God whence they came, so man, as a co-creator with God, is endowed with the gift of the sacred fire breath. And if he will use that breath for the consecration of the energy of the Holy Spirit within the chakras and within the aura, he will find himself becoming the very fullness of the Presence of God.

How can this be? you say, for the mortal mind is astounded at the very thought of being the expression of God.

Indeed, O mortal, thou canst not contain immortality! Therefore, put off thy mortality! Enter in to the consciousness of the immortals and know that your aura can be, indeed now is, the very living Presence of God—God as life pulsating, God as love innovating, God as truth energizing the soul to the fullness of its creative potential.

The very air that you breathe can be qualified with the sacred fire breath of the Holy Spirit. Indeed, the air is, as it were, the latent potential of the breath of the Holy Spirit. It is energy that is passive which can be activated by the Christ flame as the energy of the heart chakra is drawn up through the throat chakra and released as the sacred Word.

Now we come to the great indrawing. Now we come to the place where—through unswerving devotion to the Son, through the conviction to be the Christ, and through the commitment to the Holy One and the name I AM THAT I AM—you have, in the flaming potential of being itself, the opportunity to become a spiral of integration in order that the life of God as Spirit might be integrated in Matter "as above, so below."

Understand, then, that by your application to the law that I have released in the first seven of these studies, there is being built within your aura a fiery coil of life. This coil, which is approximately ten inches in diameter, you ought now to visualize rising from the base of an imaginary sundial upon which you stand.

As you look down at your feet, the coil proceeds from what would be the twelve o'clock line (positioned just in front of your feet). The coil is an electrode that winds in a clockwise direction, the coils being spaced three inches apart.

From beneath your feet to the top of your head, this coil is a pulsating white fire. And it can be focused as the action of the sacred fire of the Holy Spirit only in the aura of those who have the devotion to the Christ and the commitment to the I AM THAT I AM.

Retaining in mind and in heart the image and the awareness of this coil, let us now consider the two most important functions of the chakras: first, to be the vortex of the outbreath that is the giving-forth of God's energy as the action—the sevenfold activation —of the seven rays of the Holy Spirit; and second, to be the vortex of the inbreath, the drawing-in of the sacred fire breath as the universal essence, the passive energy of the Holy Spirit.

These functions are most obvious in the throat chakra, and therefore the purpose of this eighth study in the series is to give the devotees of the Holy Spirit a truly practical exercise and a fundamental understanding of the use of the throat chakra for the integration of the four lower bodies through the inbreathing and outbreathing of the sacred fire breath.

Just as you breathe in and breathe out through

THE FIERY COIL OF LIFE. "Understand, then, that by your application to the law that I have released in the first seven of these studies, there is being builded within your aura a fiery coil of life. This coil, which is approximately ten inches in diameter, you ought now to visualize rising from the base of an imaginary sundial upon which you stand.

"As you look down at your feet, the coil proceeds from what would be the twelve o'clock line (positioned just in front of your feet). The coil is an electrode that winds in a clockwise direction, the coils being spaced three inches apart.

"From beneath your feet to the top of your head, this coil is a pulsating white fire. And it can be focused as the action of the sacred fire of the Holy Spirit only in the aura of those who have the devotion to the Christ and the commitment to the I AM THAT I AM."

—DJWAL KUL

the throat chakra, so all of the chakras are taking in and giving forth the energies of God according to the frequency assigned to each specific chakra. As the energies that are drawn in through the chakras are of the Holy Spirit and the Mother and relate to the functions of the soul in Matter and the nourishment of the four lower bodies, so the energies that are sent forth from the chakras are of the Father and the Son and relate to the functions of the soul in Spirit and the release of its spiritually creative potential.

In the ordinary, undeveloped man and woman, the interaction of these energies is sustained at minimum levels necessary for the flow, the harmony, and the nourishment of the four lower bodies.

When man and woman, through a superior devotion and an extraordinary commitment to the Father and to the Son, begin to release a greater momentum of the energy of the Impersonal Impersonality and the Impersonal Personality of the Godhead through the chakras, then by this greater thrust of outflow there is magnetized a greater inflow of the Personal Personality and the Personal Impersonality of the energies of the Mother and of the Holy Spirit.

This is an illustration of the mathematical equation that is always present in the cosmic exchange of energy from God to man and man to God. Therefore balance, you see, is the key to the expansion of the aura—and it is the balance of plus and minus energy factors that is all important. For the aura will expand in proportion as you increase both the velocity and the vibration of energy moving into and coming forth from the seven chakras of being.

You who have been diligent in studying our instruction and who have made of that instruction the foundation of a new dimension in consciousness will find that you have already increased the outbreath—the outward thrust of Spirit, the plus factor. The following exercise will enable you to increase the inbreath—the inward thrust of Mater, the minus factor. And so you will come to know the balance of both as the regenerative action of the currents of Alpha and Omega within your form and consciousness and world.

1. First, place yourself in a meditative posture, sitting in a comfortable chair before your altar, the physical focus of your worship. If possible, you should set aside a chair that is used only during your meditations and invocations.

You should consecrate this chair by the momentum of your heart flame as a focus of the atomic accelerator that is used by the ascended masters in the Cave of Symbols. Chelas who have passed certain initiations are bidden to sit in the atomic accelerator to have the atoms and molecules of the four lower bodies stepped up by the currents of the ascension flame in preparation for the ritual of the return, the alchemical marriage that is the soul's reunion with the Spirit.

2. Place your feet flat on the floor, your hands cupped in your lap, your head erect, eyes level, chin drawn in for the disciplined flow of the energies of the heart chakra through the throat chakra.

3. The "Call to the Fire Breath," the invocation of the Goddess of Purity given to the devotees of the Holy Spirit, should now be recited three times.

Give it slowly, rhythmically, with feeling. Absorb each word and each concept with the conviction held in heart and mind that you are here and now a joint-heir with Christ. And as the beloved son, the beloved daughter, you are claiming your inheritance.[1] Yours is an inheritance of the sacred fire that issues forth from the heart of beloved Alpha and Omega, who keep the flame of the Father-Mother God in the Great Central Sun.

CALL TO THE FIRE BREATH

I AM, I AM, I AM the fire breath of God
From the heart of beloved Alpha and Omega.
This day I AM the immaculate concept
In expression everywhere I move.
Now I AM full of joy
For now I AM the full expression
Of divine love.

My beloved I AM Presence,
Seal me now
Within the very heart of
The expanding fire breath of God.
Let its purity, wholeness, and love
Manifest everywhere I AM today and forever!

(recite three times)

I accept this done right now with full power!
I AM this done right now with full power!
I AM, I AM, I AM God-Life expressing perfection
All ways at all times.
This which I call forth for myself,
I call forth for every man, woman, and child
On this planet.

The immaculate concept, the fiery blueprint according to which your soul was created in the image of the Divine One, is now impressed upon your four lower bodies. This fiery blueprint is magnetized by the coil described earlier in this lesson, which you now bring to the fore of consciousness as the pivot of your call to the fire breath. The fullness of the joy which you claim is the fullness of the expression of divine love.

4. Now visualize the buoyant energies of love being magnetized by this coil and by the energies of the heart (which from our previous exercises you hold in mind as the focus of the interlaced triangles superimposed with the name of God).

It is essential that you hang above your altar the Chart of the Presence. Your eye level when you are standing should be at the eye level of the lower figure in the chart, so that the Christ Self and the I AM Presence are above you.[2]

5.   Therefore, in all of your meditations and invocations, you should imagine through the imaging of the eye[3] that all energy released through the chakras comes forth from the I AM Presence, through the Christ Self, descending over the crystal cord into the heart chakra, thence throughout the four lower bodies.

Establish in mind, then, the concept of a perpetual flow from the heart of the individualized God Self to the heart of the Christ Self to your own threefold flame pulsating in the rhythm of God's heartbeat. The sealing of your aura within the very heart of the expanding fire breath of God is accomplished by your I AM Presence through the Christ Self in answer to your call. Remember, it is God in you who is the decreer, the decree, and the fulfillment of the decree.

6.   Visualize your aura as an ovoid of white light extending beneath your feet, beneath the coil, above your head, and above the coil. See the aura increasing in the intensity of the light as that energy is expanded from the heart chakra and thence from all of the chakras as the sacred mist that is called the

fire breath of God. Let its purity, wholeness, and love fill the ovoid of your aura, and feel your mind and heart disciplining that energy and holding it in the creative tension of your cosmic awareness.

7.   Conclude the giving of the call (three times) with the acceptance. Now you are ready for the exercise of the integration of the eighth ray.

8.   To the count of eight beats, draw in through your nostrils the sacred breath. When you first begin this exercise, you may wish to count the eight beats by the gentle tapping of your foot. The breath is drawn in through the nostrils. As you breathe in, push your abdominal muscles out, letting the air completely fill your lungs. Let your lungs be inflated like a balloon. See the air that you draw in as the pure white light.

9.   Now to the count of eight beats, hold in the air and visualize it penetrating your physical form as the essence of the Holy Spirit, which nourishes, stabilizes, and balances the interchange of energy in the physical atoms, molecules, and cells.

10.   Visualize this sacred energy flowing through your veins, moving through your nervous system, anchoring the essence of the balancing energies of the Holy Spirit in your four lower bodies and absorbing from them all impurities, which you now see being flushed out of your system as you exhale to the count of eight beats.

DEVOTEE STANDING IN THE OVOID. The action of the sacred fire can be invoked as a replica of the Cosmic Egg, sealing the pure energies flowing through purified chakras. —ECP

"Visualize your aura as an ovoid of white light extending beneath your feet, beneath the coil, above your head, and above the coil. See the aura increasing in the intensity of the light as that energy is expanded from the heart chakra and thence from all of the chakras as the sacred mist that is called the fire breath of God. Let its purity, wholeness, and love fill the ovoid of your aura, and feel your mind and heart disciplining that energy and holding it in the creative tension of your cosmic awareness." —DJWAL KUL

Let the exhalation be deliberate and disciplined as you slowly release the air as though it were a substance being pressed out of a tube. You may round your lips to increase the tension of the exhalation. Imagine that breath being pushed out from the very pit of the stomach as the abdominal muscles contract. You may lean forward if this helps to press out the last bit of air remaining in the lungs.

11. Now let your head resume an erect posture, and hold without inbreathing or outbreathing to the final count of eight beats.

12. Repeat this exercise daily, as you are physically able, until you have established a rhythm—mentally counting, if you wish, "One and two and three and four and five and six and seven and eight and one and two and three and"—and so forth. Be careful that in your zeal you do not overdo. Each one must in Christ discern his capacity, which may be anywhere from one to twelve repetitions of the exercise per daily session.

This fourfold exercise is for the balancing of the four lower bodies. The inbreath comes through the etheric body. The first hold is an action of energizing through the mental body. The outbreath is the release through the emotional body. And the final hold is for the anchoring in the physical form of the balanced action of Father, Son, Mother, and Holy Spirit.

13. When you have mastered the inbreathing,

holding, outbreathing, and holding in this fashion and the accompanying visualization of the sacred fire releasing light, energizing the consciousness, extracting impurities, and finally anchoring the energies of the Christ, then—and only then—you may add to your exercise the affirmation "I AM Alpha and Omega" to the count of eight beats.

This you mentally affirm once for each of the four steps of the exercise. This affirmation is for the establishment within you of the cloven tongues of fire, the twin flames of the Holy Spirit that are the energies of the Father-Mother God.

By thus invoking these energies and using the breath as the means to convey that energy to the four lower bodies and to anchor it in the physical form, you will be building the balanced action of the caduceus—the intertwining of the Alpha and Omega spirals along the spine that are for the ultimate victory of the masculine and feminine polarity that raises the energies of the chakras, merges in the heart as the Christ, and flowers in the crown as the Buddhic enlightenment of the thousand-petaled lotus.

Since the Fall of Man, mankind have allowed the energies of the four lower bodies to remain in a state of imbalance. Therefore, they have not had the equal flow of the currents of Alpha and Omega anchored within their forms, which are necessary to sustain the currents of regeneration, of eternal youth, and above

THE CROWN CHAKRA. The goal of self-mastery in time and space is the flowering of the "thousand-petaled lotus" of the crown. It is in the crown that man and woman are destined to know God through the mind of his Son. When we attain to that crown consciousness, true wisdom is known.

The firing of the crown with wisdom creates a magnet that draws the energies of the Mother up from the base of the spine, up through each of the successive chakras, which are the centers of our God-awareness. The enlightenment of the Buddha and of the Christ that comes with the release of the golden yellow fire of the crown chakra is the experience of knowing all things without being tutored or taught. Our awareness then includes that which is contained in the mind of God.

—ECP

yellow

all, to expand the aura to planetary and interplanetary dimensions. As a result, the unnatural law of sin, disease, decay, and death has displaced the natural law of harmony in the evolutions of earth.

Without the balance of the spirals of Alpha and Omega within you, O chelas of the sacred fire, you can go no further in the expansion of the aura. All that we have given thus far is a foundation upon which you may now build the consciousness of the Father-Mother God.

And as you increase that balance through this exercise day by day, you will come in to the awareness that you are indeed the beloved of God and that in you is the converging in the planes of Mater of the twin flames of Alpha and Omega. Behold, "I AM Alpha and Omega, the beginning and the ending, saith the Lord, which is, and which was, and which is to come, the Almighty."[4]

This, then, is the beginning of your exercise of expansion. It is also the ending of your exercise; for ultimately in the completed manifestation of the Father-Mother God, you will find that your being and consciousness has become the aura, the forcefield, of the Holy Spirit.

You will find that you have thereby magnetized that Presence of the I AM and that you are magnetized by it in a literal conflagration which is, blessed ones, the ritual of your ascension in the light. Thus from beginning to ending, the Alpha and Omega spirals within you are the fulfillment of the very living Presence of God.

I place my Electronic Presence with each one as the guardian action of the sacred fire—I AM the guard—during the period of your meditation on the fire breath and your exercise of integration through the eighth ray.

I am the willing servant of the flame.

9 THE FOUR ELEMENTS IN THE PLANES OF THE CHAKRAS

In order to master the flow of God's energy through the seven chakras, man and woman ought to consider the mastery of the four elements—of fire, air, water, and earth—as planes of God's consciousness. For by the mastery of the four elements, you will then gain the mastery of the flow of energy through the four lower bodies as these bodies serve as coordinates for the establishment of the aura of God around the soul.

The four elements, so-called, are merely word matrices used to define the planes of God's Self-awareness that the individual is capable of realizing through the four lower bodies. Thus the etheric body is the vehicle for the fire element and for man's realization of God's awareness of himself as the sacred fire.

The highest frequencies that the individual is

capable of realizing in the planes of Mater are focused through this body. The etheric, or memory, body contains both the record of the soul's evolution in the causal body in the planes of Spirit prior to its descent into Mater and the record of all of its experiences in the lower octaves after the descent.

It is through the heart chakra, where the ascending and descending triangles converge, that the soul learns to exercise the sacred fire and its uses both in the planes of Spirit and in the planes of Mater. By the fire of the heart, man and woman learn the mastery of the etheric cycles of the cosmos that spiral through the etheric body. And by the energies of the heart they do weave the deathless solar body. This is the body into which the etheric body is transformed once the karmic cycles have been fulfilled.

Thus our God who is a consuming fire[1] can be experienced in the planes of Mater through the heart chakra. And it is, of course, the threefold flame anchored in the hidden chamber of the heart that conveys this aspect of the mastery of the Christ consciousness to the soul.

Then, by the mastery and balance of the threefold flame, the disciple is able to magnetize greater and greater portions of this flame into the aura. The balanced manifestation of the threefold flame, together with the infilling of the aura with the sacred fires of the Holy Ghost, prepare the disciple to master the other six chakras through the mental, emotional, and physical bodies.

The air element and God's awareness of himself in the plane of the mind in and as the Logos are mastered in the mental body through the third eye and the seat-of-the-soul chakra. The frequency of this element is comparable to the wind that "bloweth where it listeth"[2] and to thinking and be-ness whereby the soul affirms "I am," as the expression of self-identity, drawing the conclusion "therefore I think" —or "I think, therefore I am."

For the mastery of the emotions—of God's awareness of himself as energy in *motion*—and of the water element, the disciple has the opportunity to expand and balance the energies of life and their flow in the emotional body (sometimes called the desire body) through the throat chakra and the solar plexus. But the full mastery of the physical plane and of time and space in Mater is not attained until the disciple gains the mastery of the flow of physical energies in the base-of-the-spine and the crown chakras.

In these two chakras the disciple experiences God's awareness of himself as Mother and Father united in the physical plane for the bringing-forth of the Christ consciousness. And thus the goal of the adepts of the East who meditate upon the Goddess Kundalini as the white-fire energies of the Mother coiled as the serpent fire in the base of the spine is to raise that energy through all of the chakras and to attain the merging of the energy of the Mother (which otherwise remains locked in the base of the spine) with those of the Father as these are quickened by the divine union of the Alpha-to-Omega spirals in the crown chakra.

Let us consider in this study the mastery of the flow of the sacred fire as it becomes in the throat chakra the waters of the living Word and in the solar plexus the peace-commanding Presence. Beloved Jesus, the Prince of Peace who was the Master of the Piscean age, set the example for all mankind's mastery of God's energies in motion.

So great was his mastery of the flow of fire from the heart into these two chakras that he was able to proclaim, "Heaven and earth shall pass away, but my words shall not pass away."[3] By this he meant that even though the entire forcefield of the soul's identity in the planes of Mater, together with the chakras that are used to focus the energies of heaven and earth, might cease to exist, the word of God uttered through his being would remain forever—fixed as stars in the firmament of God's being.

The mark of the Christed one is the mark of attainment whereby the energies of the chakras below the heart are uplifted and integrated with the energies of the chakras above the heart. Those above the heart carry the masculine polarity of being, and

THE SOLAR-PLEXUS CHAKRA. The "place of the sun." The solar plexus is the center of feeling where we employ the energy of emotion as God's *energy in motion* to realize the peace of God's consciousness, the peace of the ascended Jesus Christ. When your solar plexus is calm, you have the power of peace. And, using the full potential of the desire body, you have that full momentum of the "Pacific Ocean," of water molded in a matrix of love.

The flame of purple and gold is God's desiring to be God within you. And the power of God's desire comes forth as you raise the energy from the solar plexus to the level of the throat and release the fiat, as Jesus did, "Peace, be still!" Through the spoken Word, a wave of light goes over the whole planet, causing atoms and electrons to come into alignment with the flame of the Prince of Peace. The solar-plexus chakra has ten petals.

—ECP

purple and gold

those below the heart carry the feminine polarity. Once the energies of the threefold flame are balanced in the hidden chamber of the heart, the disciple can proceed to balance the points of the interlaced triangles, which are necessary for the disciple's attainment of the Christ consciousness.

Jesus is known as the Prince of Peace because he balanced the threefold flame and mastered the sixth ray, the energies of purple and gold in the solar-plexus chakra (at the navel). Holding these energies in harmony, he was able to draw upon the reserves of his solar plexus, the place of the sun, to release this energy in the power of the spoken Word.

It was in the balance of the energy flow from the desire body—which in Jesus totally reflected God's desiring for mankind—to the throat chakra that he was able to speak the word of healing, of forgiveness, of comfort. By the balanced energy flow from the throat chakra to the solar plexus, he gave forth the teaching of the Christ for the Piscean age and spoke the word that raised the dead, cast out the demons, and aligned the entire planetary body with the aura of the Cosmic Christ.

You may, then, visualize the ascending triangle of purple flecked with gold rising from the solar plexus and merging in the throat chakra with the descending triangle of royal blue for the fulfillment of the spirals of Alpha and Omega in the release of the spoken Word. These color rays, the blue and the purple, do focus the action of the beginning and the ending that seals the sacred fire breath in a matrix of completion specifically for precipitation in Mater.

If the energies in motion of these two chakras are perfectly balanced, then when the disciple speaks the word "Be thou made whole!" it is done, even as the fiat of the Lord spoken by Jesus was a rebuke to the devil who at his word departed from the lunatic boy who was "sore vexed, ofttimes falling into the fire and oft into the water."[4]

Have you ever wondered, as the disciples did, why they could not cast the demon out of the boy? Have you ever wondered why words of healing and of love spoken by the Master do not have the same effect in the planes of Mater when spoken through you as they did when he spoke them?

The answer is to be found in precisely this formula which I have given you on (1) the balancing of the threefold flame and (2) the merging of the coordinate chakras (throat and solar plexus; third eye and seat of the soul; crown and base) and their energies "as above, so below." Thus in order to be healers of mankind and to walk in the footsteps of him who commanded the wind and the wave, you must begin by learning the control—the *God-control*—of energy flow both in the solar plexus and in the spoken Word.

If you would learn the mastery of the solar plexus,

then I must remand you to the consciousness of the Elohim Peace and Aloha and their exercise of the visualization of the great sun disc over the solar plexus, calling in the name of Jesus the Christ and in the name of your own Christ Self to the Elohim of the Sixth Ray for the balancing action of their consciousness to be anchored in your solar-plexus chakra.

Visualize a circle or disc of white light the size of a dinner plate superimposed over your form at the navel. See this as a brilliant shield of armor like the white disc of the sun that appears in the sky. Then give the "Invocation to the Great Sun Disc." You may also give the "Count-to-Nine Decree" written by the Ascended Master Cuzco specifically for the mastery of the solar plexus, the throat, and the third-eye chakras.*

Always remember, blessed chelas of the sacred fire, that our instruction—and, above all, your application of that instruction—is given in order that you might prepare yourself for the initiations of the cross: the transfiguration, the crucifixion, the resurrection, and the ascension. That you might be prepared for the coming of the Lord unto the tabernacle of being is our prayer.

Thus when you have shown yourself "approved unto God, a workman rightly dividing the word of truth,"[5] the hour will come that is appointed by God

---

*See pages 229–32.

for you to be taken up "into an high mountain,"[6] into the plane of the I AM Presence apart from the world. And, in the ritual of the transfiguration, your face will "shine as the sun" and your raiment will be "white as the light."[7]

So your countenance will reflect the image and likeness of God; and your aura, as the raiment of your soul, will be filled with the white light of your own Christ Self-awareness. You will find yourself standing face to face with the ascended masters and talking with them as though with friends of old.

And if perchance there are disciples of lesser attainment standing by, they may propose the building of tabernacles[8] to commemorate the event and the spot of the converging of the energies of heaven and earth—one for you and one for each of the masters who appear conversing with you.

But you will tell them that the transfiguration is not for the exaltation of the personality, nor does the individuality of the soul equate with the human personality or the idolatrous generation. For the transfiguration is the glorying of the Lord in the soul, in the Christ Self, and in the tabernacle foursquare that has become the dwelling place of the Most High God.

The bright cloud that will overshadow you in that hour will be the cloud of the I AM Presence, the forcefield of pulsating white light into which you will one day enter through the ascension spiral. And in that bright cloud is the witness of the heavenly hosts overshadowing those who in time and space are willing to commemorate the God flame—those who are not afraid to draw forth the flame of Spirit that must be ensconced in Matter if that Matter is to be translated in the ritual of the transfiguration to the plane of its origin in Spirit. And so to all who behold the consecration of your life as the transfiguring life of the Christ, the voice out of the cloud will speak, saying, "This is my beloved Son, in whom I AM well pleased; hear ye him."[9]

If you will in earnest seek the mastery of those energies in motion anchored in the solar plexus as a reservoir of light for the release of the power of the spoken Word, the Almighty will sponsor your delivery of the Word of God in this age. And you will be the peace-commanding Presence.

And mankind will desire to hear the words that you speak; for they indeed have the authority of your sponsor from on high—the very same I AM THAT I AM who sponsored Moses, saying, "Now therefore go, and I will be with thy mouth and teach thee what thou shalt say."[10] So the same Lord will speak the word through you and will draw all mankind with the seeing of the eye and with the hearing of the ear and with the command "Hear ye him!"

I am keeping the flame for those who diligently pursue the ritual of the transfiguration.

INVOCATION TO THE GREAT SUN DISC

Beloved Mighty I AM Presence, beloved Holy Christ Self, and beloved Jesus the Christ: Blaze your dazzling light of a thousand suns in, through, and around my four lower bodies as a mighty guardian action of the light of God that never fails to protect the peaceful outpicturing of God's plan through my every thought, word, and deed.

Place your great sun disc over my solar plexus as a mighty shield of armor that shall instantaneously deflect all discord whatsoever that may ever be directed against me or the light for which I stand.

I call now in the name of my Mighty I AM Presence to the Elohim of Peace to release throughout my being and world the necessary action of the mighty flame of Cosmic Christ peace that shall sustain in me the Christ consciousness at all times, so that I may never be found engaged in a release of misqualified energy to any part of life, whether it be fear, malice, mild dislike, mistrust, censure, or disdain.

I call to beloved Saint Germain to seize all energy that I have ever released against my brethren and that has caused them any form of discomfort whatsoever. And in the name of my Mighty I AM Presence I command that that energy be removed from their worlds— cause, effect, record, and memory—and transmuted by the violet flame into the purity and perfection that is the sacred-fire essence of God, that the earth and all

(continued)

elemental life might be cut free forever from human creation and given their eternal victory in the light!

I accept this done right now with full power; I AM this done right now with full power. I AM, I AM, I AM God-life expressing perfection all ways at all times. This which I call forth for myself I call forth for every man, woman, and child on this planet!

Beloved I AM! Beloved I AM! Beloved I AM!

Mantra: O DISC OF LIGHT

> O disc of Light from heaven's height,
>   Descend with all your perfection!
> Make my aura bright with freedom's Light
>   And the Masters' love and protection!

(recite nine times)

Note: This meditation is mentioned by Djwal Kul on page 226.

SUMMIT UNIVERSITY PRESS®

Non-Profit Publisher since 1975

Tell us how you liked this book!

Book title: _____

Comments: _____

_____

_____

_____

What did you like the most? _____

How did you find this book? _____

☐ **YES! Send me FREE BOOK CATALOG**   ☐ **I'm interested in more information**

Name _____

Address _____

City _____

State _____ Zip Code _____

E-mail: _____

Phone no. _____

Your tax-deductible contributions make these publications
available to the world.

Please make your checks payable to:
Summit University Press, PO Box 5000, Gardiner, MT 59030.
Call us toll free at 1-800-245-5445.
Outside the U.S.A., call 406-848-9500.
E-mail: tslinfo@tsl.org
www.summituniversitypress.com

491-THA #1483 3/05

BUSINESS REPLY MAIL
FIRST-CLASS MAIL PERMIT NO. 20 GARDINER MT

POSTAGE WILL BE PAID BY ADDRESSEE

SUMMIT UNIVERSITY PRESS®

PO Box 5000

Gardiner, MT 59030-9900

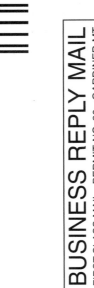

COUNT-TO-NINE DECREE

In the name of the beloved mighty victorious Presence of God, I AM in me, and my very own beloved Holy Christ Self, I am calling to the heart of the Saviour Jesus Christ and to the servant-sons of God and legions of Light who are with him in heaven, including beloved Archangel Michael and the Ascended Master Cuzco: In God's name, I decree!

Come now by love divine,
Guard thou this soul of mine, *(Visualize the white light filling the ovoid of the aura)*
Make now my world all thine,
God's light around me shine!

I count one,
It is done. *(Visualize a band of white fire around the solar plexus)*
O feeling world, be still!
Two and three,
I AM free,
Peace, it is God's will!

I count four,
I do adore *(Visualize a band of white fire around the neck and throat chakra)*
My Presence all divine!
Five and six,
O God, affix
My gaze on thee sublime!

I count seven,
Come, O heaven, *(Visualize a band of white fire around the head and third eye)*
My energies take hold!

(continued)

Eight and nine,
Completely thine,
My mental world enfold!

The white-fire light now encircles me,
All riptides are rejected!
With God's own might around me bright
I AM by love protected!

(Visualize the
white light
encircling all of
the chakras and
the four lower
bodies)

I accept this done right now with full power. I AM this done right now with full power. I AM, I AM, I AM God-life expressing perfection all ways at all times. This which I call forth for myself I call forth for every man, woman, and child on this planet.

Visualize a three-inch band of white fire encircling the body in a clockwise direction: three times around the abdomen for the solar plexus and emotional body, three times around the thyroid and throat for the physical body, and three times around the pituitary gland and head for the mental body.

Note: This decree is mentioned by Djwal Kul on page 226.

10 THE SEVEN IN THE SEVEN AND THE TEST OF THE TEN

Concentric rings of the color rays emanating from the seven chakras denote the macrocosmic-microcosmic interchange of energy within the being of the new-age man and woman. And the outflow and inflow of energy that accompanies the process marks the integration of the soul with the causal body as it enters into communion with the I AM Presence.

We have described the rings of light which in the Christed ones are continually emanating from the heart chakra. Let us also consider that there is intended to be a continual release of concentric rings of light not only from the heart chakra, but from all of the chakras. This release becomes possible as the individual consciously employs the chakras as distributing centers for the energies of the I AM Presence that circulate from the heart chakra throughout the four lower bodies.

Day by day as the aspirant gains control of the flow of life through his being, the inflow and the outflow of the life forces in the chakras increase until the hour of the transfiguration, when all of the seven chakras, together with the secondary heart chamber, are simultaneously releasing the color rings of the seven rays and the eighth ray from the base of the spine to the crown.

In other words, although the entire aura is encircled by the rings that emanate from the heart, within that aura there are released concentric rings of the color rays from each of the other chakras. And these are according to the petals and their corresponding color frequencies that are designated for each of the chakras, which are as follows:

Base of the spine: petals, 4; color frequency, white. Seat of the soul: petals, 6; color frequency, violet. Solar plexus: petals, 10; color frequency, purple and gold. Heart: petals, 12; color frequency, pink. Secondary heart chamber: petals, 8; color frequency, peach. Throat: petals, 16; color frequency, blue. Third eye: petals, 96; color frequency, green. Crown: petals, 972; color frequency, yellow.

Here we begin to see, then, the vision of the wheels within wheels that was beheld by the prophet Ezekiel.[1] Indeed, the chakras are the wheels of the law of a man's being whereby the energies of God are released to and from his being for the integration of his solar awareness in the planes of God's own Self-awareness.

Peter was the disciple who came to Jesus to learn the God-control of the flow of energy. In order to accomplish this, he was required to master fear and doubt and the questioning and curiosity of the carnal mind—all of which issue from the ego's sense of separation from God. Ultimately when Jesus' final test came—the overcoming of the last enemy[2] and the entire momentum of the records of the soul's involvement in mortality—Peter betrayed his Lord.

Jesus' triumph over death by the resurrection flame was his testimony of the law realized in the Logos for the Piscean dispensation. Those who would follow Jesus must always come face to face with these challengers—fear and doubt, death and mortality— of the flame of Christ-mastery that is the mark of the Piscean conqueror.

One day Peter asked Jesus, "Lord, how oft shall my brother sin against me, and I forgive him? till seven times?" Jesus' answer illustrates the law of the multiplication of energy by the power of ten. The Master said, "I say not unto thee, Until seven times: but, Until seventy times seven."[3]

To forgive is to free, and to free one's brother or one's sister is a gift that lies within your hand. Know

CONCENTRIC RINGS EMANATING FROM THE SEVEN CHAKRAS AND FROM THE SECONDARY HEART CHAMBER. "We have described the rings of light which in the Christed ones are continually emanating from the heart chakra. Let us also consider that there is intended to be a continual release of concentric rings of light not only from the heart chakra, but from all of the chakras. This release becomes possible as the individual consciously employs the chakras as distributing centers for the energies of the I AM Presence that circulate from the heart chakra throughout the four lower bodies.

"Day by day as the aspirant gains control of the flow of life through his being, the inflow and the outflow of the life forces in the chakras increase until the hour of the transfiguration, when all of the seven chakras, together with the secondary heart chamber, are simultaneously releasing the color rings of the seven rays and the eighth ray from the base of the spine to the crown."   —DJWAL KUL

you not that when you forgive one another and thereby free one another from bondage to the self, it is in reality you yourself who is freed? Freed from being tied through the law of karma to the one who has offended or wronged you in any way.

To forgive, one must be free of fear, of conceit and deceit, of rebellion against the law, of envy and jealousy, and especially of the retaliatory tendencies that beset the ego consciousness. To forgive and to free all parts of life, one must be free of self-pity and the agony of remorse, of ingratitude and that loathsome sense of self-righteousness. But above all, one must be free of self-love, self-condemnation, and self-hatred.

The energies of freedom are anchored in the seat-of-the-soul chakra located approximately midpoint between the navel and the base of the spine. This is the place where the action of the seventh ray of transmutation can be magnetized. And through this ray the misdemeanors of the soul enacted through a misuse of the energies of all of the chakras can be transmuted, their molds (thought matrices) melted down, and the energies used again for the building of more noble forms and for the filling of those forms with noble ideas and their corollary actions.

To forgive seven times is to forgive by the flame of the Christ the wrongs and injustices practiced by the self upon the self and other selves through its perversion of the seven planes of God's consciousness in the seven chakras. Jesus instructed Peter that this was not enough. It was not enough for the integration of the soul into the wholeness of the Christ. The Master taught his disciple that there is a need for the multiplication of the flame of forgiveness by the power of the ten as well as by the power of the seven.

Seven times seven—the period of the Buddha's enlightenment under the bo tree—is for the mastery of the seven planes of being and the mastery of these planes in the seven bodies of man—the four lower bodies and the three higher bodies (the Christ Self, the I AM Presence, and the causal body). Not just one round of seven for the anchoring of spirals of God's awareness in the wheels of the law, but the action of the seven rays in the consciousness of the Elohim multiplying the power of each of the seven chakras. And so for forty-nine days the Buddha sat under the bo tree to reach the attainment of the Enlightened One.

Now hear this: It is the requirement of the initiation of the Buddhic consciousness that you fulfill the law of the seven chakras in each of the planes of God's consciousness. Therefore, once you have gained the mastery of the heart chakra, that mastery must be transferred to each of the other chakras. This, then, will be the fulfillment of the seven rays as the mastery of the heart chakra is transferred to the others.

Likewise, once you have mastered the power of

the spoken Word in the throat chakra, the energies garnered as the Logos, as the blue fire of God-perfection, direction, and protection, must be upheld in the other six chakras. And the same holds true as you master each of the others.

Having gained the mastery of the seven in the seven, you are ready for the multiplication by the power of the ten. And now we will see why the number ten was so often a part of the ritual and the teaching of Jesus—the ten talents, the ten virgins, the ten lepers, the woman with the ten pieces of silver, and even the dragon having seven heads and ten horns and seven crowns upon his heads.[4]

The solar-plexus chakra has ten petals—five with the positive charge focusing the thrust of Alpha in the secret rays and five with a negative charge focusing the return current of Omega in the secret rays. Thus to the evolving soul consciousness, the solar plexus is the vehicle whereby the initiation of the test of the ten is passed. This is the test of selflessness, which always involves the test of the emotions and of the God-control of those emotions through the Divine Ego, which can come into prominence in the soul only as the result of the surrender of the human ego.

The desire body, as we have said, is anchored in and releases its energy through the solar plexus and the throat chakra. The desire body of mankind contains a greater amount of God's energy than any of the other three lower bodies. Whatever motives and motivational patterns are contained within the desire body, these are fulfilled both consciously and unconsciously as energy spirals are pressed into manifestation through the solar plexus and the throat chakra.

Mankind are hindered in their fulfillment of the divine plan only insofar as their desires do not reflect the desiring of God to be everywhere the fullness of life and truth and love. When, therefore, mankind, with the determination and the surrender of a Christ in the Garden of Gethsemane, surrender all lesser desires to the greater desire of the Universal Self, then the entire weight of the momentum of energy in the desire body propels the fulfillment of the will of God and the soul's own blueprint is outpictured in the four lower bodies.

It is, then, in the hour of the surrender "Nevertheless, not my will but thine be done"[5] that the full momentum of the ten petals in the solar plexus is brought to bear upon the being of man as the multiplying factor of the mastery and the attainment of the other chakras.

The reservoir of light held in the great sun disc, the magnet of the sun presence within the solar plexus, is the energy that multiplies the mastery of love in the heart, of wisdom in the crown, of purity, action, and flow in the base, of freedom in the soul, of vision in the third eye, of service in the solar plexus, and of the sacred Word in the throat.

The energies that can be drawn from the desire body of God, anchored in the solar plexus, and released for the blessing of mankind are indeed unlimited. And whether they are used for healing, for science, for abundance, or for the furthering of the arts and the culture of the Mother, they will lend the momentum of the power of the ten and of the ten-times-ten to the mastery of the other six chakras.

The twelve virtues of the heart can be multiplied individually, one by one, or as the wholeness of the balance of the threefold flame. This multiplication, whether it be of the fires of forgiveness or of the five talents, or for the healing of the lepers, is always accomplished through service to life as the true disciple ministers unto the needs of the Christ in all.

The more one recognizes the need of humanity and desires to help carry the burden of that need, the greater the energy he is able to draw from the great reservoir of life that can be pulled through the heart from the causal body and then anchored in the solar plexus, the reservoir in Mater of the energies of peace.

Realize, too, O chelas who would expand the domain of the aura by the concentric rings of the chakras, that the energies of the solar plexus may be perverted and then employed to multiply the perversions of the other chakras.

And so the seven heads of the dragon, the beast of

the carnal mind, symbolize the perversions of the seven aspects of God's consciousness through the lower mental body. The seven crowns upon those heads show the misuse of the seven rays to amplify the seven perversions. And the ten horns are used to multiply the seven-times-seven by the energies of the human will in the solar plexus. Thus, knowing the law, mankind must choose how they will use God's energy and after what manner they will release the energies of the seven chakras.

Remember, then, the parable of the man who traveled into a far country and called his servants and delivered unto them his goods.[6] The one to whom he gave the five talents is the one who required the initiation of the test of the ten in the solar plexus. The master gave to his servant the five talents as the thrust of the energy of Alpha. In the solar-plexus chakra, these talents are like five positive electrodes of the five secret rays, and they represent the thrust of the Alpha current.

It is up to the soul as it abides in time and space, far from the presence of the lord (the Christ Self and the I AM Presence), to use these electrodes as the masculine polarity of Spirit to draw unto itself through the magnetism of the Spirit the corresponding energies of Omega (the five negative electrodes of the five secret rays), the returning current of the Mother flame that rises from the base-of-the-spine chakra.

The tarrying in time and space until the lord returns is an opportunity to prove one's stewardship—one's ability to hold fast to that which is received and to use it to multiply the essence of Spirit in the planes of Mater.

And so when the lord returned to the servant, he found that the one who had received five talents came to him and brought him other five talents, saying, "Lord, thou deliveredst unto me five talents: behold, I have gained beside them five talents more." Thus, having completed the mastery of the test of the ten, the servant received the commendation of the lord, "Well done, thou good and faithful servant; thou hast been faithful over a few things, I will make thee ruler over many things: enter thou into the joy of thy lord."

The joy of the lord is the joyous energy of the sixth ray anchored in the solar plexus for the multiplication of the energies of life. Note that only five of the ten virgins passed the test of being prepared for the entering in to the chamber of the heart with the Chohan of the Sixth Ray,[7] the Master of the Piscean cycle.

This is the hour of the mastery of the feminine ray through the initiation that is called the test of the ten. And the test of the ten is the test of selflessness whereby you salute the Mother ray with the Hail Mary and thereby confirm the balance of the ten petals of the solar plexus, giving ten Hail Marys in each of the five sections of your morning rosary.[8] And the test of the ten multiplied by the action of the five secret rays that form the star of man's being is for the drawing in through the chakras of the energies of the Mother and of the Holy Spirit.

This is the age of opportunity for balance in the heart, balance in the inflow and the outflow of the sacred breath, and balance in the tests of the seven-times-seven multiplied by the power of the ten.

So fulfill the cycles of energy flow within the forcefield of being and watch how the aura will grow and grow and grow. I am focusing the geometry of the aura of the Cosmic Christ until you, by the law of balance, harmony, and congruency, are able to assume that aura.

11 THE FLAME OF FREEDOM IN THE AQUARIAN CYCLE

My beloved, hear now the story of the bondage of the souls of the Israelites—how they were freed by God from the Egyptian bondage and how they entered again into the bondage of the fleshpots of Egypt. Mankind have often wondered why the angel of the Lord or the Lord God himself did not come down from the mountain of the gods to set free the captives of the oppressors, but instead allowed the self-made law of idolatry to render that captivity captive of the law of karma.

Mankind cry out for salvation, and in the groanings of their souls they appeal to the Almighty. And yet the Almighty has appeared time and time again through his emissaries—angels, prophets, and messengers—to warn of the impending doom that hangs like the sword of Damocles over the idolatrous generation. Likewise, the hand of mercy, of justice, of prophecy, and of wisdom has appeared; and yet mankind, in the perverseness of the wicked, have defied the counsels and the counselors of the God of Israel.

To those who would know the freedom of the soul, I say, listen well! For there is a price that must be paid for that freedom. It is the surrender of your idols, of your idolatry, and of your submission to the idolatrous generation.

And so it came to pass in the days of the judges that an angel of the Lord came up from Gilgal to Bochim and said to the children of Israel: "I made you to go up out of Egypt and have brought you unto the land which I sware unto your fathers; and I said, I will never break my covenant with you. And ye shall make no league with the inhabitants of this land; ye shall throw down their altars: but ye have not obeyed my voice: why have ye done this?

"Wherefore I also said, I will not drive them out from before you; but they shall be as thorns in your sides, and their gods shall be a snare unto you. And it came to pass, when the angel of the Lord spake these words unto all the children of Israel, that the people lifted up their voice and wept."[1]

Through the hand of Moses, the Israelites were rescued from the bondage of Egypt, which represents the bondage of the soul to the cult of death and the cult of the serpent that arises out of the misuse of the sacred fire in the base-of-the-spine chakra. This is that bondage which results from the utter perversion of the Mother flame.

In order for the energies of the Israelites to rise to the plane of God-awareness in the seat-of-the-soul chakra, it was necessary that they be delivered from those who enslaved their consciousness and their energies to spirals of disintegration and death. But in order for them to retain that freedom, to receive the blessings of the Lord, and to be participants in the covenant of their Maker, it was required of them that they should not, in the words of Paul, be "unequally yoked together with unbelievers."[2]

Therefore, God warned the Israelites to be free from entanglements with those who were carnally minded, for by cosmic law the children of righteousness ought not to have fellowship—especially intermarriage and the bearing of offspring—with the children of unrighteousness. For the true Israelites are the children of reality whom God would one day use as the seed of Abraham to bring forth the Christ consciousness and that great nation which would be the fulfillment of the City Foursquare.[3]

But they would not; and their leaders did not drive out the inhabitants of the land that God had given them, nor did they throw down their altars and challenge their gods. And generations arose who knew not the Lord nor the works that he had done for Israel; and they did evil in the sight of God, forsaking the Lord and serving the false gods of Baal and Ashtaroth. Even when the Lord raised up judges among them to deliver them out of the hand of the spoilers, yet in their perverseness they would not hearken unto the judges, but "went a whoring after other gods and bowed themselves unto them."[4]

So their corruption was great, and the anger of the Lord was hot against the Israelites who departed not from their stubborn ways. And the Lord left the nations of the laggard generation without driving them out in order to prove Israel and to be the testing of her soul. These were the Philistines, the Canaanites, the Sidonians, and the Hivites.

Moreover, those who had been chosen of the Lord to carry the torch of freedom "dwelt among the Canaanites, Hittites, and Amorites, and Perizzites, and Hivites, and Jebusites: and they took their daughters to be their wives and gave their daughters to their sons and served their gods. And the children of Israel did evil in the sight of the Lord and forgat the Lord their God and served Baalim and the groves.[5]

"Come now, and let us reason together, saith the Lord: though your sins be as scarlet, they shall be as white as snow; though they be red like crimson, they shall be as wool."[6]

In the seat-of-the-soul chakra, there are anchored

in man and in woman the powers of procreation—the seed of Alpha in man, the egg of Omega in woman. And the seed and the egg contain the mandala of the Christ consciousness that is passed on from generation to generation through those who espouse the disciplines of the law and keep the commandments of their God.

The soul that is free is the soul that retains the image of the Christ and is the progenitor of that image in the raising-up of the sons and daughters of God who take dominion not only over the earth, but over the idolatrous generations who inhabit the earth. These are of the Christ consciousness, which works the works of God and bears the fruit thereof. These are they who multiply the God consciousness "as above, so below" by preserving in honor the freedom of the soul.

Some among the original Hebrews, chosen of God and to whom God gave the Promised Land, compromised their attainment in the seat-of-the-soul chakra by allowing the seed (the Christic light) of Abraham to be commingled with the Canaanites. By so doing they not only forfeited their right to be called the chosen people, but they also forfeited their vision of God in manifestation—the faculty of the third-eye chakra—which would have enabled them to recognize the Christed one who came in fulfillment of the prophecy of Isaiah.

So great was the abomination of those who had been chosen to bear the Word of the law that the Lord God allowed them to be taken into Assyrian and Babylonian captivity and ultimately to be scattered over the face of the earth. Those among the descendants of the twelve tribes of Israel who remembered their calling to free a planet and her people from idolatry and who had never compromised the law of the prophets and the patriarchs were allowed to embody upon a new continent.

They were given another land that was the fulfillment of the promise of God unto Abraham—the land of the I AM race. That race is composed of all peoples and kindreds and tongues who have the worship of the individual Christ and the one God—the God of Abraham, of Isaac, and of Jacob, who declared himself unto Moses as the principle of the I AM THAT I AM and who affirmed, "This is my name for ever, and this is my memorial unto all generations."[7]

Because the original race that was chosen to bear that name compromised the light, the very Christos of the seed of the patriarchs, the opportunity to bear the flame of freedom was widened to include all who would choose to come apart from the idolatrous generation to be a separate people who would raise up in the wilderness of the human consciousness the brazen serpent,[8] which symbolized the raising-up of

THE SEAT-OF-THE-SOUL CHAKRA. The place where the soul is anchored to the etheric (memory) and physical bodies. This chakra focuses the flame of freedom, transmutation and forgiveness—the violet flame. The violet flame is the seventh-ray aspect of the Holy Spirit that comes to us under the sponsorship of Saint Germain, the master of the imminent seventh, or Aquarian, age.

Through the science of the spoken Word, you can direct the accelerating violet flame of the Holy Spirit into the accumulation of karma recorded in the subconscious 'electronic belt'. And you can feel how the flame renews thought and feeling, liberating the soul to become all that God made it to be.

The six petals of the soul chakra represent the six-pointed star of victory. They govern the flow of light and the karmic patterns in the genes and chromosomes and in the sperm and the egg of man and woman.

—ECP

violet

the energies of the Divine Mother—the serpentine fires of the Goddess Kundalini. This is indeed the caduceus action rising as the life force, the energy that blossomed as Aaron's rod[9] through the union of the spirals of Alpha and Omega.

Thus, beloved—and I speak to all children of the I AM THAT I AM in every nation upon earth—the mastery of the seat-of-the-soul chakra is the mastery of the flame of freedom in the Aquarian cycle. It is the retaining of the energy of the seed and the egg in preparation for the bringing forth of Christed ones of the seventh root race. And it is the release of that energy in the upper chakras in creativity, in genius, in learning and innovation, and in the art, the music, the literature, and the culture of the Divine Mother.

And thus the fires of freedom anchored in the soul are not to be used in acts of immorality or for the breaking of the code of the Ten Commandments or for the desecration of the grace of the Christ and the sacred energies of the Holy Spirit.

Therefore, in the true spirit of wholeness (hol-i-ness), let the sons and daughters of God who would build the temple and the New Jerusalem[10] raise up the energies of the Mother and of the soul through the resurrection spiral. And let those energies be consecrated on the altar of the heart for the building of the golden age.

To you who would have the aura of self-mastery,

of soul freedom, I say: Let the energies of your lusts, of your pleasure seeking, of the gratification of the senses be now raised up in the wholeness of Almighty God! And with the courage, the honor, and the conviction of the Christed ones, stand before the altar of the Lord of Israel and declare:

In the name of the Messiah who has come into the
   holy of holies of my being, I consecrate my energies to the fulfillment of the spirals of Alpha and
   Omega

In the name of the Promised One whose promise is
   fulfilled in me this day, let the brazen serpent be
   raised up in the wilderness

In the name of the King of Kings and Lord of Lords,
   let the energies of my soul rise for the fulfillment
   of life

In the true name of the Lord God of Israel, I proclaim
   I AM THAT I AM
   I AM the resurrection and the life of every cell
      and atom of my four lower bodies
      now made manifest
   I AM the victory of the ascension in the light
   I AM the ascending triangle of Mater
      converging in the heart chakra and merging
      with the descending triangle of Spirit
   I AM the six-pointed star of victory
   I AM the light of all that *is real*

In my soul I AM free, for my energies are tethered to
the Holy One of Israel
And in the name of the one true God and in fulfillment of his commandment, I withdraw the seed
and the egg of Alpha
and Omega
from the unrighteous and the idolatrous generation
I AM the fulfillment of the law of love
I AM a keeper of the flame
And I AM the guardian light of the covenant of my
Maker, the Lord God of Israel

The challenge goes forth from the Lords of Karma
to those who would keep the flame of Israel in
America, in the New Jerusalem, and in every nation
upon earth: Put down your idolatry and your idolatrous generation, cast down the altars of Baal and
Ashtaroth throughout the land, and reclaim your
temples for the Lord God of hosts!

And let my people return to the sanctity of the
sacred ritual of the exchange of the sacred fire between enlightened man and woman who have come
before the altar of God to consecrate their union for
the bringing forth of the lightbearers. And let the
young who ought to be maturing in the ways of the
Christ be freed from the luciferian perversions of
life's sacred energies, from the incorrect use of the
sacred fire in sex, from premarital exchanges, and

from perverted practices that issue from the degenerate spirals of Sodom and Gomorrah.

So let these energies be restored to the place of the holy of holies. For the fiat of the Lord rings forth from Horeb this day: Let my people go![11] Set the captives free! and let the judges render judgment this day! In the name of the living Christ: Be thou made whole!

I am invoking the flaming presence of the I AM THAT I AM around all who have chosen to be the fulfillment of the promise of the Lord to Abraham, "I will make thy seed as the stars of the sky in multitude and as the sand which is by the sea shore innumerable."[12]

And I am placing the ring of freedom's fire from my consciousness as a circle of protection around the seat-of-the-soul chakra, the energies thereof, and the Christic pattern of the seed and the egg for the sealing of life within you as the life victorious and triumphant.

12 THE ENERGIES OF THE SOUL RAISED TO THE THIRD EYE

Sealed in an ovoid of light, the energies of the seat-of-the-soul chakra rise to the level of the third eye for the fulfillment of the promise of the City Foursquare. Now let the ascending triangle of the seventh ray merge with the descending triangle of the fifth ray for the alchemy of the violet flame and the precipitation of the green flame that produce the mastery of the air element in the plane of the mind.

To see is to be, and to be is to see. When you raise up the energies of the soul and of your solar awareness to the plane of the all-seeing eye and when you have the balance of love and wisdom converging at the point of reality, you become an alchemist of the Spirit in the planes of Matter. You who are the handiwork of God, by a little self-discipline, by a little self-sacrifice, can come into the inheritance of the children of Israel and behold in the tabernacle of being the coming of the City Foursquare.

In the all-seeing eye of God the Great Silent Watcher holds the immaculate concept of the inheritance of the sons and daughters of God. And the petals in the third eye are forty-eight for the outward thrust of Alpha and forty-eight for the inward thrust of Omega. In the vision of the Christ is the protection of the hereditary traits carried in the seed and the egg of man and woman. Indeed it is in the vision of the Christ that the attributes which the Lord God impressed upon the image and likeness of himself in male and female are held.

Each of the petals of the third-eye chakra focuses the guardian action of the law and the blueprint of life that is focused in the chromosomes and genes. Moreover, the forty-eight pairs of petals are for the anchoring of the twelve aspects of God's consciousness in each of the four lower bodies as they represent the four sides of the pyramid of life.[1]

Every soul that would be free must accept the challenge to be the fullness of the law of life and the balance of the threefold flame in manifestation in each of the four lower bodies. And so you see, when the twelve godly attributes have been magnetized in the heart chakra, they can be squared through the vision of the all-seeing eye of God in the third-eye

THE THIRD-EYE CHAKRA. We return to the consciousness of absolute Good through the third-eye chakra, which has ninety-six petals. The third eye, vibrating in the emerald green of the science of truth, gives us the immaculate picture of individuals, of civilizations, of the divine pattern.

Jesus said: "The light of the body is the eye." (Matt. 6:22) Through the all-seeing eye of God, the inner eye of the soul, you tune in to what should be in reality, instead of what may be occurring in the actualities of the present.

You can always tell whether or not you are looking through the third eye or through the two eyes: the third eye always gives you the immaculate concept of the blueprint of life as well as the discrimination to know Good and Evil. The two eyes give you a relative and often unclear perception and perspective on life. They do not penetrate beyond the physical plane unless in an exalted vision the faculty of sight be accelerated by miraculous intercession.

—ECP

green

chakra. And when the threefold flame and the twelve virtues are balanced in the four lower bodies, there is the converging of energy spirals in the third eye as the capstone is placed on the pyramid of life in the coming of the Christ consciousness.

The great Master Jesus gave the key to the control of the auric light in his teaching on the all-seeing eye.[2] He said, "The light of the body is the eye." And he explained to the disciples that the light of the aura is focused in the eye—the inner eye of the soul that perceives life with the spherical vision of the mind of God.

While the eyes of mankind observe the passing scenes, the scenarios of life experienced in time and space, the eye of the soul is continually interpolating patterns of causation, angles of perfection, the very building blocks of the creation that underlie all experience in the planes of Mater. Thus while the outer man takes life at its face value, the soul is evaluating the flow of energy, of karma, and of the cycles of life from the standpoint of inner reality.

The training given to the Virgin Mary as she prepared the temple for the coming of the Christed One for a mission in the womb of time and space was in the exercise of the faculty of God-vision through the power of concentration. Concentration is the focusing of the energies of the heart in the third-eye chakra as a concentrated beam of emerald hue that penetrates atomic particles, molecules of being, and cells of consciousness, drawing them into alignment with the original blueprint of the creation.

Constancy is another attribute of the overcomers that Mary learned to apply. For constancy is the ritual of applying the fifth ray to the tasks at hand in order that every deed that is done, every service that is rendered, be fulfilled according to the lines of force, the molecules of identity that govern the manifestations of Christed man and Christed woman.

Through concentration, then, as a concentrated flow of light through the forty-eight pairs of petals in the third-eye chakra, mankind may master the planes of Mater in the God-controlled release of energy from the planes of Spirit.

"If therefore thine eye be single, thy whole body shall be full of light." The single-eyed vision of which Jesus spoke is the converging of the six-pointed star of Christed awareness in the third eye.

When this is accomplished, man and woman are perpetually aware of reality; and through that awareness, life in the four octaves of selfhood is ever consecrated to the Holy Spirit. And the flow of energy through the grids and forcefields of the twelve godly attributes makes the whole body in the planes of God's consciousness—in fire, air, water, and earth— "full of light."

In order to be perfection, man must see perfection.

MEDITATION IN THE PYRAMID ON THE THIRTEEN STEPS OF INITIATION. The disciple seated in the pyramid is meditating on the thirteen steps of initiation in the Christ consciousness. The initiations of the twelve disciples, represented by the twelve signs (frequencies) of the zodiac, can be seen as twelve points on a cosmic clock; the initiations of the Christ are positioned in the center of the clock. These progressive steps on the path of personal Christhood are illustrated here by thirteen spirals, or levels of attainment, which are achieved through the seven chakras.   —ECP

THIRTY-THREE COILS OF VICTORY. The thirty-three cycles in the pyramid denote the thirty-three initiations on the path of the ascension, which was demonstrated by Jesus Christ.   —ECP

"Every soul that would be free must accept the challenge to be the fullness of the law of life and the balance of the threefold flame in manifestation in each of the four lower bodies. And so you see, when the twelve godly attributes have been magnetized in the heart chakra, they can be squared through the vision of the all-seeing eye of God in the third-eye chakra. And when the threefold flame and the twelve virtues are balanced in the four lower bodies, there is the converging of energy spirals in the third eye as the capstone is placed on the pyramid of life in the coming of the Christ consciousness."   —DJWAL KUL

The goal of those who are on the ascending spiral of being is the perfection of the original Monad, the I AM Presence. To accept perfection not only as the goal of life but as the law of life is to enter the path of initiation—*i-niche-i-action*. Initiation begins when that which affirms *I AM,* that which has an awareness of selfhood, secures itself in the *niche* of the all-seeing *eye* of God for the purpose of establishing right *action* on earth as it is in heaven.

All who would understand the miracle of the expanding circles of awareness manifest in and as the aura must come to the realization that the image and likeness of God, the pattern of the Christ out of which male and female were created,[3] is held in the third eye of each one as the potential that every living soul is destined to fulfill.

The majority of mankind fail to make contact with that potential, which is the image of the Real Self. Lifetime after lifetime, the image remains latent, the soul is not quickened, the consciousness is unmoved, and mankind go their separatist ways according to their perceptions of duality and the two-eyed vision of the outer consciousness that always perceives life as linear, as relative.

Through the sedimentation of the centuries, layer upon layer of effluvia cover over the glorious vision of the all-seeing eye of God manifest in man. And even when energies flow through the third-eye chakra, because of the energy veil that covers over this orifice of reality, mankind wrongly exercise the faculty of God-seeing.

Thus Jesus warned, "But if thine eye be evil, thy whole body shall be full of darkness"; that is, if the third eye be contaminated with the energy veil, then the four lower bodies will be filled with that darkness which manifests as the result of the misqualification, or the misuse, of the energies of the third eye.

And so the Master expounded on the consequences of the evil eye: "If therefore the light that is in thee be darkness, how great is that darkness!" He explained to his disciples: If the light which the Lord thy God giveth thee be qualified as darkness, how great is the momentum of that darkness to perpetuate life in terror and in trauma.

Finally the Master gave the formula for living in the wholeness of the City Foursquare: "No man can serve two masters: for either he will hate the one and love the other; or else he will hold to the one and despise the other. Ye cannot serve God and mammon." His inner teaching to the disciples was that no one can simultaneously hold the vision of perfection and imperfection: no one can gaze at once upon the image of Christ and the image of Satan.

This division of the consciousness between the way of God and the ways of the world is calculated ultimately to destroy the soul and its opportunity for Godward evolution. Therefore you see that the temptation to eat of the fruit of the tree of the knowledge of good and evil[4] is the first step in the plot of the fallen ones, whose *modus operandi* is always divide and conquer.

To divide the body of God upon earth, to split the consciousness of the individual, to sunder being—driving wedges between the four lower bodies and the soul, causing schism within and without, and ultimately the destruction of both the human and the divine personality through a loss of contact with the material as well as the spiritual environments—this is the intent of the fallen ones bent on the destruction, one by one, of each individual framework of identity.

It is not possible for mankind to serve the carnal mind and the Christed One simultaneously. Therefore the challenge is given to the stalwart and the true to purify the center that has been established for the anchoring of the vision of God and of the perfect pattern of being and to let the energies that have been trained to focus on duality be raised to the plane of oneness. As the Psalmist said: "I will lift up mine eyes unto the hills, from whence cometh my help. My help cometh from the Lord [the impersonal-personal law], which made heaven and earth."[5]

Let vision flow from the upper reaches of consciousness! Let vision flow back to God and be tethered to the blueprint out of which all things were made!

And know, O disciples of the law, that he that keepeth the house of reality is ever beholding perfection within you, through you, as the consciousness of the all-seeing eye. Indeed, the Lord, the Christed One of yourself, is thy keeper[6]—keeping the way of the Tree of Life, keeping the flow of energy, keeping the flame within the hidden chamber of the heart.

Thus that Christed One within you *is* the all-seeing, all-knowing, all-loving One who preserves thee from all aspects of the energy veil that would becloud the mind and the consciousness. The Christ consciousness *is* the preserver of thy soul.

And thus the Lord shall preserve the going-out of the energies of divine vision from the third-eye chakra—of that constancy which manifests as concentration upon and consecration to the immaculate concept of all life. The Christ Self shall preserve the coming-in into the temple of the soul of the energies of the Mother and the Holy Spirit for the balanced manifestation of the City Foursquare "from this time forth and even for evermore."

Therefore, let all flesh, all carnality, and all carnal-mindedness be silent before the Lord; for his energies are raised up out of the holy habitation of the Divine Mother (the base-of-the-spine chakra) and of the soul (the seat-of-the-soul chakra) unto the vision of the all-seeing eye (the third-eye chakra).

O chelas of the sacred fire, behold, as the prophet Zechariah saw through the all-seeing eye, the vision of Joshua the high priest standing before the angel of the Lord and Satan standing at his right hand to resist him.[7] Thus it is in the arena of action, in the flow of time and space, that the carnal mind, the dragon of self-indulgence, comes forth to challenge the soul as it prepares to merge with the image of the Real Self, the Only Begotten of God.

But the Lord, as the law of being, rebukes the energies misqualified in the self-centeredness of the ego. And although the soul, as Joshua, may be clothed with the filthy garments, representing its former involvement with the world, the Lord speaks the fiat of the cleansing unto the fiery angels who stand before him, saying, "Take away the filthy garments from him."

And unto the soul the declaration of the law of forgiveness in the changing of garments is given: "Behold, I have caused thine iniquity to pass from thee, and I will clothe thee with change of raiment." And so in answer to the command of the Lord, they set a fair mitre upon his head and clothed him with garments as the angel of the Lord stood by.

And now comes the covenant of the Lord of hosts made unto every soul who will slay the dragon of the not-self, the false identity that has claimed the kingdom of the seat-of-the-soul chakra and perverted there the image of the True Self held in the all-seeing eye of God:

"If thou wilt walk in my ways and if thou wilt keep my charge, then thou shalt also judge my house and shalt also keep my courts, and I will give thee places to walk among these that stand by. Hear now, O Joshua the high priest, thou and thy fellows that sit before thee: for they are men wondered at: for, behold, I will bring forth my servant the BRANCH." This is the promise to every soul who will overcome idolatry in the seat of the soul and who will return to one God and one Christ perceived as the law of immaculate selfhood.

"For behold the stone that I have laid before [the soul of] Joshua; upon one stone [the rock of Christ] shall be seven eyes." This is the Lord's promise of the transformation of the soul consciousness into the Christ consciousness through the raising-up of the energies from the level of the seat-of-the-soul chakra to the level of the third eye.

Therefore Christ—the Promised One, the Messiah —shall come into thy being, into the citadel of thy consciousness. And the seven eyes indicate the mastery of the seven rays of the Christ consciousness in the seven chakras that comes about through the mastery of the single-eyed vision of the Lord.

"Behold, I will engrave the graving thereof, saith the Lord of hosts, and I will remove the iniquity of that land in one day." And so in one cycle as the fulfillment of the round of the expression of God's consciousness through the seven rays shall the transmutation of the sin of the Israelites be accomplished.

And in that day, when the souls of the true Israelites accept the covenant of their Maker, then shall they call every man neighbor in the confraternity of souls who recognize the flame of life as held in common by all. In that day shall the members of the body of God in the house of Israel be found under the vine of the Christ and under the direction of the individual Christ Self. And they shall make supplication unto the Lord of being under the fig tree— the I AM THAT I AM—the great Presence of the Monad of Life revealed as the one true God.

Then shall Joshua the high priest—the soul that has been vindicated in the sacred fires of the Holy Spirit—be made the true head of the Church as he takes dominion in the New Jerusalem through the single-eyed vision of the Christ. And Zerubbabel, representing the state, the energies of Mater conquered in the soul and converging in the third eye as the City Foursquare, fulfills the balance of the foundations of the law as the head of the state.

Now God-government reigns throughout the world of the individual and the nations because mankind have conquered the enemy within and without "not by might nor by power, but by my

Spirit [the I AM Presence], saith the Lord of hosts."[8]

Thus in the mastery of the air element through the seat-of-the-soul chakra and the third eye, heart and head, church and state, Spirit and Matter, are one in the harmony of the six-pointed star.

And the two anointed ones stand by the Lord of the whole earth with those seven which are the eyes of the Lord—the seven chakras that are the windows of the soul—while the seven Elohim, the seven Spirits of God, anchor in mankind and in the planetary body the energies of the seven rays "which run [flow] to and fro through the whole earth."[9] The olive trees are the messengers of the Lord who in every age proclaim the balance of Alpha and Omega in church and in state and in the life of God lived triumphantly here and now.

I am for the balanced manifestation of the light within an expanding auric forcefield destined to be of planetary dimension.

13 THE RAISING-UP OF THE ENERGIES OF THE MOTHER

From the fount of the Mother arise the energies of the Trinity—of Mother, Son, and Holy Spirit—sacred Mater-realization of the law, the Logos, and the life.

In the four petals of the base-of-the-spine chakra is the opportunity for the mastery of self in Matter, for taking dominion over earth, air, fire, and water. The base of the spine is the very foundation of life in form. It is the square of the base of the pyramid that is built line upon line by the wise master builders who have learned to focus the threefold flame not only in the center of the pyramid, but also in the center of every stone that is laid according to the chief cornerstone, the Christ consciousness without which no other stone is laid that is laid.

The four petals of the Mother are for the anchoring in Matter-form of the action of the squaring of the fires of the heart chakra whereby the circle of infinity becomes the cube of God Self-awareness in time and space. The four petals form the base of the figure-eight pattern—even the flow of the caduceus—that crosses in the heart chakra and reaches its culmination in the crown of life.

These four petals symbolize twin flames mastering the energies of life "as above, so below"—plus and minus in Alpha, plus and minus in Omega. Whether in Spirit or in Mater, in the flame of the Divine Mother twin flames converge for the union of the energies of life that are for the emancipation of the Christ consciousness in all. White light bursts forth as a thousand suns signal across the skies the fohatic emanations of the eternal Logos.

> In the base of the spine,
> A geometry of harmony sublime,
> The Mother cradles primal essence
> For the realization here and now
> Of Father, Son, and Holy Spirit's vow.
> In the cradle of the Mother
> Is the Manchild's sphere.
> In the cradle of the Mother
> Are the hieroglyphs of Spirit
> And the lexicon of the law.
> In the cradle of the Mother

THE BASE-OF-THE-SPINE CHAKRA. The cradle of the Mother. Four petals set the pattern for the flowering of the Mother flame in each of the four lower bodies. Our entire physical universe is a manifestation of Mother because it is Spirit's point of focalization in Matter. From that point, the soul (the feminine potential of man and woman) rises for the reunion of Mother with Father in the crown, which brings forth the Son, the Christ, in the center of the heart.

When you have the mastery of the base chakra, you attain the omnipresent consciousness of Mother Mary. And it is the white fire of the Mother that gives you the power to be everywhere on earth simultaneously. Self-mastery of the base-of-the-spine chakra is the secret of the bilocation and levitation of the saints. In the East, its fire is known as the Kundalini.   —ECP

white

CADUCEUS ACTION THROUGH PURIFIED CHAKRAS.

"The four petals of the Mother are for the anchoring in Matter-form of the action of the squaring of the fires of the heart whereby the circle of infinity becomes the cube of God Self-awareness in time and space. The four petals form the base of the figure-eight pattern—even the flow of the caduceus—that crosses in the heart of man and reaches its culmination in the crown of life.

"These four petals symbolize twin flames mastering the energies of life 'as above, so below'—plus and minus in Alpha, plus and minus in Omega. Whether in Spirit or in Mater, in the flame of the Divine Mother twin flames converge for the union of the energies of life that are for the emancipation of the Christ consciousness in all. White light bursts forth as a thousand suns signal across the skies the fohatic emanations of the eternal Logos."   —DJWAL KUL

Is a diamond without flaw
And the crystal-clear water
Flowing as the river of life.
In the cradle of the Mother
Is child-man waiting to be born.
In the cradle of the Mother
Is the coming of a golden morn.

When the Holy Ghost came upon the virgin consciousness of Mary as she exemplified the Mother ray
[Ma-ray] and the power of the Highest overshad-
owed her, there was the converging in her womb of
the energies of Alpha and Omega for the fulfillment
of the promise of the coming of Messias.[1] By her
devotion to the Mother ray and to the immaculate
concept of the soul of Christ, Mary had magnetized
in her four lower bodies and in her chakras an intense concentration of the polarity of Omega.

The awareness of God as Mother was so real
within the consciousness of Mary and her identification of self in and as the Mother flame was so complete that in the true understanding of the self as
God, she became in the plane of Mater God's own
awareness of Self as Mother. Hence the salutation of
Gabriel, "Hail, thou that art highly favoured, *the
Lord is with thee:* blessed art thou among women."[2]

Among the generations of the *womb man*ifestation, Mary excelled and was highly favored with

grace—the grace of Spirit, of Alpha. But this favoring was the fulfillment of the law; for that portion of the Cosmic Virgin which she had garnered in Matter was the magnetization factor whereby the Holy Ghost and the seed of the Most High God converged in her womb for the immaculate conception of Jesus, the Christed One.

The Magnificat of Mary recorded in the first chapter of the Book of Luke* is the praise of this daughter of Israel whose soul (anchored in the seat-of-the-soul chakra) magnifies the law of the Lord, the Word of the Lord, and the seed of the Holy Ghost. And the rejoicing of her spirit is the buoyant energy of the I AM Presence flowing through her being and throughout all of her centers—the light of her God and her Saviour.

In the Magnificat, Mary utters forth her praise of the I AM Presence, who has regarded the "low estate of his handmaiden." This blessed one realized that but for the Spirit of the I AM THAT I AM, the energies of the Mother in the base of the spine would remain quiescent. But with the moving of that Spirit in her being, she recognized the fountain of life springing forth—with all generations, all cyclings of energies from the chakras, affirming the blessedness of the rising flow of the Mother flame.

Mary, a true daughter of Israel, sanctifies the name

*Luke 1:46–55. See page 287.

of God "I AM THAT I AM" and affirms that name as the power of the conception of the Christ. And thereby she confirms the vision of his great mercy and strength, of his judgments, and of the scattering of the proud who have misused the energies of God in the imaginations of their hearts.

She acknowledges the exaltation of the energies of life and the putting-down of the mighty from their seats—from their positions of worldly power gained by the positioning of the ego in the seats of the chakras where Christ ought to be enthroned. In the true Spirit of prophecy, she foretells the time when those who anchor in life and in life's sacred centers the dark energies of the ego and the energy veil with which it surrounds itself will be utterly cast down.

And in those who hunger for the truth and righteousness of the law, she foresees the filling of the aura and of the centers with goodly virtue. But those whose auras and chakras are already filled with the miasma of mechanization are sent empty away—devoid of the Holy Spirit. And so Mary, by her acceptance of the covenant that the I AM Presence had made with Abraham and with the seed of the Christ that he bore, became the instrument of the culmination of the Christ consciousness in the sons and daughters of Israel.

When you give the salutation to the Mother ray in the recitation of the Hail Mary, you are giving praise to the energies of the Mother locked within the flame in the hidden chamber of the heart and sealed in the base-of-the-spine chakra. In this gentle yet powerful salutation, you are day by day drawing the energies of the white-fire core and the base of the spine—yes, even the serpentine fires of the Goddess Kundalini—up the spinal altar for the nourishment and the wholeness of life in all of its centers.

And so, you see, down through the centuries, the precious rosary given by the saints as an offering to the holy Mother has been the means whereby the ascended masters have introduced into Western culture an aspect of the science practiced by the yogis of the Himalayas in the raising of the Kundalini and the purification of consciousness thereby. The personification of the Mother in Mary in the West, and the adoration of that Mother image by all who acknowledge her Son as the Christed One, is the means, altogether safe, whereby the soul might experience the reunion with the Father-Mother God in the tabernacle of being.

This ritual can be actualized in this very life here on earth without forcing the chakras and without disturbing the delicate balance of karmic cycles. On a parallel with this experience is the transmutation by the fires of the Holy Spirit of the energy layers of the electronic belt, which is comprised of the records, held in the subconscious strata of the mind, of individual causation and the memory of the soul's previous incarnations since the descent into Matter.

The New-Age Rosary,[3] with scriptural meditations on the life of Jesus and Mary combined with affirmations and adorations of the Spirit, provides the seeker after the divine union with a masterful yet moderate method of communion for the raising-up of the energies of the Mother through the chakras to that union in the crown which is the attainment of the God consciousness, the Buddhic light, in the petals (virtues) of the thousand-petaled lotus.

To all who are enamored with the Mother flame, I say: The Lord hath need of thee. For to saturate the planes of fire, air, water, and earth with the devotion of the Mother ray—this is the goal of life on earth.

To raise up a culture and a civilization that is saturated with light, light's dimension, and light's intention to be the fullness of God as "thy kingdom come on earth as it is in heaven"[4]—this indeed is the true destiny of the soul. The more mankind come to the feet of the Divine Mother with praise and with glory, the more they will magnetize the light of Father and Son for the converging of the fires of the Holy Spirit in all.

The world is often devoid of the Spirit of the Christ Mass and of the true Spirit of the law, because they have forsaken the true image of the Mother and erected in her place the great whore and the lusts of Babylon the

Great.[5] These idols continually drain the chakras and the aura of mankind of that light which flows from the I AM Presence, the light of the Christ "which lighteth every man that cometh into the world."[6] What a pity that mankind who are the recipients of that wondrous light of the star of his appearing "consume it," as James said, "upon their lusts."[7]

In order for mankind to expand layer upon layer, sphere within sphere, the light of the aura, the old momentums of the carnal mind must be broken and the energies of the Mother raised step by step, initiation by initiation, up the spinal ladder through each of the chakras until the rippling of life in the ecstasy of communion is experienced in the resurrection of being and the transfiguration from mortality to immortality.

Those who truly acknowledge the Father acknowledge the Son. Those who truly acknowledge the Son acknowledge the Mother. It is the light of the Son, the living joy of the Son manifest in the threefold flame, that magnetizes the energies of the Mother from the base of the spine to the heart.

And therefore, those who have developed a more-than-ordinary expanse of the Christ consciousness do magnetize the flame of the Mother, which, when drawn up through being and consciousness, does ultimately merge with the light of the Father in the crown. When this occurs, the Holy Ghost fills the tabernacle of being with a peculiar witness of the wholeness of God.

The ascending triangle of white fire (the energy of Omega in the base chakra) that converges with the descending triangle of yellow fire (the energy of Alpha in the crown) in the crown and in the heart is the fusion of the energies of the Father-Mother God in the Star of David, the star of every man's victory, and the promise of the Messiah. All who strive for this union and practice the ritual of daily offering their energies upon the altar of the heart will increase the aura to its maximum potential, until the aura itself, focusing the Great Central Sun magnet, draws forth the living, breathing essence of the Holy Spirit, and man and woman walk the earth filled with the Presence of our God.

This is the goal of life for you. To achieve it you must follow the meditations and exercises recommended by the ascended masters, including those given in this series. But above all, you must become love, all love, that you might fulfill the law of your being and thereby transcend the law of time and space.

I am fitting you for the goal of the alchemical marriage, and I shall give you an exercise for the marriage of the soul to the Spirit of God in my final release in this series.

I am and I remain in the center of the star of your being.

THE MAGNIFICAT OF MARY

My soul doth magnify the Lord,
And my spirit hath rejoiced in God my Saviour.
For He hath regarded the low estate
     of His handmaiden:
For, behold, from henceforth
     all generations shall call me blessed.
For He that is mighty hath done to me great things;
     and holy is His name.
And His mercy is on them that fear Him
     from generation to generation.
He hath shewed strength with His arm;
He hath scattered the proud
     in the imagination of their hearts.
He hath put down the mighty from their seats
     and exalted them of low degree.
He hath filled the hungry with good things;
     and the rich He hath sent empty away.
He hath holpen His servant Israel
     in remembrance of His mercy;
As He spake to our fathers,
     to Abraham, and to his seed for ever.

Note: This meditation is mentioned by Djwal Kul on pages 281–82.

14 THE RITUAL OF THE ALCHEMICAL UNION

Thirty-three centuries ago, one Ikhnaton[1] beheld the sun as the focal point for God's consciousness and adored the light radiating forth from the great sun disc. The pharaoh of Egypt described the universe as a giant egg, a great cell of being in which he conceived the nucleus as the source of that creative force which he acknowledged as the life energy of God.

Long before Jesus came to grace the earth with the flame of the Christ, Ikhnaton proclaimed himself a son of God and affirmed the presence of that God within his heart. Not only was Ikhnaton among the first of the monotheists to come to the fore in the history of the Fertile Crescent following the sinking of Atlantis, but he was also among the first of the joint-heirs with Christ to proclaim himself in the identity of the Flaming One, which he acknowledged as sonship.

Perceiving God in nature and in every form of life, Ikhnaton was of the lineage of the ancient priesthood of the order of Melchizedek, which included in its descent Enoch, Elijah, Zarathustra, John the Baptist, Jesus, and many others. These priests of the sacred fire were one and all filled with the Holy Spirit and the fire of the I AM THAT I AM, which prepares the way for the coming of the Sun King and the Sun Queen.

Ikhnaton was among the first of the great prophets of the Middle East to acknowledge that God was a part of all that he had created, to affirm the great mystery of the Word incarnate. In truth he proclaimed the integration of the spirals of Spirit with the cycles of Mater. Indeed, he understood the light as the flow of energy, of love and truth and law, in and out of material form and consciousness as the very flow of God himself, God the Spirit who dwelt in the Sun behind the sun and in the mystical center of the Cosmic Egg.

All of these revelations, which went against the mainstream of current religious thought and practice, including his development of culture and the arts in the realism of a living flame—these came to the fore in Ikhnaton because of the purity of his heart and mind and soul, the clarity of the crystal stream of water of life flowing through his chakras, and above all, through his deep devotion to the Mother flame whom he honored in his consort, the beautiful Queen Nefertiti, and in their seven daughters outpicturing the seven rays of the Christ consciousness in the Mother flame.

We bow, then, before the flame of one who was true to his Real Self, who was indeed living truth, and who left a mark of truth upon the sands of time. And we call to your attention that the measure of this man or of any man who would be the Christ is the measure of purity and of the flow of purity in being and consciousness.

By the flow of purity, the soul can bring forth the full complement of that which otherwise remains sealed in the causal body, the spheres within spheres of pulsating life energy surrounding the Divine Monad of the Higher Self. The soul that swims in the sunlight of God, content to absorb the energies of the higher sphere, the causal body of life, is the soul that comes forth in Mater with attainment, with mastery, and with the gifts of the Spirit to impart to a world impoverished, darkened, and disjointed.

Ikhnaton knew God by the impulse of the soul, even as his soul, adorned in the veil of innocence, was the bride of his Spirit prepared for the alchemical union, for the merger of the pearl of the lower self with the crystal of the Higher Self. And so the alchemical marriage which the priest (the Christ Self) officiating at the altar of the heart is prepared to perform—that is, the wedding of the soul to Spirit—will take place in the tabernacle of being in the hour of the ascension. But along life's way there is indeed opportunity for the precelebration of the ritual of the return.

Each day as you come before your God and before the Son that is the light of the heart, your soul, with the layers of consciousness that make up the fragile pearl, can don the wedding garment in the communion ritual commemorating the hour of the transfiguration and of the crystallization of energies in Spirit when that soul, veiled in Mater energies, will rise from the plane of being through all of the centers, gathering unto itself, as the fire infolding itself,[2] the net gain of the rounds of rebirth.

You see, precious hearts yearning also for soul freedom, the soul is the feminine potential, the negative polarity, of Spirit that went forth from the center of being to increase the awareness, the aura of creativity. And by the very nature of its nonpermanence, the soul must fulfill a certain cycling and recycling of energies as layer upon layer its *id*-entity is formed through experience and experimentation with free will in the dimensions of time and space.

Deep within the conscious knowing, that point of awareness which is in the nucleus of the pearl, the soul is aware of its tenuousness and of the temporal nature of all aspects of selfhood that is realized in the planes of Mater. And thus the yearning of the soul for freedom—freedom to create, freedom to express, freedom to be the truth—reaches a mounting crescendo, an orchestrated movement wherein all of the energies of life vested in that soul potential move with the primal spiritual urge. For the soul knows that the preservation of its life can occur only in the union of the soul with the Spirit, the I AM Presence.

The quest for God on earth is the quest of the soul in search of that permanent identity that can be realized only in the presence of the living God. Through the alchemical marriage the soul becomes a permanent atom in the body of God. And the laws of decay and death and the disintegration of the soul itself no longer apply; for the soul that was corruptible has put on incorruption,[3] and immortality is the sealing of mortality as the place where evil dwells.

The first step in the alchemical marriage is the rising of the primal essence of Mother life from the base-of-the-spine chakra to the level of the seat of the soul. In this action the soul, as the negative polarity of being, increases its awareness of self to the level of awareness of being as Mother.

And thus the way back Home is found
As the soul listens to the call of the Mother—
To her song and her whistle,

Her lullaby and her discipline.
Having descended to the farthest descent
In the densification of God's energy,
The soul experiences God as Mother,
And the twain rise to the center
Where God's energy in motion
Is the victory of peace and a flaming sword.
Here in the solar plexus
God's desiring to be creator and creativity
Is found to be the impetus of striving.

And with a mighty heave and a ho
And a laughter and "Here I go,"
Soul in the mantle of the Mother
Reaches the plane of the Christ,
Adoring the flame of God as threefold wonder
Anchored in the hidden chamber—
Mother and Son and a new dimension of life begun.

Whereas it is written,
"The soul that sinneth, it shall die,"[4]
It is also written,
"The soul that winneth, it shall fly."
Soaring sunward to the fiery core
Of the heart's universal store,
The pearled one is attired
In all-transforming fires.

And the transfiguration is the mark
Of the rising of the soul

Clothed upon with the raiment of the Mother
To the plane of the heart
Where the fire of earth and the fire of heaven meet.
Here the union of the triangles
Of all of the chakras
Is found to be the twenty-four
As each star of victory
Reveals a point of identity
On the cosmic clock of Alpha and Omega.

In the transfiguration
The whirling stars
Of victory, reality, fulfillment, vision, and peace
Release the energy
For the transformation
Of every particle of selfhood,
Every nook and cranny of the four lower bodies;
And life below is imbued with life above.
At last the soul has found
The plane of oneness.
No more to go the round
Of the toilers and the spoilers,
The soul confirms the equality
Of Christ-conformity.

Now the Mother Goddess, Flame of Life,
With threefold essence of the Son,
Escorts the bride, the glowing one,
To the upper planes of Spirit;

And the fire infolding itself
Draws into the pearl and into the sacred whirl
The weavings of the Word
And of every word
That proceedeth out of the mouth of God.

Rising to the vision of the whole of creation,
The procession becomes the ritual of the sphere
Reentering the seed and the molecule of life.
And all at once freedom from all strife!
Mother, Son, and soul
Find the oneness of the whole
In the thousand-petaled lotus of the mind of God.
Our Father, our Father, we are one
In the petaled rays of flaming yod!
AUM—AUM—AUM!

Now the trinity of Holy Family,
Father, Mother, and sacred Son,
Merges with the soul to make it whole:
This is the promise and the goal.
At this very moment, the moment of the homing,
The Holy Spirit sparked in the
    union of Father-Mother
Attends the temple and the altar,
And a flame rises in the heart
To ignite the whole
With the afflatus of the Oversoul.

I have painted for you with words and the frequencies of my love the image of the ritual of the rising of the Mother in the soul and the upward flow of caduceus spirals. At the conclusion of this sacred ritual—which you can accomplish by visualization, invocation, and meditation on the thoughtforms I have given—the energies recede to the plane of the heart where they are anchored. And there in the inner inn of being, the Virgin Mother rocks the Christ Child, the soul held in arms, tutored by the Mother during the tarrying in time and space until the soul becomes the fullness of the grace of the only begotten Son, the Christed One of the incarnation.

The ritual of the alchemical union as it is reenacted on earth takes place in the manner described. But the ultimate release of the soul from the mortal coil occurs when the soul as the full complement of God-realized being takes flight and the jewel in the heart of the lotus is released unto the everlasting arms of the I AM Presence. And all of the modes of identity, aspects of selfhood, vehicles for the soul's expression in the various dimensions of Matter and of Spirit, converge at the point of spiritual cognition that we have termed the I AM Presence.

And at the moment when in ceremonial rite the Christ Self gives the bride of the soul to the bridegroom of the Spirit, the words are spoken, "They are no more twain, but One."[5] This is being androgynous, being fulfilled, being God-willed in the wholeness of the union of twin flames that converge as the I AM Presence of each of the souls that have issued forth from the Divine Monad.

Those who are students of the ascended masters need not practice the traditional forms of yoga to attain the immortal reunion. Nevertheless, they will find in these sciences the presaging of the higher way of fulfillment through the energies of the Holy Spirit invoked as the fires of transmutation and liberation.

When your aura becomes filled with the fire of God through daily invocations made in the name of the I AM Presence, fiats of the Word, and decrees of definition, there is a pressure that is brought to bear upon the soul and consciousness whereby its true identity, its individuality, is literally catapulted into the Holy of Holies, the secret place of the Most High God that is the I AM Presence.

Pursue, then, your decrees with all diligence. And know that when decrees are merged with effective meditation, such as that which has been given in the eightfold exercise of the sacred fire breath and other specifics released from the ascended-master octave, including visualization and affirmation of the immaculate concept, you have within your hand the most effective means of securing permanent selfhood at the close of this embodiment.

And for the daily balancing of karma and the

transmutation of decadent energies of the past, for
the spiritual irrigation of the chakras with the flowing Word of Life, for the filling of the aura with light,
for the expansion and the holding of the expansion
of the aura, there is no system, ancient or modern,
that can replace the science of the spoken Word[6]
revealed by Lord Maitreya, demonstrated by the
messengers, and prescribed by the chohans of the
rays for their chelas who would make the most rapid
advances on the path to self-mastery.

The statement "Thou shalt decree a thing, and it
shall be established unto thee"[7] from the Book of Job
is corollary to the law "The call compels the answer."
You, then, who are advancing in these studies of the
human aura, understand that the purpose of this intermediate series has been to acquaint you with the
specifics of the application of the law and the light for
the surrender of the lesser self, for the sacrifice of all
forms of self-indulgence, and for the affirmation of
true being here and now in the very plane of awareness
where you find yourself a son or a daughter of God.

Wherever you are, whoever you are, O aspirant
on the path, hear my word! Take my hand—but not
only my hand. My heart also I extend in love and in
that divine friendship which is grounded in the life
that is not afraid to lay down itself for the Friend.[8]

Consider the calling and the cause that we share.
Consider that in the simple act of compelling light to

flow and to glow in the aura and in the centers that God has provided as anchoring points for his consciousness evolving in man, you can contribute to the universal scheme, to cosmic purpose.

And by the application of the law—whatever the cost, whatever the price in the giving-up of the little self—the Higher Self can be won, and omnipotence, omnipresence, and omniscience can reign in the temple of the heart. And then the cell of life that you are as a microcosmic world can blend with and become the cell of God that is the Macrocosmic Egg. Think on this awhile.

As I take my leave of you,
I quote the ancient bard,
Now the hierarch of the age:
"But if the while I think on thee, dear friend,
All losses are restor'd and sorrows end."[9]
Think then upon a friend
Who walked the earth thirty-three rounds ago—
Ikhnaton, a pharaoh of pharaohs,
A prophet of the future and the ancient past,
The seer of a cosmos vast,
Artist and architect of reality,
God's overman who wielded power
For peace and energy, for enlightenment.

For this friend, as the ascended messenger of the gods, stands ready with the invisible yet visible hosts of the Lord to take your hand, to walk and talk with you, and to bequeath to you innocence of soul, purity of flow, and the integration of the stars of your chakras for the creation of the permanent aura of being, the mansion of God-being, the house of the Lord in which is centered the permanent atom of selfhood—the soul that is truly free.

> I walk with him along life's way.
> I am also yours to have.
> And to you I say,
> Won't you come our way?
> For our way is his way;
> And because he has made it his own,
> You, too, can make it your own.

I am for the victory of life everlasting in the aura of the cosmos.

D.K.

EXAMPLES OF
HOW THE AURA LOOKS
WHEN MUDDIED BY
THE HUMAN
CONSCIOUSNESS

MUDDIED AURA I. We have free will, and therefore we can do exactly what we will with the energies of our chakras, the centers of light in our body that govern the flow of energy to all levels of our being. Through our chakras we are intended to simultaneously release God's light into the world, filling our auras with Spirit, and to take in God's light, taking in prana, or the Holy Spirit. We release God's light as Father, a masculine action; we take in God's light as Mother, a feminine action. This is the balance of the T'ai Chi in each chakra. It forms a basket-weave effect as these spiritual centers are whirling.

This person is misusing each of his seven chakras. The crown, which should be the crown of life, is releasing nothing but the human consciousness, adding to the mass consciousness of the race. By the mass consciousness we mean the sea of humanity who are not enlightened. In this drawing you can see the uncontrolled release of energy in the thought and feeling worlds. Energy is being raised, but it is flowing through the crown and third eye imperfectly. There is a mental explosion going on in this person's consciousness. That mental explosion is the misuse of the third eye in the sending forth of images that are incorrect.

You can also see the misuse of the spoken Word through the throat chakra as the flame of blue descending in a tirade of energy. You can see the misuse of the heart chakra, where there is a stirring up of the emotions, as well as the misuse of the solar plexus, seat of the soul and base of the spine.   —ECP

MUDDIED AURA 2. This is another form of misqualification, filling the aura with brown. That sinking feeling
you get in the belly when you contact human creation
sinks all of the energy down, down, and down.

These lines from the heart indicate a direct action
of psychic consciousness coming out as a psychic hook.
A psychic hook hooks you into someone's human
consciousness through sympathy.

The impure heart colors all of the other chakras.
It is dripping with human sympathy that is going to affect
the emotions, color the soul and the soul awareness, and
finally result in the misuse of the base-of-the-spine
chakra.   —ECP

MUDDIED AURA 3. This is a typical aura of those who are part of the mass consciousness. The auras of people like this are filled with brown and green like the muck you see at the bottom of a river. They move in the astral plane. They do not invoke the tube of light or the violet flame, and so their auras take on and are colored by their surroundings.

The vertical lines of red and orange show that people like this are powder kegs—they are ready to become angry the moment their egos are offended. Put them in contact with someone who has separated from the mass consciousness and they are likely to explode because they cannot bear the contact with light. Put them in contact with people who are part of the milling crowd, part of the herd, and they get along just fine. They move in between one another's angers and passions and prides, and they get along and tolerate one another's human effluvia.

Such individuals are largely dominated by what is called the moon consciousness. The moon as an orange focal point or cap above the crown completely obliterates the contact of God through the crown chakra. The moon as a black focus of the crescent at the base of the spine cuts off the contact with the Divine Mother and the purity of the Mother light. These people are governed by the cycles of the moon. As the moon goes through the twelve signs of the zodiac about each twenty-eight days, they tend to take on the misuses of God's energy through lunar substance, which is the emotional misuse of the sacred fire.   —ECP

MUDDIED AURA 4. This is another aura of the mass consciousness. This person has a considerable amount of faith, as denoted by the blue halo around his head. He might be a very religious person who has a bit of illumination in his aura gleaned from his faith, as denoted by the yellow vertical lines around his head. But his heart is a sympathetic heart. The energies of the heart, instead of coming out in a direct line, are tending to fall because he has not discerned the difference between compassion and sympathy. He is always in sympathy with someone who is the underdog, and that sympathy falls to the solar plexus.

This kind of person identifies with other people's human consciousness. Instead of exalting the Christ, he sinks to the level of whomever he is with, whomever has a problem. Instead of using the light of the heart to uplift, to ennoble, to instill others with Christ awareness, he tends to use the heart energy to be "in agreement with"—which is what sympathy means—someone's human consciousness.

Among mankind there are very sincere people, but because they have not invoked the action of the Holy Spirit, their auras have not been purged of this sympathetic substance. Auras change very quickly. The moment this person comes in contact with the violet flame of the Holy Spirit, that quickening fire passing through his aura will begin to transmute this substance and give him an entirely new awareness of God.

There are many layers of misqualified energy to be

(continued)

consumed, and the scrubbing action of the violet flame works both from the surface of the aura to the chakras and from the threefold flame within the secret chamber of the heart to the surface. Once the violet flame begins to do its work, his chakras will become more aligned and his aura will show a more intense radiation—beginning as a trickle, then intensifying as a beacon of light through all of the chakras.   —ECP

MUDDIED AURA 5. Here the misuse of the sacred fire of God is centered in the crown and the third eye. This is the aura of someone who is mentally polarized but not Christ-polarized. His mind is not filled with the Christ consciousness.

This kind of person can be steeped in any kind of philosophy or carnal or intellectual accomplishment, but he will not have the corona, the crown of the Christ, the halo of life. His crown and head area will be marked by the type of manifestation you see here. The other chakras are also impure, but most of the energy this person receives from God is misused mentally.   —ECP

MUDDIED AURA 6. In this drawing we see the misuse of the sacred fire through the power of the spoken word. This is mortal cursing and malice. It is being completely out of control in the throat chakra. It is sending forth arrows and barbs and psychic wedges. The red arrows at the throat and red zigzags around the legs denote passion. The black arrows and spirals denote the total misuse of the Word of God.

This person is in a state of anger. I am certain you have seen people like this, even in public places. They become slightly irritated and go into a tirade. They start swearing at the nearest person they think has done something wrong to them. They are polluting the aura of their own world as well as the aura of the earth. This is where pollution starts. If you ever have a tantrum, this is what you look like. All of the chakras are discolored, but here you can especially see what the throat chakra would look like. The beautiful flow of God's pure blue energy in the Word of God through the throat chakra is desecrated and compromised beyond recognition.

The karma of the misuse of this energy settles. It settles in the "electronic belt," which surrounds the chakras below the heart. It takes time to clean up the residue of misqualified energy that settles in the electronic belt. It takes meditation, it takes invocation, it takes the violet flame. The immediate, surface vibration of the aura may be cleaned quickly, but the misuse of energy that piles up century after century takes certain cycles to clear.

—ECP

MUDDIED AURA 7. This figure shows the aura of
a black magician misusing the energies of the third eye
and the solar plexus. You can see the demons of the mind
that he is projecting to carry out his will. The person
I took this reading from was actually a figure well placed
in our government; and that aura shows a master-minded
manipulation of forces, of nations, and of the planet itself.

When we are confronted by this energy, how does
it affect us? We may feel as if we had been hypnotized.
Almost trembling, we may feel that we have been totally
subjugated by intimidation.

People like this have an almost overpowering will.
They put out their ideas, their policies, whatever they
are going to put out, with an intense use of the third-eye
chakra. They become so strong in their misuse of energy
that it takes people who have a corresponding momentum of Christ consciousness in the same chakra to see
through them and overcome them.

Most people have not misused the sacred fire to this
degree, nor have they attained a corresponding level
of the Christ consciousness. So they become victimized
by those who are black magicians. Until they do attain
a corresponding level of the Christ consciousness, they
are defenseless, except through invocation to the I AM
Presence and the Christ Self, who will immediately overshadow the soul who is confronted by the "accuser
of the brethren."   —ECP

MUDDIED AURA 8. This drawing shows the total mechanization concept—an individual totally dominated by the mass mind. It is not unusual for people to have this kind of aura.

The kundalini is nothing but an orange coil rising from the base of the spine. In all of the chakras, energy is misused and perverted, put out as a net of materialism and mechanization.

This is not pretty, but this entire plane of the human consciousness is not pretty. Yet God, as the flame of life within, will clean this up when we diligently invoke his sacred fire. The snakelike form at this person's feet indicates animal magnetism and its calcification in the planes of the subconscious mind. —ECP

NOTES

BOOK ONE

CHAPTER 1
The Perfecting of the Aura

1. Matt. 5:8.
2. Matt. 18:12–14; Luke 15:3–7.
3. Matt. 10:26; Mark 4:22; Luke 12:2.
4. Matt. 13:12; 25:29; Mark 4:25; Luke 8:18; 19:26.
5. Matt. 18:10.
6. Matt. 25:40.
7. Col. 2:9.
8. John 8:12; 9:5; 12:46.

CHAPTER 2
The Susceptibility of the Aura

1. Overlaid with his imperfect thoughts and feelings.
2. Gen. 2:9; 3:22, 24; Rev. 2:7; 22:2, 14.
3. Luke 16:8.
4. John 14:12.
5. This refers to the teachings of the ascended masters, available in weekly *Pearls of Wisdom*, Keepers of the Flame lessons, and books published by Summit University Press. They provide an excellent foundation for those taking up Kuthumi's studies of the human aura.

CHAPTER 3
The Colorations of the Aura

1. Ps. 1:2; Josh. 1:8.
2. Col. 2:9.
3. Rom. 8:14–17; Gal. 3:26–29; 4:6, 7.
4. Matt. 7:3–5; Luke 6:41, 42.

CHAPTER 4
The Reading of the Aura

1. Isa. 30:20.
2. I Cor. 6:20.
3. Matt. 7:1.
4. The Ascended Master Kuthumi maintains a spiritual home, or retreat, in the heaven-world over Shigatse, Tibet.
5. John 10:30.
6. Gen. 37:3, 23, 32.
7. John 19:23.
8. Matt. 27:19.
9. Luke 23:4, 14; John 18:38; 19:4, 6.
10. Isa. 55:1.

CHAPTER 5
The Intensification of the Aura

1. Heb. 12:1.
2. John 1:5.
3. John 10:1.
4. John 8:12.
5. Isa. 1:28.

CHAPTER 6
The Strengthening of the Aura

1. The threefold flame, anchored in the eight-petaled chakra called the hidden, or secret, chamber of the heart, has three "plumes" that embody the three primary attributes of God. The blue plume (on your left) embodies God's power. The yellow plume (in the center) embodies God's wisdom. The pink plume (on your right) embodies God's love. See also pp. 140–45 and glossary, s.vv. "Chart of Your Divine Self" (p. 355), "Christ" (pp. 362–64), "Power, Wisdom, and Love," and "Threefold flame."
2. Matt. 18:3, 4; 19:14; Mark 10:14, 15; Luke 18:16, 17.
3. Acts 2:1–4.
4. Ps. 18:30, 32.

CHAPTER 7
The Expansion of the Aura

1. Prov. 23:7.
2. Jude 3.
3. Prov. 13:15.
4. Ps. 91:11, 12.
5. Matt. 4:3, 4; Luke 4:3, 4.
6. I Cor. 2:9.
7. Matt. 5:16.

8. John 5:30; 14:10.
9. Matt. 21:44; Luke 20:18.
10. William Shakespeare, *Hamlet,* act 1, sc. 5, lines 166–67.

CHAPTER 8
The Shield of the Aura

1. Ps. 91:5.
2. William Shakespeare, *Hamlet,* act 3, sc. 1, line 58.
3. Matt. 16:23; Mark 8:33; Luke 4:8.
4. Matt. 27:13, 14; Mark 15:4, 5; Luke 23:8, 9; John 19:8, 9.
5. Rev. 21:6; 22:1, 17.
6. Matt. 10:8.
7. Heb. 12:1.
8. John 14:1, 27.

CHAPTER 9
The Protection of the Aura

1. Matt. 26:53.
2. Kuthumi was embodied as Francis of Assisi (c. 1181–1226), founder of the Franciscan order, canonized 1228.
3. Luke 2:14.

CHAPTER 10
The Purification of the Aura

1. Matt. 5:14, 15.
2. Isa. 1:18.
3. Luke 12:3.
4. Luke 15:7.
5. Matt. 22:1–14.
6. The Master is speaking of the death process, given to man as an act of mercy that he might have a reprieve from the vanity of this world and partake of the light and wisdom of higher realms between embodiments. Moreover, the forfeiting at birth of the memory of previous lives enables the hope of heavenly spheres to replace the seemingly endless records of mortal involvement.
7. Ps. 2:7; Acts 13:33; Heb. 1:5; 5:5.
8. Isa. 25:8; I Cor. 15:54.

CHAPTER 11
The Star of the Aura

1. I Cor. 15:41.
2. I John 2:15.
3. Eccles. 3:1–8.

4. I Cor. 15:52.
5. II Cor. 5:17.
6. Rev. 22:1, 17; 21:6.

CHAPTER 12
*The Crystal Flowing
Stream of the Aura*

1. Luke 3:17.
2. Ps. 23:4.
3. Matt. 7:1.
4. Matt. 9:2; 14:27; Mark
   6:50; John 16:33.
5. Matt. 5:16.

BOOK TWO

CHAPTER 1
*The Pulsation
of Life Becoming Life*

1. Phil. 2:5.
2. Prov. 4:23.
3. The Ascended Masters El
   Morya, Kuthumi, and
   Djwal Kul were embodied
   as Melchior, Balthazar,
   and Caspar—the three
   wise men who paid hom-
   age to the Christ Child
   (see Matt. 2:1–12).
4. Matt. 22:37.
5. Acts 1:9.
6. I Cor. 3:11; 10:4; Eph.
   2:20.

7. Matt. 22:39; Mark 12:31.
8. Exod. 3:13–15.
9. Mal. 2:1, 2.
10. Matt. 10:33.
11. Isa. 40:7, 8.
12. Gen. 3:19.

CHAPTER 2
*The Name of God
Is the Key*

1. I Pet. 3:4.
2. Rom. 8:5.
3. The word *Christ* is derived
   from the Greek *Christos,*
   meaning "anointed."
4. Jer. 31:33; Heb. 8:10;
   10:16.
5. Rom. 8:2.
6. Rom. 8:6.
7. Josh. 24:15.
8. Rev. 1:18.
9. Rom. 8:7.
10. Prov. 16:25.
11. Mal. 4:1.
12. Mal. 4:2.
13. Gen. 3:15.
14. Matt. 22:1–14.

CHAPTER 3
The Interlaced Triangles

1. James 4:8.
2. Isa. 55:8.
3. Phil. 2:5.

4. Rom. 8:14–17; Gal. 3:26–29; 4:4–7.
5. See Mark L. Prophet, *Cosmic Consciousness: One Man's Search for God,* published by Summit University Press.
6. John 1:9.
7. I Cor. 13:12.

CHAPTER 4
The Challenge of the Mind

1. Luke 16:15.
2. Luke 16:9.
3. I Cor. 15:47–49.
4. I Cor. 3:1, 2.
5. Matt. 5:25.
6. James 4:7.
7. Matt. 16:23; Mark 8:33; Luke 4:8.
8. Matt. 18:21, 22.
9. Matt. 18:6; Mark 9:42; Luke 17:2.
10. Luke 16:16.
11. Luke 17:21.
12. Ps. 23:6.
13. Ps. 23:1.
14. Ps. 1:2.
15. Ps. 1:3.
16. I John 3:2.
17. Matt. 5:8.

CHAPTER 5
The Hidden Chamber of the Heart

1. For the teachings and past lives of the seven chohans, see Mark L. Prophet and Elizabeth Clare Prophet, *Lords of the Seven Rays: Mirror of Consciousness,* published by Summit University Press.
2. The seven rays as they are released on the seven days of the week are as follows: Monday, third ray (pink); Tuesday, first ray (blue); Wednesday, fifth ray (green); Thursday, sixth ray (purple and gold); Friday, fourth ray (white); Saturday, seventh ray (violet); and Sunday, second ray (yellow).
3. Matt. 25:40.
4. The decree is the most powerful of all applications to the Godhead. It is the command of the son or daughter of God made in the name of the I AM Presence and the Christ for the will of the Almighty to come into manifestation as above, so

below. It is the means whereby the kingdom of God becomes a reality here and now through the power of the spoken Word. It may be short or long and usually is marked by a formal preamble and a closing, or acceptance. See Mark L. Prophet and Elizabeth Clare Prophet, *The Science of the Spoken Word*, published by Summit University Press.

5. I Pet. 5:8.

CHAPTER 6
*The Spectrum
of God's Consciousness*

1. John 1:14.
2. Acts 2:3.
3. II Pet. 1:19.
4. Acts 2:2.
5. Deut. 4:24; 9:3; Heb. 12:29.
6. Gen. 4:9.
7. Gen. 14:18; Ps. 110:4; Heb. 5:5–10; 6:20; 7.
8. Deut. 10:17; Ps. 136:2; Dan. 2:47.
9. Gen. 1:26, 27.
10. Ps. 37:37.
11. Matt. 12:31, 32; Mark 3:28, 29; Luke 12:10.

12. Rev. 13:16–18; 14:9–11; 15:2; 16:2; 19:19, 20; 20:4.
13. Rev. 21:16.
14. Ps. 2:1.
15. Rev. 12:15, 16.
16. Matt. 24:24; Mark 13:22.
17. Gen. 1:3.
18. Matt. 12:36, 37.
19. Rev. 12:10, 11.
20. Mark 16:20.
21. Matt. 6:19, 20.
22. Rev. 1:13–16.
23. Rev. 1:17, 18.

CHAPTER 7
The Law of Congruency

1. To help you visualize the concentric rings of light emanating from the heart, see the illustration on the front cover. It shows an aura filled with the violet light of the Holy Spirit, which purifies and transmutes negativity in the aura. The illustration also depicts the seven major chakras as they appear in their perfected state. A 2-1/4" x 3-1/2" laminated card of this chakra illustration is available from Summit University Press.
2. See the following rosaries

to Mother Mary, published by Summit University Press: Mother Mary's Scriptural Rosary for the New Age, eight scriptural rosaries dictated by Mary to Elizabeth Clare Prophet, published on 8 audiocassettes and in *My Soul Doth Magnify the Lord! Mother Mary's New Age Teachings and Rosary with a Challenge to Christendom. A Child's Rosary to Mother Mary,* 15-minute rosaries with scriptural readings from the New Testament for adults and children, 5 albums, 3 audiocassettes each, and on CD. *The Fourteenth Rosary: The Mystery of Surrender,* 2-audiocassette album.

3. Matt. 6:22, 23; Luke 11:34, 35.

4. Ps. 82:6; John 10:34.

CHAPTER 8
The Sacred Fire Breath

1. Rom. 8:14–17; Gal. 3:26-29; 4:4–7; Eph. 1:5, 10, 11; Heb. 9:15; I John 3:2.

2. The Chart of Your Divine Self is available as a 15" x 26" full-color poster. Altar set of 3 posters: Chart, 15" x 26" (to hang in the center), portraits of Jesus Christ and Saint Germain (to hang to the left and right of the Chart), 12" x 16" each, published by Summit University Press.

3. See discussion of eye magic by Mark L. Prophet and Elizabeth Clare Prophet on pp. 48–49 of *Climb the Highest Mountain,* 2d ed., published by Summit University Press.

4. Rev. 1:8.

CHAPTER 9
The Four Elements in the Planes of the Chakras

1. Deut. 4:24; 9:3; Heb. 12:29.

2. John 3:8.

3. Matt. 24:35; Mark 13:31; Luke 21:33.

4. Matt. 17:14–21.

5. II Tim. 2:15.

6. Matt. 17:1, 2; Mark 9:2, 3; Luke 9:28, 29.

7. Matt. 17:2.

8. Matt. 17:3, 4; Mark 9:4, 5;

Luke 9:30–33.
9. Matt. 17:5.
10. Exod. 4:12.

CHAPTER 10
*The Seven in the Seven
and the Test of the Ten*

1. Ezek. 1:16.
2. I Cor. 15:26.
3. Matt. 18:21, 22.
4. Matt. 25:28, 1; Luke 17:12; 15:8; Rev. 12:3.
5. Luke 22:42.
6. Matt. 25:14–30.
7. Jesus was chohan of the sixth ray during the Piscean age. When Jesus and his disciple Saint Francis (Kuthumi) assumed the office of World Teacher on January 1, 1956, the Ascended Lady Master Nada assumed the chohanship of the sixth ray in Jesus' stead.
8. See pp. 198 and 323, ch. 7 n. 2.

CHAPTER 11
*The Flame of Freedom
in the Aquarian Cycle*

1. Judg. 2:1–4.
2. II Cor. 6:14.
3. Rev. 21:16.

4. Judg. 2:10–13, 16, 17.
5. Judg. 2:19–22; 3:1, 3–7.
6. Isa. 1:18.
7. Exod. 3:13–15.
8. Num. 21:8, 9; John 3:14.
9. Num. 17:8.
10. Rev. 3:12; 21:2.
11. Exod. 7:16.
12. Gen. 22:17; 26:4; Heb. 11:12.

CHAPTER 12
*The Energies of the Soul
Raised to the Third Eye*

1. You will note that there are forty-six chromosomes in man. These contain the genes (the DNA) of his heredity, which are intended to convey the Christic patterns of the soul blueprint from generation to generation. The forty-eight pairs of petals in the third-eye chakra are for the anchoring of the flame of life in each of the forty-six chromosomes. The two that remain unmanifest are the white-fire lodes of Alpha and Omega, which are anchored in the etheric body as electrodes for the androgynous conscious-

ness that is aware of the wholeness of the Father-Mother God in Christed man and Christed woman.

2. Matt. 6:22–24; Luke 11:34–36.
3. Gen. 1:27; 5:1, 2.
4. Gen. 2:9, 16, 17.
5. Ps. 121:1, 2.
6. Ps. 121:4–8.
7. Zech. 3.
8. Zech. 4:6–10.
9. Zech. 4:1–5, 10–14; Rev. 11:3, 4.

CHAPTER 13
The Raising-Up of the Energies of the Mother

1. John 4:25, 26.
2. Luke 1:28.
3. See p. 323, ch. 7 n. 2.
4. Matt. 6:10; Luke 11:2.
5. Rev. 17, 18.
6. John 1:9.
7. James 4:3.

CHAPTER 14
The Ritual of the Alchemical Union

1. Ikhnaton: I acknowledge the at-one-ness of God. Ikhnaton (Amenhotep IV) was pharaoh of Egypt c. 1375–1358 B.C. Ikhnaton introduced a revolutionary monotheism based on the worship of the one God, whom he called Aton. He represented Aton in the symbol of a sun disc or orb with diverging rays, each of which ended in a hand bestowing blessings upon all life.
2. Ezek. 1:4.
3. I Cor. 15:53.
4. Ezek. 18:4, 20.
5. Matt. 19:6.
6. See p. 322, ch. 5 n. 4 and glossary, s.vv. "Spoken Word," "Decree," and "Mantra."
7. Job 22:28.
8. John 15:13.
9. William Shakespeare, Sonnet 30, lines 13–14.

To order books, tapes, CDs, and posters from Summit University Press, call 1-800-245-5445 or 406-848-9500.

INCARNATIONS
OF THE ASCENDED
MASTER KUTHUMI

Thutmose III, reigned c. 1503–1450 B.C., pharaoh, prophet, and high priest in the period of the New Kingdom. Thutmose expanded the Egyptian kingdom to include most of the Middle East. His most decisive victory was on a battlefield near Mt. Carmel. There he led the entire army single file through narrow Megiddo Pass to surprise and defeat an alliance of 330 rebellious Asian princes—a daring maneuver protested by the pharaoh's terrified officers. Thutmose alone was assured of his plan and rode ahead holding aloft the image of Amon-Ra, the Sun God who had promised him the victory.

Pythagoras, c. 582–c. 507 B.C., Greek philosopher, the "fair-haired Samian" who was regarded as the son of Apollo. As a youth, Pythagoras conferred freely with priests and scholars, eagerly seeking scientific proof of the inner law revealed to him in meditation upon Demeter, the Mother of the Earth. His quest for the great synthesis of truth led him to Palestine, Arabia, India, and finally to the temples of Egypt, where he won the confidence of the priests of Memphis and was gradually accepted into the mysteries of Isis at Thebes.

When Asian conqueror Cambyses launched a savage invasion of Egypt c. 529 B.C., Pythagoras was exiled to Babylon, where the prophet Daniel still served as king's minister. Here rabbis revealed to him the inner teachings of the I AM THAT I AM given to Moses. Zoroastrian magi tutored him in music, astronomy, and the sacred science of invocation. After twelve years, Pythagoras left Babylon and founded a brotherhood of initiates at Crotona, a busy Dorian seaport in southern Italy. His "city of the elect" was a mystery school of the Great White Brotherhood.

At Crotona, carefully selected men and women pursued a philosophy based upon the mathematical expression of universal law, illustrated in music and in the rhythm and harmony of a highly disciplined way of life. After a five-year

THE MASTER KOOT HOOMI (1884)

probation of strict silence, Pythagorean "mathe-maticians" progressed through a series of initiations, developing the intuitive faculties of the heart whereby the son or daughter of God may become, as Pythagoras' *Golden Verses* state, "a deathless God divine, mortal no more."

Pythagoras delivered his lectures from behind a screen in a veiled language that could be fully comprehended only by the most advanced initi-ates. The most significant phase of his instruc-tion concerned the fundamental concept that number is both the form and the essence of cre-ation. He formulated the essential parts of Euclid's geometry and advanced astronomical ideas that led to Copernicus' hypotheses. It is recorded that two thousand citizens of Crotona gave up their customary lifestyle and assembled together in the Pythagorean community under the wise administration of the Council of Three Hundred—a governmental, scientific, and reli-gious order that later exercised great political influence throughout Magna Grecia.

Pythagoras, the "indefatigable adept," was killed when Cylon, a rejected candidate of the mystery school, incited a violent persecution. Standing in the courtyard of Crotona, Cylon read aloud from a secret book of Pythagoras, *Hieros Logos*

(Holy Word), distorting and ridiculing the teaching. When Pythagoras and forty of the leading members of the Order were assembled, Cylon set fire to the building and all but two of the council members died. As a result, the community was destroyed and much of the original teaching was lost. Nevertheless, "the Master" has influenced many great philosophers, including Plato, Aristotle, Augustine, Thomas Aquinas, and Francis Bacon.

Balthazar, first century, one of the three Magi (astronomer/adepts) who followed the star (the I AM Presence) of the Manchild born to the Virgin Mary. Believed to have been the King of Ethiopia, Balthazar brought the treasure of his realm, the gift of frankincense, to Christ.

Saint Francis of Assisi, c. 1181–1226, the divine poverello, who renounced family and wealth and embraced "Lady Poverty." He lived among the poor and the lepers, finding unspeakable joy in imitating the compassion of Christ. While kneeling at Mass on the feast of St. Matthias in 1209, he heard the gospel of Jesus read by the priest and the Lord's command to his apostles, "Go, preach." Francis left the little church and began evangelizing and converting many. Among them was the noble Lady Clare, who later left her home dressed as the bride of Christ and presented herself to Francis for admittance to the mendicant order.

One of the many legends surrounding the lives of Francis and Clare describes their meal at Santa Maria degli Angeli, where Francis spoke so lovingly of God that all were enraptured in Him. Suddenly the people of the village saw the convent and the woods ablaze. Running hastily to quench the flames, they beheld the little company enfolded in brilliant light with arms uplifted to heaven.

God revealed to St. Francis the divine presence in "brother sun" and "sister moon" and rewarded his devotion with the stigmata of Christ crucified. The prayer of St. Francis is yet spoken by people of all faiths throughout the world: "Lord, make me an instrument of thy peace!..."

Shah Jahan, 1592–1666, Mogul emperor of India, who overthrew the corrupt government of his father, Jahangir, and restored in part the noble ethics of his grandfather Akbar the Great. During his enlightened reign, the splendor of the Mogul court reached its zenith and India entered her golden age of art and architecture. Shah

Jahan lavished the imperial treasury on music, paintings, and the construction of awesome monuments, mosques, public buildings, and thrones throughout India, some of which may still be seen today.

The famous Taj Mahal, "the miracle of miracles, the final wonder of the world," was built as a tomb for his beloved wife, Mumtaz Mahal. She had ruled by his side almost as an equal and died in 1631 giving birth to their fourteenth child. Shah Jahan spared no effort in making the monument "as beautiful as she was beautiful." It is the symbol of the Mother principle and celebrates his eternal love for Mumtaz.

Koot Hoomi Lal Singh, nineteenth-century Kashmiri Brahman, Shigatse, Tibet; also called K.H. In 1875 he founded with El Morya the Theosophical Society to reacquaint mankind with the ancient wisdom that underlies all the world's religions.

Ascended Master Kuthumi, serves with Jesus as World Teacher; formerly Chohan of the Second Ray of Divine Illumination. Kuthumi is known as the Master Psychologist and a sponsor of youth. He is hierarch of the etheric Temple of Illumination in Kashmir, India, also called the

Cathedral of Nature, and head of the Brothers and Sisters of the Golden Robe.

Kuthumi maintains his retreat in the heaven-world over Shigatse, Tibet, where he plays his grand organ—drawing the harmony of cosmos by the sacred fires of his heart. With this celestial music, he sends healing and peace throughout the planetary body to souls in transition (especially at the hour of death) and guides them to the etheric retreats of the Great White Brotherhood for tutoring in preparation for their next earthly life. He inspires architects, poets, and scientists with the mystical remembrance of their own soul's harmony in the celestial geometry and the rhythm of the stars.

GLOSSARY

Words set in italics are defined elsewhere in the glossary.

Adept. A true adept is an initiate of the *Great White Brotherhood* of a high degree of attainment, especially in the control of *Matter*, physical forces, nature spirits, and bodily functions; fully the alchemist undergoing advanced initiations of the *sacred fire* on the path of the *ascension*.

Akashic records. All that transpires in an individual's world and all events in the physical universe are recorded in an *etheric* substance and dimension known as akasha (Sanskrit, from the root *kās* 'to be visible, appear', 'to shine brightly', 'to see clearly'). Akasha is primary substance, the subtlest, ethereal essence, which fills the whole of space; "etheric" energy vibrating at a certain frequency so as to absorb, or record, all of the impressions of life. The akashic records can be read by *adepts* or those whose *soul*

For information on publications and cassettes cited in this glossary, write Summit University Press, PO Box 5000, Corwin Springs, MT 59030-5000 USA, call 1-800-245-5445 or 406-848-9500, or fax 1-800-221-8307 or 406-848-9555.

(psychic) faculties are developed. The *Messenger* has explained that an *Ascended Master* or an unascended adept can look at a record just the way an archaeologist would look through layers of the earth. He can look through layers of records and pinpoint any age or time since the earth was created and read the record of what happened at that particular point in time and space. The Messenger Mark L. Prophet said: "Man makes a record every time he thinks or speaks or feels. Just like a clock ticking twenty-four hours a day, the computers of heaven are ticking off and recording the events of our lives and bringing back to our own personal doorstep exactly what we send out."

Alpha and Omega. The Divine Wholeness of the Father-*Mother* God affirmed as "the beginning and the ending" by the Lord *Christ* in Revelation. Ascended *twin flames* of the Cosmic *Christ consciousness* who hold the balance of the masculine-feminine polarity of the Godhead in the Great *Central Sun* of *cosmos.* Thus, through the Universal Christ, the *Word* incarnate, the Father is the origin and the Mother is the fulfillment of the cycles of God's consciousness expressed throughout the *Spirit-Matter* creation. *See also* Mother.

(Rev. 1:8, 11; 21:6; 22:13. Compare the Hindu Puruṣa and Prakṛti.)

Angel. Divine spirit, herald, forerunner; messenger sent by God to deliver his Word to his children.

Ministering spirits sent forth to tend the heirs of *Christ*—to comfort, protect, guide, strengthen, teach, counsel, and warn. Cohorts of *Light* in the service of the Christed ones, the *sons and daughters of God,* throughout *cosmos.* An 'angle' of God's consciousness—an aspect of his Self-awareness; a being fashioned by God out of his own flaming Presence to minister unto his Life in form. "And of the angels he saith, 'Who maketh his angels spirits and his ministers a flame of fire.'" The angelic hosts comprise an evolution set apart from mankind by their flaming selfhood and their purity of devotion to the Godhead and to the *Archangels* and hierarchs under whose command they serve. Their function is to concentrate, accelerate, and amplify the attributes of God on behalf of his creation. They minister to the needs of mankind by magnetizing Light to their *auras,* intensifying feelings of hope, faith, and charity, honor, integrity, courage, truth and freedom, mercy and justice, and every aspect of the crystal clarity of the Mind of God. Because of the blessedness of their unseen presence, the author of Hebrews said, "Be not forgetful to entertain strangers: for thereby some have entertained angels unawares"—and in so saying made a point for the case that angels do take embodiment and move among us as our best friends and helpers, even when total strangers.

Metaphorically speaking, angels are electrons revolving around the Sun Presence that is God—electrons who have elected, by his will innate within them, to expand his consciousness in every plane of being. Angels are electrons who have been 'charged' with the light/energy/consciousness of the Great *Central Sun* to be 'electrodes', i.e., pillars of God's fiery presence acting as 'step-down transformers' of the ineffable Light, that his children might receive some hope of the glory that is to come midst the dark night of their karmic condition upon earth. Angels can assume human form or that of 'rods' and 'cones' or spirals and coils of concentrated energy that can be released for personal and planetary healing in answer to the call of the Christed ones as a literal transfusion of the Body and Blood of the Cosmic Christ wherever and whenever there is a need. There are angels of healing, protection, love, comfort and compassion, angels attending the cycles of birth and death, angels of the All-Seeing Eye of God who wield the flaming sword of Truth to cleave asunder the Real from the Unreal. There are types and orders of angels who perform specific services in the *cosmic hierarchy*, such as *seraphim* and *cherubim*, and angel devas who serve with the nature spirits and *elementals* of fire, air, water, and earth.

(Ps. 104:4; Heb. 1:7; 13:2. Elizabeth Clare Prophet, audio and video lecture series *How to Contact Angels—Your Guides, Guardians and Friends*.)

The fallen angels are those who followed Lucifer in the Great Rebellion and whose consciousness therefore "fell" to lower levels of vibration and awareness as they were by law "cast out into the earth" at the hand of Archangel *Michael*—constrained, by the *karma* of their disobedience to God and his Christ and their blasphemy of his children, to take on and evolve through dense *physical bodies*. Here they walk about, as Peter said, seeking whosesoever *souls* and minds and bodies they may devour, sowing seeds of unrest and the Luciferian rebellion among the people through the subculture of rock music and drugs, the media, and their Babylonian cult of idolatry. They are known variously as the fallen ones, Luciferians, Watchers, Nephilim, "giants in the earth," Satanists, Serpents, sons of Belial, etc.

(Rev. 12:9; Gen. 6:1–7. See Elizabeth Clare Prophet, *Forbidden Mysteries of Enoch: Fallen Angels and the Origins of Evil,* containing all the Enoch texts, including the Book of Enoch and the Book of the Secrets of Enoch.)

Angel of the LORD. The presence of the Deity in angelic form. The Seven *Archangels* and their *Archeiai* ministering on the *seven rays* together with the five of the secret *rays* and the hierarchs of the thirteenth are the Angels of the LORD that "stand in the Presence of God" and are "sent from God" as his messengers to transmit the *Light (Christ consciousness)* of that I AM THAT I AM to his sons and daughters for the accomplishment of those dispensations that they announce. Unto Moses was revealed the *I AM Presence* through "the angel of the LORD who appeared unto him in a flame of fire," which was the actual presence and personification of the I AM THAT I AM by

Archangel *Michael*. This truth confirms the initiation conferred by God upon certain beings advanced in the heavenly *hierarchy* to actually bear in their person—in their *chakras* and auric field—the weight of God's Presence. Even so have his prophets, *messengers* and Christed ones borne this "burden" of the LORD, as they were called to be his visible evangels in form, taking embodiment to minister with the *angels,* Archangels, *cherubim,* and *seraphim* on behalf of *souls* evolving in the earth planes.
(Luke 1:19; Exod. 3:2; Jer. 23:30–40; Zech. 9:1; 12:1; Hab. 1:1; Mal. 1:1.)

Antahkarana. (Skt. for "internal sense organ.") The web of life. The net of *light* spanning *Spirit* and *Matter* connecting and sensitizing the whole of creation within itself and to the heart of God.

Antichrist. *n.* When capitalized, the specific embodiment of Absolute *Evil,* the Evil One. The planetary dweller-on-the-threshold. "Little children, it is the last time: and as ye have heard that Antichrist shall come, even now are there many antichrists; whereby we know that it is the last time." The term is also applied to such as Lucifer, *Satan,* the Watchers, Nephilim, and other fallen *angels* who "kept not their first estate," who stand in opposition to Absolute Good. These betrayers of the *Word* have sworn allegiance to the powers of Death and Hell and vowed to destroy God incarnate in his Church, his saints and his little ones. When lowercased, a person or power antagonistic to the *Christ,* or *Light,* in *Jesus* and his own. *adj.* Having the characteristics of Antichrist, denying the Christ potential in the children of God, destroying *souls* by the perversion of the Person and Light of Christ.

(I John 2:18, 22; 4:3; II John 7; Gen. 6:1–7; Jude 6.)

Archangel. Hierarch of angelic hosts; the highest rank in the orders of *angels.* Each of the *seven rays* has a presiding Archangel who, with his divine complement, an *Archeia,* embodies the *God consciousness* of the *ray* and directs the bands of angels serving in their command on that ray. The Archangels and Archeiai of the rays and the location of their retreats are as follows: First Ray, blue, Archangel *Michael* and **Faith,** Banff, near Lake Louise, Canada. Second Ray, yellow, Archangel **Jophiel** and **Christine,** south of the Great Wall near Lanchow, north central China. Third Ray, petal pink, deep rose and ruby, Archangel **Chamuel** and **Charity,** St. Louis, Missouri, USA. Fourth Ray, white and mother-of-pearl, Archangel **Gabriel** and **Hope,** between Sacramento and Mount Shasta, California, USA. Fifth Ray, green, Archangel **Raphael** and *Mary,* Fátima, Portugal. Sixth Ray, purple and gold, Archangel **Uriel** and **Aurora,** Tatra Mountains, south of Cracow, Poland. Seventh Ray, violet and purple, Archangel **Zadkiel** and **Holy Amethyst,** Cuba.

(See *Vials of the Seven Last Plagues: The Judgments of Almighty God Delivered by the Seven Archangels.* Archangel Gabriel, *Mysteries of the Holy Grail.* "The Class of the

Archangels," in *Pearls of Wisdom,* 1981, vol. 24, Book I, nos. 4–15; 8-audiocassette album. "The Healing Power of Angels," in *Pearls of Wisdom,* 1986, vol. 29, Book I, nos. 25–34; Book II, nos. 51–57; 2 videocassette albums, 2 cassettes each; 2 audiocassette albums, 12 cassettes each. Elizabeth Clare Prophet, "Self-Healing Workshop with the Healing Power of Angels," 3 audiocassettes; "On the Healing Power of Angels: Christ Wholeness—the Seven Rays of God," 2 videocassettes; 3 audiocassettes. *On Wings of Angels,* songs to the Archangels and their consorts, audiocassette.)

Archangel Michael. *See* Michael, Archangel.

Archeia (pl. **Archeiai**). Divine complement and *twin flame* (feminine polarity) of an *Archangel.*

Arhat. A Buddhist monk who has attained nirvana; one undergoing the initiations of the *Buddha.*

Ascended being. *See* Ascended Master.

Ascended Master. One who, through *Christ* and the putting on of that Mind which was in Christ *Jesus,* has mastered time and space and in the process gained the mastery of the self in the *four lower bodies* and the four quadrants of *Matter,* in the *chakras* and the balanced *threefold flame.* An Ascended Master has also transmuted at least 51 percent of his *karma,* fulfilled his divine plan, and taken the initiations of the Ruby *Ray* unto the ritual of the *ascension*— acceleration by the *sacred fire* into the *Presence* of the I AM THAT I AM. An Ascended Master is one who inhabits the planes of *Spirit,* the kingdom of God (God's consciousness), and may teach unascended *souls* in an *etheric* retreat or in the etheric cities on the etheric plane (the kingdom of heaven). (Phil. 2:5.)

Ascension. The ritual whereby the *soul* reunites with the *Spirit* of the Living God, the *I AM Presence*. The ascension is the culmination of the soul's God-victorious sojourn in time and space. It is the reward of the righteous that is the gift of God after the last judgment before the great white throne in which every *man* is judged "according to their works." The ascension was experienced by Enoch, of whom it is written that he "walked with God: and he was not, for God took him"; by Elijah, who went up by a whirlwind into heaven; and by *Jesus,* although his ascension did not take place on the occasion when scripture records that he was taken up into a cloud into heaven. The *Ascended Master El Morya* has revealed that Jesus made his ascension from Shamballa after his passing in Kashmir at the age of 81 in A.D. 77. The reunion with God in the ascension, signifying the end of the rounds of *karma* and rebirth and the return to the LORD's glory, is the goal of life for the *sons and daughters of God.* Jesus said, "No man hath ascended up to heaven but he that came down from heaven, even the Son of man." The soul—by salvation ('Self-elevation'), the conscious raising up of the Son of God within her temple— puts on her wedding garment to fulfill the office of the **Son** (Sun, or *Light*) of manifestation. The soul is made worthy by Jesus' grace to be the bearer of his cross and his crown. Following the initiatic path of Jesus, the soul ascends through the *Christ Self* to her LORD, the I AM Presence, whence she descended. (Rev. 20:12, 13; Gen. 5:24; II Kings 2:11; Luke 24:50, 51; Acts 1:9–11; John 3:13. See Serapis Bey, *Dossier on the Ascension.* Elizabeth Clare Prophet, *A Retreat on the Ascension—an Experience with God,* 8-audiocassette album.)

Aspirant. One who aspires; specifically, one who aspires to reunion with God through the ritual of the *ascension.* One who aspires to overcome the conditions and limitations of time and space to fulfill the cycles of *karma* and one's reason for being through the sacred labor.

Astral. *adj.* Having or carrying the characteristics of the astral plane. *n.* A frequency of time and space beyond the physical yet below the mental, corresponding with the *emotional body* of *man* and the collective unconscious of the race. The astral plane is the repository of the collective thought and feeling patterns, conscious and unconscious, of mankind. Because the astral plane has been muddied by impure human thought and feeling, the term "astral" is also used in a negative context to refer to that which is impure or "*psychic.*" *See also* Psychic.

Astral body. *See* Emotional body.

Aura. A luminous emanation or 'electromagnetic' field surrounding the *physical body,* often equated with the *astral body.* A halo or nimbus associated with the saints, originating in the *soul* and soul blueprint, which mirrors by *free will* the heavenly or the earthly patterns. The distinctive radiation of sentient life and inorganic objects as captured in Kirlian photography. Breath or atmosphere surrounding and interpenetrating the four lower *bodies of man* and his *chakras* upon which the impressions, thoughts, feelings, words, and actions of the individual are registered, including his *karma* and the records of past lives. A spiritual corona, referred to as the L-field or Life-field (*astral/etheric* sheath) surrounding mankind and organic life that both regulates and reflects the health, vitality, and longevity of the physical body or organism. The highly charged circle of *sacred fire* surrounding *Christ,* an *Ascended Master, angel, Elohim* or Cosmic Being, transferable as 'grace' to whomsoever they will it.

(See Kuthumi and Djwal Kul, *The Human Aura.* Elizabeth Clare Prophet, *The Control of the Human Aura through the Science of the Spoken Word,* 2-audiocassette album.)

Bodies of man. The four lower bodies are four sheaths consisting of four distinct frequencies that surround the *soul*—the physical, emotional, mental, and *etheric*—providing vehicles for the soul in her journey through time and space. The etheric sheath, highest in vibration, is the gateway to the three higher bodies, which are the *Christ Self,* the *I AM Presence,* and the *Causal Body. See also* Chart of Your Divine Self, Etheric body, Mental body, Emotional body, and Physical body.

(See Mark L. Prophet and Elizabeth Clare Prophet, *Climb the Highest Mountain,* 2d ed., pp. 164–73; *The Lost Teachings of Jesus I,* softbound, pp. 224–26, or pocketbook, Book Two, pp. 66–69.)

Body elemental. A being of nature (ordinarily invisible and functioning unnoticed in the physical octave) that serves the *soul* from the moment of its first incarnation in the planes of *Mater* to tend the *physical body.* About three feet high and resembling the individual whom he serves, the body elemental, working with the guardian *angel* under the regenerative *Christ Self,* is the unseen friend and helper of *man.* See also Elementals.
(See Mark L. Prophet and Elizabeth Clare Prophet, *Climb the Highest Mountain,* 2d ed., pp. 455–64.)

Brotherhood. *See* Great White Brotherhood.

Brothers and Sisters of the Golden Robe. An order of *ascended* and *unascended beings* dedicated to the illumination of mankind through the flame of wisdom, headed by the *Ascended Master Kuthumi,* with retreats on the *etheric* plane in *Shigatse* and Kashmir.
(See Kuthumi, "The 'Second Coming' of the Saints," in *Pearls of Wisdom,* 1989, vol. 32, pp. 781–82, 786.)

Buddha. (From Skt. *budh* 'awake', 'know', 'perceive'.) Buddha means "the enlightened one." It denotes an office in the spiritual *hierarchy* of worlds that is attained by passing certain initiations of the *sacred fire,* including those of the *seven rays* of the *Holy Spirit* and of the five secret *rays,* the raising of the

Feminine Ray (sacred fire of the Kundalini), and the "mastery of the seven in the seven multiplied by the power of the ten."

(See "The Seven in the Seven and the Test of the Ten," in Kuthumi and Djwal Kul, *The Human Aura,* bk. 2, chap. 10.)

Gautama attained the enlightenment of the Buddha twenty-five centuries ago, a path he had pursued through many previous embodiments culminating in his forty-nine-day meditation under the Bo tree; hence he is called Gautama, the Buddha. He holds the office of Lord of the World, sustaining, by his *Causal Body* and *threefold flame,* the divine spark and consciousness in the evolutions of earth approaching the path of personal Christhood. His *aura* of Love/Wisdom ensouling the planet issues from his incomparable devotion to the Divine *Mother.* He is the hierarch of Shamballa, the original retreat of Sanat Kumara now on the *etheric* plane over the Gobi Desert. On April 18, 1981, the beloved Gautama Buddha established his Western Shamballa in America's wilderness at the northern border of Yellowstone National Park at the Inner Retreat of the Royal Teton Ranch.

(See Gautama Buddha, "Quietly Comes the Buddha," in *Pearls of Wisdom,* 1975, vol. 18, nos. 17–29; *Pearls of Wisdom,* 1983, vol. 26. *Peace in the Flame of Buddha,* 2-audio-cassette album. Elizabeth Clare Prophet, "The Message of the Inner Buddha," in *Pearls of Wisdom,* 1989, vol. 32, nos. 28–30; *A Message of Perfect Love from the Heart of Gautama Buddha,* 3-audiocassette album; *The Buddha and the Mother,* 6-audiocassette album; "Insatiable Desire: The

Enemy Within" and "The Eightfold Path of Self-Mastery," two 1-hr. TV shows on video, 2 audiocassettes; "The Buddhic Essence," two 1-hr. TV shows on video, 4-audiocassette album.)

Lord Maitreya, the Cosmic *Christ,* has also passed the initiations of the Buddha. He is the long-awaited Coming Buddha who has come to the fore to teach all who have departed from the way of the Great Guru, Sanat Kumara, from whose lineage both he and Gautama descended. In the history of the planet, there have been numerous Buddhas who have served the evolutions of mankind through the steps and stages of the path of the Bodhisattva. In the East *Jesus* is referred to as the Buddha Issa. He is the World Saviour by the Love/Wisdom of the Godhead. *See also* Lord Maitreya.

(See the following by Elizabeth Clare Prophet: *The Lost Years of Jesus.* "Lord Maitreya: The Coming Buddha Who Has Come" and "The Path of the Bodhisattva: The Historical Maitreya," in *Pearls of Wisdom,* 1984, vol. 27, Book I, pp. *1– 76;* Book II, pp. *1–74.* "The Path of the Bodhisattva: The Historical Maitreya," 2 audiocassettes.)

In the 1960s, nine unascended *lifestreams* who had passed the initiations of the Buddha volunteered to embody to assist the evolutions of earth during their difficult and dangerous transition into the age of Aquarius. Their world service will be recognized when they have reached the age of the Christic and Buddhic example, age thirty-three to thirty-six. On January 1, 1983, Gautama Buddha announced that nine Buddhas who had been in nirvana for nine hundred years were descending the shaft of *light* to enter the hearts of nine individuals upon this planet and, by their Electronic Presence, to enter the forcefield of thousands of dedicated hearts. Gautama also released the dispensation that every prayer, *mantra,* and chant of devotees of Christ and Buddha from that time on would be multiplied by the power of the heart of Gautama and the nine Buddhas.

Carnal mind. The *human ego,* the human will, and the human intellect; self-awareness without the *Christ;* the animal nature of *man,* called mechanization man and the mechanization concept by the Master R; called the dweller-on-the-threshold in esoteric tradition. For the apostle Paul, "the carnal mind is enmity against God: for it is not subject to the law of God, neither indeed can be."
(Rom. 8:7. See Elizabeth Clare Prophet, "The Lost Teachings of Jesus: On the Enemy Within," 2 audiocassettes. *Pearls of Wisdom,* 1983, vol. 26, pp. 50, 383–91, 429–54; 1985, vol. 28, Book I, pp. 84, 85–93, 97; 1986, vol. 29, Book I, pp. 199, 203, 210–12.)

Causal Body. The Body of First Cause; interpenetrating spheres of *light* and consciousness surrounding the *I AM Presence* in the higher levels of *Spirit*. The Causal Body is the place where we "lay up treasure in heaven." It is the storehouse of every good and perfect thing that is a part of our true identity. The spheres of the Causal Body contain the records of the virtuous acts we have performed to the glory of God and the blessing of *man* through our many incarnations on earth. One's spiritual resources and creativity —talents, graces, gifts and genius, garnered through exemplary service on the seven *rays*—may be drawn forth from the Causal Body through invocation made to the I AM Presence in the name of the *Christ Self.*

In addition, the great spheres of the Causal Body are the dwelling place of the Most High God to which *Jesus* referred when he said, "In my Father's house are many mansions . . . . I go to prepare a place for you . . . . I will come again and receive you unto myself; that where I AM [where I, the incarnate Christ, AM in the I AM Presence], there ye may be also." The Causal Body is the mansion, or habitation, of the Spirit of the I AM THAT I AM to which the soul returns through Christ Jesus and the individual Christ Self in the ritual of the *ascension.* The Causal Body as the star of each man's individualization of the God Flame was referred to by Paul when he said, "One star differeth from another star in glory." *See also* Chart of Your Divine Self.
(Matt. 6:19–21; John 14:2, 3; I Cor. 15:41.)

Central sun. A vortex of energy, physical or spiritual, central to systems of worlds that it thrusts from itself or gathers unto itself by the central sun magnet. Whether in the *microcosm* or the *Macrocosm,* the central sun is the principal energy source, vortex, or nexus of energy interchange in atoms, cells, *man* (the heart center), amidst plant life and the core of the

earth. The **Great Central Sun,** also called the **Great Hub,** is the center of *cosmos;* the point of integration of the *Spirit-Matter* cosmos; the point of origin of all physical-spiritual creation; the nucleus, or white fire core, of the *Cosmic Egg.* (The God Star, Sirius, is the focus of the Great Central Sun in our sector of the galaxy.) The **Sun behind the sun** is the spiritual Cause behind the physical effect we see as our own physical sun and all other stars and star systems, seen or unseen, including the Great Central Sun. The Sun behind the sun of cosmos is perceived as the Cosmic *Christ*—the *Word* by whom the formless was endowed with form and spiritual worlds were draped with physicality. Likewise, the Sun behind the sun is the Son of God individualized in the *Christ Self,* shining in all his splendor behind the *soul* and its interpenetrating sheaths of consciousness called the *four lower bodies.* It is the Son of man—the 'Sun' of every *man*ifestation of God. The Sun behind the sun is referred to as the "Sun of righteousness," which does heal the mind, illumine the soul and light all her house, and as "the glory of God," the *Light* of the City Foursquare.
(Mal. 4:2; Rev. 21:23.)

Chakra. (Skt. for "wheel," "disc," "circle.") Term used to denote the centers of *light* anchored in the *etheric body* and governing the flow of energy to the four lower *bodies of man.* There are seven major chakras corresponding to the *seven rays,* five minor chakras corresponding to the five secret *rays,* and a total of 144 light centers in the body of man. The seven major chakras, their rays, Sanskrit names, and colors are as follows: First Ray, **throat,** Vishuddha, blue; Second Ray, **crown,** Sahasrāra, yellow; Third Ray, **heart,** Anāhata, pink; Fourth Ray, **base-of-the-spine,** Mūlādhāra, white; Fifth Ray, **third eye,** Ājñā, green; Sixth Ray, **solar plexus,** Maṇipūra, purple and gold; Seventh Ray, **seat-of-the-soul,** Svādhish-ṭhāna, violet.

(See Djwal Kul, *Intermediate Studies of the Human Aura* (with color plates of the chakras), also published in *The Human Aura.* Mark L. Prophet and Elizabeth Clare Prophet, *The Lost Teachings of Jesus I,* softbound, pp. 261–91, color plates following p. 260, or pocketbook, Book Two, pp. 114–55. Elizabeth Clare Prophet, *Mother's Chakra Meditations —From My Heart to Buddha,* 8-audiocassette album; *Saint Germain's Heart Meditation I,* audiocassette.)

Chamuel. *See* Archangel.

Chart of Your Divine Self. There are three figures represented in the Chart of Your Divine Self. We refer to them as the upper figure, the middle figure and the lower figure. These three correspond to the Christian Trinity: The upper corresponds to the Father, who is one with the Mother, the middle to the Son, and the lower to the temple of the *Holy Spirit.*

We address our Father-Mother God as the *I AM Presence.* This is the I AM THAT I AM, whom God revealed to Moses and individualized for every son and daughter of God. Your I AM Presence is

THE CHART OF YOUR DIVINE SELF

surrounded by seven concentric spheres of rainbow *light*. These make up your *Causal Body*, the biding place of your I AM Presence. In Buddhism it is called the Dharmakaya—the body of the Lawgiver (the I AM Presence) and the Law (the Causal Body).

The spheres of your Causal Body are successive planes of God's consciousness that make up your heaven-world. They are the "many mansions" of your Father's house, where you lay up your "treasures in heaven." Your treasures are your words and works worthy of your Creator, constructive thoughts and feelings, your victories for the right, and the virtues you have embodied to the glory of God. When you judiciously exercise your *free will* to daily use the energies of God in love and in harmony, these energies automatically ascend to your Causal Body. They accrue to your *soul* as "talents," which you may then multiply as you put them to good use lifetime after lifetime.

The middle figure in the Chart represents the "only begotten Son" of the Father-Mother God, the Universal *Christ*. He is your personal Mediator and your soul's Advocate before God. He is your *Higher Self*, whom you appropriately address as your beloved *Holy Christ Self*. John spoke of this individualized presence of the Son of God as "the true Light, which lighteth every *man* that cometh into the world." He is your Inner Teacher, your Divine Spouse, your dearest Friend and is most often recognized as the

Guardian *Angel.* He overshadows you every hour of the day and night. Draw nigh to him and he will draw nigh to you.

The lower figure in the Chart is a representation of yourself as a disciple on the *path* of reunion with God. It is your soul evolving through the planes of *Matter* using the vehicles of the *four lower bodies* to balance *karma* and fulfill her divine plan. The four lower bodies are the etheric, or memory, body; the mental body; the desire, or emotional, body; and the physical body.

The lower figure is surrounded by a *tube of light,* which is projected from the heart of the I AM Presence in answer to your call. It is a cylinder of white light that sustains a forcefield of protection 24 hours a day, so long as you maintain your harmony in thought, feeling, word and deed.

Sealed in the secret chamber of your heart is the *threefold flame* of Life. It is your divine spark, the gift of life, consciousness and free will from your beloved I AM Presence. Through the Love, Wisdom and Power of the Godhead anchored in your threefold flame, your soul can fulfill her reason for being on earth. Also called the Christ flame and the liberty flame, or fleur-de-lis, the threefold flame is the spark of the soul's Divinity, her potential for Christhood.

The silver (or crystal) cord is the stream of life, or *"lifestream,"* which descends from the heart of the

I AM Presence through the Holy Christ Self to nourish and sustain (through the seven *chakras* and the secret chamber of the heart) the soul and her four lower bodies. It is over this 'umbilical' cord that the light of the Presence flows, entering the being of man at the crown chakra and giving impetus for the pulsation of the threefold flame in the secret chamber of the heart

The lower figure represents the son of man or child of the Light evolving beneath his own 'Tree of Life'. The lower figure corresponds to the Holy Spirit, for the soul and the four lower bodies are intended to be the temple of the Holy Spirit. The *violet flame,* the spiritual fire of the Holy Spirit, envelops the soul as it purifies. This is how you should visualize yourself standing in the violet flame. You can invoke the violet flame daily in the name of your I AM Presence and Holy Christ Self to purify your four lower bodies and consume negative thoughts, negative feelings and negative karma in preparation for the ritual of the alchemical marriage—your soul's union with the Beloved, your Holy Christ Self.

Shown just above the head of the Christ is the dove of the Holy Spirit descending in the benediction of the Father-Mother God. When your soul has achieved the alchemical marriage, she is ready for the baptism of the Holy Spirit. And she may hear the Father-Mother God pronounce the approbation: "This is my beloved Son in whom I AM well pleased."

When your soul concludes a lifetime on earth, the I AM Presence withdraws the silver cord, whereupon your threefold flame returns to the heart of your Holy Christ Self. Your soul, clothed in her etheric garment, gravitates to the highest level of consciousness to which she has attained in all of her past incarnations. Between embodiments she is schooled in the etheric retreats until her final incarnation when the great law decrees she shall return to the Great God Source to go out no more.

Your soul is the nonpermanent aspect of your being, which you make permanent through the *ascension* process. By this process your soul balances her karma, bonds to your Holy Christ Self, fulfills her divine plan and returns at last to the living Presence of the I AM THAT I AM. Thus the cycles of her going out into the Matter *Cosmos* are completed. In attaining union with God she has become the Incorruptible One, a permanent atom in the Body of God. The Chart of Your Divine Self is therefore a diagram of yourself—past, present and future.

(Matt. 3:17. See Mark L. Prophet and Elizabeth Clare Prophet, *Climb the Highest Mountain; The Lost Teachings of Jesus I*, softbound, pp. 205–59, 267–68, or pocketbook, Book Two, pp. 43–110, 126–27. Elizabeth Clare Prophet, *The Astrology of the Four Horsemen,* chap. 37.)

Chela. (Hindi *celā* from Skt. *ceṭa* 'slave', i.e., 'servant'.) In India, a disciple of a religious teacher or guru. A term used generally to refer to a student of the *Ascended Masters* and their teachings. Specifically, a student of more than ordinary self-discipline and devotion initiated by an Ascended Master and serving the cause of the *Great White Brotherhood. See also* Discipleship. (See El Morya, *The Chela and the Path: Meeting the Challenge of Life in the Twentieth Century*.)

Cherub (pl. **cherubim**). Member of an order of angelic beings devoted to the expansion and protection of the flame of love, wielding the sword and the judgment of the Ruby *Ray* and the *Holy Spirit*. Hence the LORD God "placed at the east [gate] (the gate of the *Christ consciousness*) of the garden of Eden Cherubims and a flaming sword which turned every way, to keep the way of the *Tree of Life.*" Even so the LORD instructed Moses to fashion cherubim of gold as focuses of these true angelic guardians of the mercy seat of the ark of the covenant. Traditionally, God dwelt between the cherubim and spoke to Moses from the mercy seat—the altar of the *I AM Presence,* whose Law, engraven on tablets of stone, was carried in the ark from place to place in their wilderness wanderings. David describes the LORD riding upon a cherub, flying upon the wings of the wind. Ezekiel portrays the cherubim as four-winged, four-faced creatures accompanied by whirling wheels. The cherub may be identified with the winged *karibu,* "intercessor" in Mesopotamian texts, portrayed as a sphinx, griffin, or winged human creature. Throughout *cosmos,* the wise and strong cherubim are found in manifold aspects of service to God and his offspring. (Gen. 3:24; Exod. 25:17–22; II Sam. 22:11; Ezek. 1, 10.)

Chohan. Lord or master; a chief. Each of the *seven rays* has a Chohan who focuses the *Christ consciousness* of the *ray,* which is indeed the law of the ray governing its righteous use in *man*. Each Chohan is an *Ascended Master*. Having ensouled and demonstrated the law of the ray throughout numerous incarnations, and taken initiations both before and after the *ascension,* he or she is appointed to the office of Chohan by the Maha Chohan, "Great Lord." The Maha Chohan is the representative of the *Holy Spirit* on all the rays. The names of the Chohans, the rays they represent and the locations of their physical/*etheric* focuses are as follows: First Ray, *El Morya,* Retreat of God's Will, Darjeeling, India. Second Ray, **Lanto,** Royal Teton Retreat, Grand Teton, Jackson Hole, Wyoming, USA. Third Ray, **Paul the Venetian,** Château de Liberté, southern France, with a focus of the *threefold flame* at the Washington Monument, Washington, D.C. Fourth Ray, **Serapis Bey,** the Ascension Temple and Retreat at Luxor, Egypt. Fifth Ray, **Hilarion** (the apostle Paul), Temple of Truth, Crete. Sixth Ray, *Nada,* Arabian Retreat, Saudi Arabia. Seventh Ray, *Saint Germain,* Royal Teton Retreat, Grand Teton, Wyoming; Cave of Symbols, Table Mountain, Wyoming. Saint Germain also works out of the Great Divine Director's focuses—the Cave of Light in India and the Rakoczy mansion in Transylvania, where Saint Germain presides as hierarch. (See "Messages from the Seven Chohans of the Rays," in *Pearls of Wisdom,* 1968, vol. 11, nos. 1–7. The Seven

Chohans, the Maha Chohan, and the World Teachers, "The Opening of the Temple Doors," in *Pearls of Wisdom,* 1973, vol. 16, nos. 10–19. The Seven Chohans, "Retreat of the Seven Chohans of the Rays," in *Pearls of Wisdom,* 1982, vol. 25, Book II, nos. 56–63. Mark L. Prophet and Elizabeth Clare Prophet, *Lords of the Seven Rays; The Lost Teachings of Jesus II,* softbound, pp. 149–226, or pocketbook, Book Three, pp. 105–200. Elizabeth Clare Prophet, "Lords of the Seven Rays on Crystals, with Chakra Initiations," 4 audiocassettes; "Lords of the Seven Rays: Find the Perfect Master and Crystal for You," two 1-hr. TV shows on video. *Ten Songs to the Seven Chohans and the Maha Chohan,* 2 audiocassettes.)

Christ. (From the Gk. *Christos* 'anointed'.) **Messiah** (Heb., Aram. 'anointed'); **'Christed one',** one fully endued and infilled—anointed—by the *Light* (the Son) of God. The *Word,* the Logos, the Second Person of the Trinity, "And the Word was made flesh and dwelt among us (and we beheld his glory, the glory as of the only begotten of the Father), full of grace and truth. . . . *That was the true Light which lighteth every man that cometh into the world.* He was in the world, and the world was made by him, and the world knew him not." In the Hindu Trinity of Brahma, Vishnu, and Shiva, the term "Christ" corresponds to or is the incarnation of Vishnu, the Preserver; Avatara, God-man, Dispeller of Darkness, Guru.

The **Universal Christ** is the mediator between the planes of *Spirit* and the planes of *Matter;* personified as the *Christ Self,* he is the mediator between the Spirit of God and the *soul* of *man.* The Universal Christ sustains the nexus of the figure-eight flow of consciousness through which the energies of the Father (Spirit) pass to his children for the crystallization (Christ-realization) of the *God Flame* by their souls' strivings in the cosmic womb (matrix) of the *Mother* (Matter). This process is called materialization (*Mater*-realization), "The Descent." The process whereby the soul's coalesced energies of the Mother pass through the nexus of the *Christ consciousness* to the Father is the acceleration called spiritualization (Spirit-realization), "The Ascent." Another name for the process whereby the soul's energy returns from Matter to Spirit is sublimation (sublime action), or transmutation. The consummation of this process is experienced by the soul, now one with the Son, as the *ascension*—union with the Spirit of the *I AM Presence,* the Father. The ascension is the fulfillment in heaven of *Jesus'* promise on earth: "At that day ye shall know that I am in my Father, and ye in me, and I in you.... If a man love me, he will keep my words: and my Father will love him, and we will come unto him, and make our abode with him."

The fusion of the energies of the positive and negative polarity of the Godhead in the creation takes place through the Universal Christ, the Logos without whom "was not any thing made that was made." The flow of light from the *Macrocosm* to the *microcosm,* from the Spirit (the I AM Presence) to the soul and back again over the figure-eight spiral, is fulfilled through this blessed mediator, who is Christ, the

LORD, the true incarnation of the I AM THAT I AM. Because Jesus Christ is that embodied Word he can say: "I AM [the I AM in me is] the Open Door [to heaven and earth] which no man can shut." "All Power is given unto me [through the I AM in me] in heaven and in earth." "Behold, I AM [the I AM in me is] alive forevermore, as Above so below, and have the keys of the kingdom of heaven and the keys of hell and death, and to whomsoever the Father wills, I give it, and it is given in his name." This which is affirmed even today by the *Ascended Master* Jesus Christ is also affirmed in your behalf by your beloved Christ Self. Thus the Universal Christ of the one Son and the many does indeed mediate the Presence of the I AM to you through your very own beloved Holy Christ Self. This is the true Communion of the Cosmic Christ whose Body (Consciousness) was 'broken', shared, individualized, for every child of the Father's heart. The Sons of God hold the Maxim Light in trust for the babes in Christ.

The term "Christ" or "Christed one" also denotes an office in *hierarchy* held by those who have attained self-mastery on the *seven rays* and the seven *chakras* of the *Holy Spirit*. Christ-mastery includes the balancing of the *threefold flame* — the divine attributes of *Power, Wisdom, and Love* — for the harmonization of consciousness and the implementation of the mastery of

THE THREEFOLD FLAME OF LIFE:
YOUR OPPORTUNITY TO BECOME THE CHRIST

the seven rays in the chakras and in the *four lower bodies* through the Mother Flame (raised Kundalini). At the hour designated for the ascension, the soul thus anointed raises the spiral of the threefold flame from beneath the feet through the entire form for the transmutation of every atom and cell of her being, consciousness, and world. The saturation and acceleration of the four lower bodies and the soul by this transfiguring light of the Christ Flame takes place in part during the initiation of the *transfiguration,* increasing through the resurrection and gaining full intensity in the ritual of the ascension.

The individual Christ Self, the personal Christ, is the initiator of every living soul. When the individual passes these several initiations on the path of Christhood, including the "slaying of the dweller-on-the-threshold," he earns the right to be called a Christed one and gains the title of *son or daughter of God.* Some who have earned that title in past ages have either compromised that attainment altogether or failed to manifest it in subsequent incarnations. In this age the Logos requires them to bring forth their inner God-mastery and to perfect it on the physical plane while in physical embodiment. Therefore, to assist the sons and daughters of God in making their manifestation commensurate with their inner Light, the Masters of the *Great White Brotherhood* have released their teachings through the Ascended Masters and their *Messengers* in this century. And *Saint Germain* founded the Keepers of the Flame Fraternity providing graded monthly lessons to the members of this order, dedicated to keep the flame of Life throughout the world. Prior to the successful passing of the initiations of *discipleship,* the individual is referred to as a child of God in contrast to the term "Son of God," which denotes full Christhood wherein the soul in and as the Son of man is become one in the Son of God after the example of Christ Jesus.

Expanding the consciousness of the Christ, the Christed one moves on to attain the realization of the Christ consciousness at a planetary level and is able to hold the balance of the Christ Flame on behalf of the evolutions of the planet. When this is achieved, he assists members of the heavenly hierarchy who serve under the office of the *World Teachers* and the planetary Christ. *See also* Chart of Your Divine Self, Jesus. (John 1:1–14; 14:20, 23. Compare Rev. 3:8; Matt. 28:18; Rev. 1:18.)

Christ consciousness. The consciousness or awareness of the self in and as the *Christ;* the attainment of a level of consciousness commensurate with that which was realized by *Jesus,* the Christ. The Christ consciousness is the realization within the *soul* of that Mind which was in Christ Jesus. It is the attainment of the balanced action of *Power, Wisdom, and Love*—of Father, Son, and *Holy Spirit*—and the purity of the *Mother* through the balanced *threefold flame* within the heart. It is Faith perfected in the desire to

do God's Will, Hope in the salvation of Christ Jesus by the path of his righteousness performed in us, and Charity's excellence in purest Love of giving and receiving in the LORD.
(Phil. 2:5.)

Christ Self. The individualized focus of "the only begotten of the Father full of grace and truth." The Universal *Christ* individualized as the true identity of the *soul;* the *Real Self* of every man, woman, and child to which the soul must rise. The Christ Self is the mediator between a man and his God. He is a man's own personal Teacher, Master, and Prophet who officiates as High Priest before the altar of the Holy of Holies *(I AM Presence)* of every man's temple made without hands. The advent of the universal awareness of the Christ Self in God's people on earth is foretold by the prophets as the descent of THE LORD OUR RIGHTEOUSNESS, also called the BRANCH, in the Universal Age at hand. When one achieves the fullness of soul-identification with the Christ Self, he is called a Christed, or anointed, one, and the Son of God is seen shining through the Son of man.
(John 1:14; Isa. 11:1; Jer. 23:5, 6; 33:15, 16; Zech. 3:8; 6:12. See Mark L. Prophet and Elizabeth Clare Prophet, *Climb the Highest Mountain,* 2d ed., pp. 148–60, 340–41, 368–69; *The Lost Teachings of Jesus I,* softbound, pp. 240–45, or pocketbook, Book Two, pp. 86–92. Elizabeth Clare Prophet, *The Astrology of the Four Horsemen,* pp. 53–57, 479–86, 494–98; "Jesus Christ, Avatar of the Ages," 1 videocassette, 2 audiocassettes.)

Color rays. *See* Seven rays.

Cosmic consciousness. (1) God's awareness of himself in and as the *cosmos*. (2) *Man's* awareness of himself as he lives, moves, and has being within the spheres of God's cosmic Self-awareness. The awareness of oneself fulfilling the cycles of the cosmos in and through the Great *God Self;* the awareness of the self as a part of God in cosmic dimensions; the attainment of initiations through the blessedness of the Cosmic *Christ* leading to God Self-realization in the Universal One.

Cosmic Egg. The spiritual-material universe, including a seemingly endless chain of galaxies, star systems, worlds known and unknown, whose center, or white fire core, is called the Great *Central Sun.* The Cosmic Egg has both a spiritual and a material center. Although we may discover and observe the Cosmic Egg from the standpoint of our physical senses and perspective, all of the dimensions of *Spirit* can also be known and experienced within the Cosmic Egg. For the God who created the Cosmic Egg and holds it in the hollow of his hand is also the *God Flame* expanding hour by hour within his very own sons and daughters. The Cosmic Egg represents the bounds of *man's* habitation in this cosmic cycle. Yet, as God is everywhere throughout and beyond the Cosmic Egg, so by his Spirit within us we daily awaken to new dimensions of Being, *soul*-satisfied in conformity with his Likeness.

Cosmic hierarchy. The universal chain of individualized God-free beings fulfilling the attributes and aspects of God's infinite Selfhood. Included in the cosmic hierarchical scheme are Solar Logoi, *Elohim, Sons and Daughters of God, ascended* and unascended *Masters* with their circles of *chelas,* Cosmic Beings, the twelve solar hierarchies, *Archangels* and *angels* of the *sacred fire,* children of the *Light,* nature spirits (called *elementals*) and *twin flames* of the *Alpha-Omega* polarity sponsoring planetary and galactic systems. This universal order of the Father's own Self-expression is the means whereby God in the Great *Central Sun* steps down the Presence and Power of his Universal Being/Consciousness in order that succeeding evolutions in time and space, from the least unto the greatest, might come to know the wonder of his Love. The criterion that establishes one's placement on this ladder of life called hierarchy is the level of one's spiritual/physical attainment. This is measured by one's balanced self-awareness "hid with *Christ* in God" and one's demonstration of his Law, by his Love, in the *Spirit-Matter cosmos.*

In the third century, Origen of Alexandria set forth his conception of a hierarchy of beings, ranging from angels to human beings to demons and beasts. This renowned scholar and theologian of the early Church, who set forth the chief cornerstone of Christ's doctrine and upon whose works subsequent Church fathers, doctors, and theologians built their traditions, taught that *souls* are assigned to their respective offices and duties based on previous actions and merits, and that each one has the opportunity to ascend or descend in rank. Many beings of the heavenly hierarchy are named in the Book of Revelation. Apart from the false hierarchy of *Antichrist,* including the reprobate angels, some of the members of the *Great White Brotherhood* accounted for by *Jesus* are Alpha and Omega, the Seven Spirits, the angels of the seven churches, the Four and Twenty Elders, the four beasts, the saints robed in white, the Two Witnesses, the God of the Earth, the Woman clothed with the Sun and her *Manchild,* Archangel *Michael* and his angels, the Lamb and his wife, the one hundred and forty-four thousand who have the Father's name written in their foreheads, the angel of the Everlasting Gospel, the seven angels (i.e., the Archangels of the *seven rays*) who stood before God, the angel clothed with a cloud and a rainbow upon his head, the seven thunders, the Faithful and True and his armies, and him that sat upon the great white throne. *See also* Elohim.

(Rev. 1:4, 8, 11, 20; 2:1, 8, 12, 18; 3:1, 4, 5, 7, 14; 4:2–10; 5:2, 6, 11; 6:9–11; 7:1, 2, 9, 13, 14; 8:2; 10:1, 3, 7; 11:3, 4; 12:1, 5, 7; 14:1, 3–6, 14–19; 15:1; 16:1–4, 8, 10, 12, 17; 17:1; 18:1, 21; 19:4, 7, 11–17; 20:1; 21:6, 9; 22:13. See Elizabeth Clare Prophet, *The Great White Brotherhood in the Culture, History and Religion of America,* pp. 83–101. Origen, *On First Principles.*)

Cosmic law. That law which governs mathematically, yet with the spontaneity of mercy's flame, all manifestation throughout the *cosmos* in the planes of *Spirit* and *Matter.*

Cosmos. The universe conceived as an orderly, harmonious system; a complex orderly self-inclusive system. All that exists in time and space including spectra of *light,* forces of bodies, cycles of the elements—life, intelligence, memory, record and dimensions beyond physical perception—mathematically calculated as the evidence of things not seen as yet, but which do appear in the *Spirit* cosmos that coexists with and interpenetrates the *Matter* cosmos as a grid of light. Our *Mother's* Matter cosmos consists of the entire physical/*astral* creation of universes known and unknown. Our Father's Spirit cosmos all around us veils the inner blueprint and motion of First Cause and causation by which worlds are framed and hung by his Universal Mind and the planes of effect *(karma)* in which we abide are sustained for a season.

Darjeeling Council. A council of the *Great White Brotherhood* consisting of *Ascended Masters* and unascended *chelas* headed up by *El Morya,* its chief, headquartered in Darjeeling, India, at the Master's *etheric* retreat. Members include *Mother Mary,* Kuan Yin, Archangel *Michael,* the Great Divine Director, *Serapis Bey, Kuthumi,* Djwal Kul and numerous others whose objective is to train *souls* for world service in God-government and the economy, through international relations and the establishment of the inner *Christ* as the foundation for religion, education, and a return to golden-age culture in music and the arts.

Decree. *n.* a foreordaining will, an edict or fiat, an authoritative decision, declaration, a law, ordinance or religious rule; a command or commandment. *v.* to decide, to declare, to determine or order; to ordain, to command or enjoin; to invoke the presence of God, his *light*/energy/consciousness, his power and protection, purity and perfection.

It is written in the Book of Job, "Thou shalt decree a thing, and it shall be established unto thee: and the light shall shine upon thy ways." The decree is the most powerful of all applications to the Godhead. It is the "Command ye me" of Isaiah 45:11, the original command to Light, which, as the "Lux fiat," is the birthright of the *sons and daughters of God.* It is the authoritative Word of God spoken in *man* by the name of the *I AM Presence* and the living *Christ* to bring about constructive change on earth through the will of God and his consciousness come, on earth as it is in heaven—in manifestation here below as Above. The dynamic decree offered as praise and petition to the LORD God in the science of the *spoken Word* is the "effectual fervent prayer of the righteous" that availeth much. The dynamic decree is the means whereby the supplicant identifies with the Word of God, even the original fiat of the Creator "Let there be light: and there was light." Through the dynamic decree spoken with joy and love, faith and hope in God's covenants fulfilled, the supplicant receives the engrafting of the *Word* and experiences the transmutation by the *sacred fire* of the *Holy Spirit,* the "trial by fire" whereby all *sin,* disease, and death are consumed, yet the righteous *soul* is preserved. The decree is the alchemist's tool and technique for personal and planetary transmutation and self-transcendence. The decree may be short or long and is usually marked by a formal preamble and a closing or acceptance.

(Job 22:28; Gen. 1:3; James 1:21; 5:16; I Cor. 3:13–15; I Pet. 1:7. See Mark L. Prophet and Elizabeth Clare Prophet, *The Science of the Spoken Word.* Jesus and Kuthumi, *Prayer and Meditation. Prayers, Meditations and Dynamic Decrees for the Coming Revolution in Higher Consciousness,* Sections I and II. Elizabeth Clare Prophet, *The Astrology of the Four Horsemen,* chaps. 38–40. Mark L. Prophet and Elizabeth Clare Prophet, *The Science of the Spoken Word: Why and How to Decree Effectively,* 4-audiocassette album. Elizabeth Clare Prophet, *"I'm Stumping for the Coming Revolution in Higher Consciousness!"* 3-audiocassette album. Call or write for information on audiocassettes of decrees, songs, mantras and rosaries, including decrees to Archangel Michael, El Morya and Lord Lanto and healing, love and violet-flame decrees.)

Desire body. *See* Emotional body.

Discipleship. The state of being an adherent of the *Christ* and of the Teachings of the *Great White Brotherhood;* the process of attaining self-mastery through self-discipline in the initiations of the *Buddha,* the *World Teachers,* and the *Ascended Masters.*

Steps of initiation in discipleship under the Living *Word:* (1) **Student:** Under this phase the individual studies, becomes a student of the writings and the teachings of the Master. He is free to come and go in his community, enjoying fellowship with his followers and the fruits of their dedication but has declared no particular responsibility to the person of the Master. He has taken no vows, made no commitment, but may be studying to "show himself approved" in order to be accepted as a servant, or co-server (otherwise known as *"chela"*), sharing the joy of the Master's world mission. (2) **Disciple** (chela): The individual desires to enter into a bond with the Master—to be taught directly by the Master rather than through his published writings alone. The disciple answers the call of the Master to leave his nets of karmic entanglements and worldly desire and follow him: "Come leave your nets, I will make you fishers of men." The disciple receives the initiations of the Cosmic Christ in the course of his service to the Master. His heart, mind, and *soul* have begun to unfold a greater love as appreciation and gratitude for the teachings received in the previous level of student. This love is translated into action as self-sacrifice, selflessness, service, and surrender to the Person of the Christ, the Sun behind the Son of man of the Master; when this step has been accelerated to the level of the "acceptable offering," and the chela is engaged in balancing his *threefold flame* and his *karma,* he may be considered for the next step. (3) **Friend:** Those counted as friend of the Master enter by invitation—"Henceforth I call you no more servants but friends"—into a relationship as companion and co-worker, bearing increased responsibilities for the Master's path as world saviour. The friend bears the cross as well as the burden of *Light* of the Master; he demonstrates the qualities of friendship as in the life of Abraham and other chelas who have risen to a level of understanding the very heart and the experience of the Master—providing comfort, consolation, advice, and support out of loyalty to both the purposes and the person of the Master. (4) **Brother:** The degree of brother is the level where the oneness of the Guru-chela, *Alpha-Omega* relationship is complete through the horizontal figure-eight exchange heart-to-heart; the Guru has actually made his disciple a part of his own flesh and blood and offered to him the full momentum of his attainment and portions of his mantle and authority in preparation for the Master's *ascension* and the disciple's assuming of the part or whole of the Master's office. This is the love relationship exemplified between *Jesus* and John, his *Mother, Mary,* and perhaps his own flesh-and-blood brother (or cousin) James. (5) **Christ,** or **Christed one:** the Anointed of the Incarnate Word. (II Tim. 2:15; Matt. 4:19; Mark 1:17; John 15. See Jesus and Kuthumi, *Corona Class Lessons,* chaps. 25–30.)

Divine Ego. Awareness of true selfhood in and as the *Christ Self,* the God Self, or the *I AM Presence;* the Higher Consciousness; the Source or Origin of *man.* One's sense of selfhood at the point of origination; *Divine Monad.*

Divine Manchild. The Manchild born to the Woman clothed with the Sun is the incarnation of the Universal *Christ* for the Aquarian age in the one and the many *sons and daughters of God* whose destiny it is to focus the *Christ consciousness* to the evolutions of earth. Lowercased, the term "manchild" refers to the child who has the *Holy Spirit* from his mother's womb, e.g., John the Baptist and *Jesus.* (Rev. 12.)

Divine Monad. *See* Chart of Your Divine Self.

Divine Mother. *See* Mother.

El Morya. The *Ascended Master.* Lord *(Chohan)* of the First *Ray* of God's Will, Chief of the *Darjeeling Council* of the *Great White Brotherhood,* founder of *The Summit Lighthouse,* teacher and sponsor of the *Messengers* Mark L. Prophet and Elizabeth Clare Prophet. The Master's extraordinary devotion to God's Word and Work is a powerful stream that runs throughout his *soul's* incarnations on earth as he has stood staunch in the role of Advocate, Teacher, and Exemplar before our spirits soaring unto Love.

As the Rajput prince El Morya Khan, he worked closely with *Kuthumi,* Djwal Kul, *Serapis Bey, Saint Germain* and others to found the Theosophical Society in 1875. He was Abraham, the ancient patriarch who emerged from Ur of the Chaldees to become the prototype and progenitor of the twelve tribes of Israel. Returning as Melchior, one of the three wise men of the East, he followed the star that portended the birth of the best of his seed who would fulfill all the promises of God unto his spiritual descendants.

As Arthur, king of the Britons, he beckoned knights of the Round Table to quest the Holy Grail and summoned the knights and ladies of the court of Camelot to attain through initiation the inner mysteries of *Christ*. Appearing again on Britain's soil as Thomas Becket as well as Thomas More, both martyred, he twice played the role of defender of the Faith and challenger of King Henry—also twice born (Henry II and VIII), and twice the oppressor. In the sixteenth century, his soul's journey took him to the East in the person of Akbar, greatest of Mogul emperors, and in the nineteenth to Ireland to be her poet laureate Thomas Moore. In 1898 the renowned "Mahatma of the Himavat," El Morya Khan, ascended to the heart of God.

During the 1920s and 1930s the Ascended Master El Morya worked with Nicholas and Helena Roerich, who set forth his writings in numerous published works. In 1958 he called Mark L. Prophet to disseminate the Teachings of the Ascended Masters as *Pearls of Wisdom*, published by the newly founded Summit Lighthouse. With Saint Germain and *Mother Mary,* he also trained Elizabeth Clare Prophet as his Messenger. Through the embodied Messenger he delivers the Teachings of the Universal Christ for the Aquarian age and conducts retreats on practical spiritual techniques for meeting the personal and planetary challenges posed by the prophecies of Saint John's Revelation. El Morya's musical keynote, capturing the frequencies of his Electronic Presence, was set forth in part by Sir Edward Elgar in his *Pomp and Circumstance.*

(See the following works by El Morya: *The Chela and the Path; The Sacred Adventure; Morya: The Darjeeling Master Speaks to His Chelas on the Quest for the Holy Grail; Ashram Notes; Ashram Rituals,* booklet and 2 audiocassettes; *El Morya: Chohan of the First Ray,* 2-audiocassette album. Mark L. Prophet and Elizabeth Clare Prophet, *Lords of the Seven Rays,* Book One, chap. 1; Book Two, chap. 1. *El Morya, Lord of the First Ray: Dynamic Decrees with Prayers and Ballads for Chelas of the Will of God 1–4,* audiocassettes. *Hail to the Chief! A Salute to El Morya,* songs on CD and audiocassette.)

Elementals. Beings of earth, air, fire, and water; nature spirits who are the servants of God and *man* in the planes of *Matter* for the establishment and maintenance of the physical plane as the platform for the *soul's* evolution. Elementals who serve the fire element are called salamanders; those who serve the air element, sylphs; those who serve the water element, undines; those who serve the earth element, gnomes. *See also* Body elemental.

(See Mark L. Prophet and Elizabeth Clare Prophet, *Climb the Highest Mountain,* 2d ed., pp. 444–70, 548–55. *Saint Germain On Prophecy,* Book Three. Jesus and Kuthumi, *Corona Class Lessons,* pp. 371–76. *Violet Flame for Elemental Life — Fire, Air, Water and Earth 1* and *2,* audiocassettes of decrees and songs.)

Elohim. (Plural of Heb. *Eloah* 'God'.) One of the Hebrew names of God, or of the gods; used in the Old
Testament about 2,500 times, meaning "Mighty
One" or "Strong One." *Elohim* is a uniplural noun re-
ferring to the *twin flames* of the Godhead that comprise the "Divine Us." When speaking specifically
of either the masculine or feminine half, the plural
form is retained because of the understanding that
one half of the Divine Whole contains and is the androgynous Self (the Divine Us). The Seven Mighty
Elohim and their feminine counterparts are the
builders of form; hence, Elohim is the name of God
used in the first verse of the Bible, "In the beginning
God created the heaven and the earth." Serving directly under the Elohim are the four beings of the
elements, "the Four Cosmic Forces," who have dominion over the *elementals*—gnomes, salamanders,
sylphs, and undines.

The Seven Mighty Elohim are the "seven Spirits of
God" named in Revelation and the "morning stars"
that sang together in the beginning, as the LORD
revealed them to his servant Job. There are also five
Elohim who surround the white fire core of the
Great *Central Sun*. In the order of *hierarchy,* the
Elohim and Cosmic Beings carry the greatest concentration, the highest vibration, of *Light* that we
can comprehend in our state of evolution. They represent, with the four beings of nature, their consorts
and the elemental builders of form, the power of our

Father as the Creator (the blue *ray*). The Seven *Arch-angels* and their divine complements, the great *seraphim, cherubim,* and all the angelic hosts represent the love of God in the fiery intensity of the Holy Ghost (the pink ray). The Seven *Chohans* of the Rays and all *Ascended Masters,* together with unascended *sons and daughters of God,* represent the wisdom of the Law of the Logos under the office of the Son (the yellow ray). These three kingdoms form a triad of manifestation, working in balance to step down the energies of the Trinity. The intonation of the sacred sound "Elohim" releases the tremendous power of their God Self-awareness stepped down for our blessed use through the Cosmic *Christ.*

Following are the names of the Seven Elohim, the rays they serve on, and the locations of their *etheric* retreats: First Ray, **Hercules and Amazonia,** Half Dome, Sierra Nevada, Yosemite National Park, California, USA. Second Ray, **Apollo and Lumina,** western Lower Saxony, Germany. Third Ray, **Heros and Amora,** Lake Winnipeg, Canada. Fourth Ray, **Purity and Astrea,** near Gulf of Archangel, southeast arm of White Sea, Russia. Fifth Ray, **Cyclopea and Virginia,** Altai Range where China, Siberia, and Mongolia meet, near Tabun Bogdo. Sixth Ray, **Peace and Aloha,** Hawaiian Islands. Seventh Ray, **Arcturus and Victoria,** near Luanda, Angola, Africa. (Rev. 1:4; 3:1; 4:5; 5:6; Job 38:7. See *Spoken by Elohim, Pearls of Wisdom,* 1978, vol. 21. The Seven Mighty Elohim, "The Chalice of Elohim," in *Pearls of Wisdom,* 1989, vol. 32, nos. 9–15; 5 audiocassettes. *The Seven Elohim in the Power of the Spoken Word,* 4-audiocassette album.)

Emotional body. One of the four lower *bodies of man,* corresponding to the water element and the third quadrant of *Matter;* the vehicle of the desires and feelings of God made manifest in the being of *man.* Also called the astral body, the desire body, and the feeling body.

Etheric. Of or relating to the highest plane of the *Matter cosmos,* i.e., the heaven world. The etheric frequency and its correspondent plane of consciousness is the repository of the fiery blueprint of the entire physical universe.

Etheric body. One of the four lower *bodies of man,* corresponding to the fire element and the first quadrant of *Matter;* called the envelope of the *soul,* holding the blueprint of the divine plan and the image of *Christ*-perfection to be outpictured in the world of form. Also called the memory body. Sanat Kumara announced on New Year's Day 1985 that the earth received a new *etheric* sheath containing the record and blueprint of the planet's original divine plan and that the opportunity for the world to renew the golden age had never been greater.
(See Sanat Kumara, "The Turning Point of Life on Earth: A Dispensation of the Solar Logoi," in *Pearls of Wisdom,* 1985, vol. 28, Book I, pp. 60–61.)

Evil. *Energy-veil;* the veil of misqualified energy that *man* imposes upon *Matter* through his misuse of the *sacred fire;* maya, illusion. The consciousness of relative good and evil, embodied by *lifestreams* moving against the current of God's will, is the consequence of the *freewill* experiment adopted by *souls* who chose to descend in plane and consciousness below the level and frequency of the Christ Mind. Absolute Evil, embodied by fallen *angels,* is the state of those who declared war against Almighty God, his *Christ* and his offspring in the Great Rebellion, who have not ceased their warfare against the seed of the Divine *Mother,* will not bend the knee before the *Light* and will be defeated in Armageddon by the LORD's Judgment through his hosts—the forces of Absolute Good, God-identified in heaven and earth. As a consequence of the victory of Light over Darkness, souls who have lost the Edenic bliss may be saved from all evil and the Evil One by conscious freewill election in Christ to return to his reign under the Law of God.

(See the following by Elizabeth Clare Prophet: *Forbidden Mysteries of Enoch: Fallen Angels and the Origins of Evil.* "The Origin of Evil," in *Kabbalah: Key to Your Hidden Power,* published in *Pearls of Wisdom,* 1992, vol. 35, Book II, pp. 159–91. "The Origin of Evil," 1-hr. TV show on video, part 4 of "Keys from Judaism: The Kabbalah and the Temple of Man," also on audio.)

Four lower bodies. *See* Bodies of man, Physical body, Mental body, Emotional body, and Etheric body.

Free will. The freedom to create; the option to choose the right- or the left-handed path, Life or Death, the positive or the negative spirals of consciousness. Having the gift of free will, the *soul* may choose to dwell in the plane of the relative, where good and *evil* are relative to one's perspective in time and space; or she may choose the plane of the Absolute, where Good is real and Evil is unreal and the soul beholds God as living Truth "face-to-face." Free will means that the individual may accept or reject the divine plan, the laws of God, and the opportunity to live in the consciousness of Love.

God's gift of free will carries with it a certain span of consciousness known as the life span, a series of embodiments, and the "bounds of *man's* habitation." The soul, therefore, is not only confined to time and space during the period of her experimentation with free will, but she is also limited to a certain number of life cycles. At the end of this opportunity (compartmentalized in days, years, and dimensions), the use that the soul has made of the gift of free will determines her fate. The soul that has chosen to glorify the *Divine Ego* (Reality) ascends into the *Presence* of the I AM THAT I AM. The soul that has chosen to glorify the *human ego* (unreality) passes through the second death, her Self-denying consciousness permanently self-canceled; and all of her energies, simultaneously passed through the *sacred fire,* are returned to the Great *Central Sun* for repolarization.

(Rev. 20:6, 11–15; 21:8; Acts 17:26.)

Gabriel. *See* Archangel.

Gautama Buddha. *See* Buddha.

Goal-fitting. A term used by *El Morya, Chohan* of the First *Ray,* to describe the fitting of the evolving *soul* consciousness for the goal of reunion with God; a process of discipline and initiation through service and application of the *sacred fire* that souls preparing for the *ascension* undergo under the loving direction of the *Ascended Masters.*

(See *The Chela and the Path* for the Master's fundamentals on goal-fittedness for meeting the challenges of the twentieth century.)

God consciousness. The consciousness, or awareness, of one's true self as the manifestation of God; the awareness of the I AM THAT I AM, or the *I AM Presence,* in and through and beyond oneself in universal manifestation; the ability to maintain this conscious God Self-awareness—omnipotent, omniscient and omnipresent—wherever oneself, as Being, is and declares in the fullness of the *Light,* "Lo, because Thou art, I AM." The state of God Self-mastery whereby one maintains this vibration in Divine Wholeness of the *Alpha-Omega* principle in the planes of *Spirit-Matter.* The plane of God's consciousness is the kingdom of God. And all who dwell therein (beyond the earth/heaven realms) are truly extensions of God's own consciousness—only his in the highest expression of Love. *See also* Cosmic consciousness. (Ps. 82:6; John 10:34.)

God Flame. The flame of God; the *sacred fire;* the identity, being, and consciousness of God in and as the white fire core of being. Moses declared, "For the LORD thy God is a consuming fire." Wherever the flame of God is or is invoked by his offspring, the sacred fire descends to consume (transmute by its white fire and Seventh *Ray* action, the *violet flame*) all unlike itself. From the sacred fire of Ahura Mazda revealed by Zarathustra, to *Jesus'* baptism by the Holy Ghost "with fire," to the apostle's perception of the trial by fire, to the eternal flame of the sevenfold lights of the Hebrews, all children of the One who would return to the flame have revered God's flaming Presence and beheld him in the very midst of the Shekhinah glory. And in their hearts they accept the reality of his promise unto the *soul,* the waiting Bride, "For I, saith the LORD, will be unto her a wall of fire round about, and will be the glory in the midst of her."
(Deut. 4:24; Matt. 3:11, 12; I Cor. 3:13–15; I Pet. 1:7; Exod. 25:31–40; 37:17–24; Zech. 2:5.)

God Presence. *See* I AM Presence.

God Self. *See* I AM Presence.

Great Central Sun. *See* Central sun.

Great Hub. *See* Central sun.

Great White Brotherhood. A spiritual order of Western saints and Eastern *adepts* who have reunited with the *Spirit* of the living God and who comprise the heavenly hosts. They have transcended the cycles of *karma* and rebirth and ascended (accelerated) into that higher reality which is the eternal abode of the *soul*. The *Ascended Masters* of the Great White Brotherhood, united for the highest purposes of the brotherhood of *man* under the Fatherhood of God, have risen in every age from every culture and religion to inspire creative achievement in education, the arts and sciences, God-government and the abundant Life through the economies of the nations. The word "white" refers not to race but to the *aura* (halo) of white *light* surrounding their forms. The Brotherhood also includes in its ranks certain unascended *chelas* of the Ascended Masters. *Jesus Christ* revealed this heavenly order of saints "robed in white" to his servant John in Revelation. *See also* Cosmic hierarchy.

(Rev. 3:4, 5; 6:9–11; 7:9, 13, 14; 19:14. See Elizabeth Clare Prophet, *The Great White Brotherhood in the Culture, History and Religion of America.*)

Hierarchy. *See* Cosmic hierarchy.

Higher Self. The *I AM Presence;* the *Christ Self;* the exalted aspect of selfhood. Used in contrast to the term *"lower self,"* or "little self," which indicates the *soul* that went forth from and may elect by *free will* to return to the Divine Whole through the realization of the oneness of the self in God. Higher consciousness.

Hilarion. *See* Chohan.

Holy Christ Self. *See* Christ Self.

Holy Spirit. Third Person of the Trinity; the omnipresence of God; the cloven tongues of fire that focus the Father-*Mother* God, also called the *sacred fire;* the energies of Life that infuse a *cosmos.* In the Hindu Trinity of Brahma, Vishnu, and Shiva, the Holy Spirit corresponds to Shiva, known as the Destroyer/ Deliverer because his all-consuming Love, when invoked in the planes of *Matter,* binds the forces of *evil* and transmutes the cause and effect of *man's* miscreations, thus delivering him from the prison house of *karma* and its dark denizens. Prana is the essence of the Holy Spirit that we take in by the sacred fire breath through the *chakras* to nourish the *four lower bodies.* The Holy Spirit focuses the balance of the Father-Mother God in the white fire core of being. The exorcism of foul spirits and unclean entities is accomplished by the sacred fire of the Holy Spirit in the name of *Christ* and the I AM THAT I AM. The nine gifts of the Spirit are powers conveyed to the Lord's servants to bind death and hell and work his works on earth.

The Person and the Flame of the Holy Spirit is the Comforter whom *Jesus* promised would come when our Lord took his leave—to enlighten us, to teach us, and to bring all things to our remembrance that beloved Jesus has taught us, both in heaven and on earth. Each time a *son or daughter of God* ascends into the *Presence* of the I AM THAT I AM, the Holy Spirit descends to fill the void and to magnify the

Lord's Presence on earth. This is the ritual of the descent of the Holy Ghost promised by Jesus to his disciples when the Master said, "Tarry ye in the city of Jerusalem, until ye be endued with power from on high," which took place on Pentecost.

The representative of the flame of the Holy Spirit to earth's evolutions is the *Ascended Master* who occupies the office of Maha *Chohan*. The Holy Spirit is the Personal Impersonality of the Godhead and is positioned on the west side of the City Foursquare. *See also* Chart of Your Divine Self.
(I Cor. 12:4–11; John 14:16, 26; 16:7; Luke 24:49, 51; Mark 16:19; Acts 2:1–4. See Mark L. Prophet and Elizabeth Clare Prophet, *Climb the Highest Mountain,* 2d ed., pp. 386–88, 408–44, 555–62; *The Lost Teachings of Jesus II,* softbound, pp. 158–63, or pocketbook, Book Three, pp. 116–22; *Lords of the Seven Rays,* Book One, pp. 15–20, Book Two, pp. 277–97. Elizabeth Clare Prophet, audio and video lecture series on the Holy Spirit: "Who and What Is the Holy Spirit," "How to Become a Disciple of the Holy Spirit," "How to Earn the Anointings by the Holy Spirit," "The Gifts of the Holy Spirit Are for You—Today" and "The Gifts of Healing from the Holy Spirit." *The Holy Spirit Streameth: Meditations for the Purification of the Eighth-Ray Chakra,* audiocassette of songs. *Come, Holy Dove! Mystical Union through the Names of God,* audiocassette of song.)

Human consciousness. That consciousness which is aware of the self as human—limited, mortal, fallen, sinful, subject to error and the passions of the senses —and therefore declares with the Son of *man:* "I of mine own (human) self can do nothing. It is the

Father (the *I AM Presence*) in me that doeth the Work of the LORD."
(John 5:30; 14:10.)

Human ego. That point of the personality which embraces the *human consciousness* and all that it stands for as true selfhood; the anti-self, the synthetic image. Nevertheless, the positive ego, successful and having a healthy self-image, is the very vital ingredient that enables the human to fearlessly reach for the *Divine Ego,* step by step letting go of itself, forsaking the past until that human mask is no longer a vice or device. And pure joy as radiant being becomes one's new definition of selfhood and perspective on Reality. It is proverbial that a healthy ego is essential to a healthy surrender unto God — the true and only Ego of us all.

Human monad. The entire forcefield of self, the interconnecting spheres of influences — hereditary, environmental, karmic — which make up that self-awareness which identifies itself as human. The reference point of lesser- or non-awareness out of which all mankind must evolve to the realization of the *Real Self* as the *Christ Self.*

I AM Presence. The I AM THAT I AM; the individualized Presence of God focused for each individual *soul.* The God-identity of the individual; the *Divine Monad;* the individual Source. The origin of the soul focused in the planes of *Spirit* just above the physical form; the personification of the *God Flame* for the individual. *See also* Chart of Your Divine Self. (Exod. 3:13–15.)

Immaculate concept. The pure concept or image of the *soul* held in the Mind of God; any pure thought held by one part of life for and on behalf of another part of life. The essential ingredient to every alchemical experiment without which it will not succeed. The ability to hold the image of the perfect pattern to be precipitated, to see the vision of a project complete, to draw a mental picture, to retain it and to fill it in with *light* and love and joy—these are keys to the science of the immaculate concept taught by *Mother Mary* as well as the Master Alchemist. The exercise of the inner sight through the third eye is a process of purification whereby, as *Jesus* said, "If thine eye be single—and singly, one-pointedly focused upon the Beloved God—thy whole body shall be full of Light" —i.e., of *Christ's* illumining Presence.

"God is the supreme practitioner of the science of the immaculate concept. No matter how far *man* might wander from his individuality, God ever beholds man in the image of Reality in which He created him.... This science of the immaculate concept is practiced by every *angel* in heaven. It is that law which is written in the inward parts of man, known by his very heart of hearts, yet dim in the memory of his outer mind. It is based on the visualization of a perfect idea which then becomes a magnet that attracts the creative energies of the *Holy Spirit* to his

being to fulfill the pattern held in mind."
(Matt. 6:22; Jer. 31:33; Heb. 8:10. See Mark L. Prophet and
Elizabeth Clare Prophet, *Climb the Highest Mountain*, 2d
ed., pp. 48–50, 155.)

Jesus. The *Ascended Master* Jesus *Christ.* The avatar of
the Piscean age; the incarnation of the *Word*, the
Universal Christ; the example of the *Christ consciousness* that was to have been outpictured by the children of God in the two-thousand-year dispensation
of the Piscean age; one who realized the fullness of
the *Christ Self* and was therefore called Jesus, the
Christ. He came to reveal the individual Christ Self
to all mankind and to show the works of the Father
(the *I AM Presence*) that can be accomplished by his
sons and daughters in and through the flame of the
individual Christ Self. Jesus holds the office in *hierarchy* of *World Teacher*, which he shares with the
Ascended Master *Kuthumi*, who was embodied as
Saint Francis. Jesus' retreat is the Resurrection Tem-
ple, located in the *etheric* realm over the Holy Land.
He also serves in the Arabian Retreat in the Arabian
Desert northeast of the Red Sea. *See also* Ascension.
(See Jesus and Kuthumi, *Prayer and Meditation; Corona
Class Lessons.* Mark L. Prophet and Elizabeth Clare Prophet,
The Lost Teachings of Jesus. The following by Elizabeth Clare
Prophet: *The Lost Years of Jesus.* "The Lost Years and the
Lost Teachings of Jesus," 1-hr. TV show on video. "The
Golden Age of Jesus Christ on Atlantis," 2 videocassettes; 2
audiocassettes. "Jesus Christ, Avatar of the Ages," 1 video-
cassette; 2 audiocassettes. "Roots of Christian Mysticism,"
five 1-hr. TV shows on video; 6 audiocassettes. For additional

lectures on the lost years and lost teachings of Jesus, including teachings on Gnostic texts, send for a Summit University Press catalog.)

Jophiel. *See* Archangel.

Karma. (Skt. *karman,* nominative *karma,* 'act', 'deed', 'work'.) Karma is energy/consciousness in action; the law of cause and effect and retribution. Also called the law of the circle, which decrees that whatever we do comes full circle to our doorstep for resolution. Paul said, "Whatsoever a man soweth, that shall he also reap." Newton observed, "For every action there is an equal and opposite reaction." The law of karma necessitates the *soul's* reincarnation until all karmic cycles are balanced. Thus, from lifetime to lifetime *man* determines his fate by his actions, including his thoughts, feelings, words, and deeds. *Saint Germain* teaches the accelerated path of transmutation of karma by the *violet flame* of the *Holy Spirit* and the transcending of the rounds of rebirth through the path of individual Christhood leading to the *ascension* demonstrated by *Jesus.*
(Gal. 6:7. See Mark L. Prophet and Elizabeth Clare Prophet, *The Lost Teachings of Jesus I,* softbound, pp. 129–33; or pocketbook, Book One, pp. 173–77. *The Lost Teachings of Jesus II,* softbound, pp. 44–50; or pocketbook, Book Two, pp. 240–47. The following by Elizabeth Clare Prophet: *The Astrology of the Four Horsemen,* pp. 3–19, 65–71, 491–98. "Prophecy for the 1990s," in *Pearls of Wisdom,* 1988, vol. 31, Book I, pp. 1–91; Book II, pp. 1–123. "Prophecy for the 1990s III," in *Pearls of Wisdom,* 1990, vol. 33, nos. 4–12.

"Karma, Reincarnation and Christianity," in *Pearls of Wisdom*, 1992, vol. 35, nos. 11–14, 17, 22; 2 videocassettes; 3 audiocassettes.)

Karmic Board. *See* Lords of Karma.

Karmic Lords. *See* Lords of Karma.

Kuthumi. The *Ascended Master.* Serves with *Jesus* in the office of *World Teacher;* formerly *Chohan* of the Second *Ray;* master psychologist; sponsor of youth; head of the Order of the *Brothers and Sisters of the Golden Robe* and of the *etheric* Temple of Illumination in Kashmir, also known as the Cathedral of Nature. The Master maintains a focus at *Shigatse,* Tibet, where he plays his grand organ—drawing the harmony of *cosmos* by the *sacred fires* of his heart. With this celestial music, he sends healing and peace throughout the planetary body to *souls* in transition (especially at the hour of death) and guides them to the etheric retreats of the *Great White Brotherhood* for tutoring in preparation for their next earthly life. He inspires architects, poets, and scientists with the mystical remembrance of their own soul's harmony in the celestial geometry and the rhythm of the stars. *See also* "Incarnations of the Ascended Master Kuthumi," pp. 327–34.

(See Kuthumi, *Studies of the Human Aura,* also published in *The Human Aura.* Jesus and Kuthumi, *Prayer and Meditation; Corona Class Lessons.* Kuthumi, Lanto, and Meru, *Understanding Yourself,* also published in *Kuthumi On Selfhood—Consciousness: The Doorway to Reality, Pearls of Wisdom,* 1969, vol. 12, nos. 25–40.)

Lanto. *See* Chohan.

Lifestream. The stream of life that comes forth from the one Source, from the *I AM Presence* in the planes of *Spirit,* and descends to the planes of *Matter* where it manifests as the *threefold flame* anchored in the heart *chakra* for the sustainment of the *soul* in Matter and the nourishment of the *four lower bodies.* Used to denote souls evolving as individual "lifestreams" and hence synonymous with the term "individual." Denotes the ongoing nature of the individual through the cycles of individualization.

Light. Spiritual light is the energy of God, the potential of the *Christ.* As the personification of *Spirit,* the term "Light" can be used synonymously with the terms "God" and "Christ." As the essence of Spirit it is synonymous with *"sacred fire."* It is the emanation of the Great *Central Sun* and the individualized *I AM Presence*—and the Source of all life. It is that which kindles the divine spark, for the true Light lights every *man*ifestation of God who must descend into a darkened world. The Lightbearer is the dispeller of Darkness and the Light of his I AM Presence is from the realms of the Eternal Day.
(John 1:7–9.)

Lord Maitreya. The *Ascended Master.* Together with Gautama, Maitreya followed the disciplines of the *Buddha* under Sanat Kumara. He holds the office of Cosmic *Christ* and Planetary Buddha, serving in *hierarchy* under Lord Gautama, directing the office of the *World Teachers*. He demonstrates on behalf of an evolving humanity the *cosmic consciousness* of the Christ in all areas of human endeavor and its universality throughout *cosmos*. He is known as the Great Initiator and was, in fact, the initiator of *Jesus* in his individualization of the Christ Flame in his final embodiment as world saviour and exemplar of the Way, the Truth, and the Life to all *aspirants* on the path of personal Christhood. Beloved Maitreya was the LORD God in Eden, Guru of *twin flames*. The long-awaited "Coming Buddha," he has indeed come to reopen his Mystery School to assist *Saint Germain* and Portia, twin flames of the Seventh *Ray* and hierarchs of Aquarius, to usher in the new age. On May 31, 1984, he dedicated the Heart of the Inner Retreat and the entire Royal Teton Ranch to the Path and Teaching of the Cosmic Christ in order that those who departed from his tutelage, going the way of Serpents (the fallen *angels* who led Eve astray), might be restored and the children of the *Light* follow the Son of God in the regeneration. As the sponsor of twin flames he is the friend of all initiates of the *sacred fire*. When called upon, he will give the illumination of the Christ and the strength of the *Word* to pass the initiations that come under his sponsorship. *See also* Buddha.

(See Lord Maitreya, "On Initiation," in *Pearls of Wisdom*, 1975, vol. 18, nos. 49–53; *Maitreya On the Image of God: A Study in Christhood by the Great Initiator, Pearls of Wisdom*, 1984, vol. 27, Books I and II. Elizabeth Clare Prophet,

"Darshan with the Cosmic Christ," 2 audiocassettes; "The Path of the Bodhisattva: The Historical Maitreya," 2 audiocassettes; "The Age of Maitreya," 1 videocassette, 2 audiocassettes.)

Lords of Karma. The *ascended beings* who comprise the Karmic Board. Their names and the *rays* that they represent on the board are as follows: **Great Divine Director,** First Ray; **Goddess of Liberty,** Second Ray; **Ascended Lady Master** *Nada,* Third Ray; *Elohim* **Cyclopea,** Fourth Ray; **Pallas Athena,** Goddess of Truth, Fifth Ray; **Portia,** Goddess of Justice, Sixth Ray; **Kuan Yin,** Goddess of Mercy, Seventh Ray; **Dhyani Buddha Vairochana,** newly appointed eighth member. The Lords of Karma dispense justice to this system of worlds, adjudicating *karma,* mercy, and judgment on behalf of every *lifestream.* All *souls* must pass before the Karmic Board before and after each incarnation on earth, receiving their assignment and karmic allotment for each lifetime beforehand and the review of their performance at its conclusion. Through the Keeper of the Scrolls and the *recording angels,* the Lords of Karma have access to the complete records of every lifestream's incarnations on earth. They determine who shall embody, as well as when and where. They assign souls to families and communities, measuring out the weights of karma that must be balanced as the "jot and tittle" of the law. The Karmic Board, acting in consonance with the individual *I AM Presence* and *Christ Self,* determines when the soul has earned the right to be free from the wheel of karma and the round of rebirth.

The Lords of Karma meet at the Royal Teton Retreat twice yearly, at winter and summer solstice, to review petitions from unascended mankind and to grant dispensations for their assistance.

(See Mark L. Prophet and Elizabeth Clare Prophet, *Climb the Highest Mountain*, 2d ed., pp. 529–35. *Pearls of Wisdom*, 1994, vol. 37, no. 3, pp. 30–31.)

Lords of the Seven Rays. *See* Chohan.

Lower self. *See* Chart of Your Divine Self, Higher Self.

Macrocosm. (From the Gk., meaning "great world.") The larger *cosmos;* the entire warp and woof of creation, which we call the *Cosmic Egg.* Also used to contrast *man* as the *microcosm,* "the little world," against the backdrop of the larger world in which he lives. *See also* Microcosm.

Maitreya. *See* Lord Maitreya.

Man. The *man*ifestation of God; male and female made in the image and likeness of God *(Elohim).* Mankind or the human race; Homo sapiens.

Manchild. *See* Divine Manchild.

Mantra. A mystical formula or invocation; a word or formula, often in Sanskrit, to be recited or sung for the purpose of intensifying the action of the *Spirit* of God in *man.* A form of prayer consisting of a word or a group of words that is chanted over and over again to magnetize a particular aspect of the Deity or of a being who has actualized that aspect of the Deity. *See also* Decree.

(See Mark L. Prophet and Elizabeth Clare Prophet, *The Lost Teachings of Jesus II,* softbound, pp. 141–46, 450–51, or pocketbooks, Book Three, pp. 79–85, Book Four, pp. 192–93; "The Efficacy of Decrees," with instruction on Indian mantras and bhajans, 1 audiocassette. Elizabeth Clare Prophet, *The Liberating Power of the Word,* album 1, 6 audiocassettes. *Devotions to Lord Krishna: The Maha Mantra and Bhajans,* audiocassette and booklet.)

Mary. *See* Mother Mary.

Mass consciousness. The collective consciousness of humanity; the collective unconscious of the race; the lowest common denominator of mankind's collective awareness vibrating at the level of the *astral* plane. The mass mind is the collective, computerized, programmed mind of humanity.

Mater. (Lat. for "mother.") Mater is the *mater*-ialization of the *God Flame,* the means whereby *Spirit* acquires, 'physically', fourfold dimension and form through the feminine, or negative, polarity of the Godhead. The term used interchangeably with "Matter" to describe the planes of being that conform to and comprise the universal chalice, or matrix, for the descent of that *Light* of God which is perceived as *Mother.* It is through this Mother aspect of himself that the Spirit of God, the Father, evolves the consciousness of the *Christ,* the only begotten Son of God, in his children as a developing *Christ-Self* awareness through the *threefold flame*—divine spark and signet of their joint-heirship to be. The *soul* that descends from the plane of Spirit abides in time and space in Mater for the purpose of its spiritual/physical evolution that necessitates self-mastery of the energies of God through the judicious exercise of *free will*. The four lower *bodies of man,* of a planet, and of systems of worlds—as the four planes, quadrants and cosmic forces—occupy and make up the frequencies of Matter. *See also* Spirit.

Matter. *See* Mater.

Mental body. One of the four lower *bodies of man,* corresponding to the air element and the second quadrant of *Matter;* the body that is intended to be the vehicle, or vessel, for the Mind of God or the *Christ* Mind. "Let this [Universal] Mind be in you which was also in Christ *Jesus.*" Until quickened, this body remains the vehicle for the *carnal mind,* often called the lower mental body in contrast to the Higher Mental Body, a synonym for the *Christ Self* or *Christ consciousness.*
(Phil. 2:5.)

Messenger. Evangelist. One who goes before the *angels* bearing to the people of earth the good news of the gospel of *Jesus* Christ and, at the appointed time, the Everlasting Gospel. The Messengers of the *Great White Brotherhood* are anointed by the *hierarchy* as their apostles ("one sent on a mission"). They deliver through the dictations (prophecies) of the *Ascended Masters* the testimony and lost teachings of Jesus Christ in the power of the *Holy Spirit* to the seed of

Christ, the lost sheep of the house of Israel, and to every nation. A Messenger is one who is trained by an Ascended Master to receive by various methods the words, concepts, teachings, and messages of the Great White Brotherhood; one who delivers the law, the prophecies, and the dispensations of God for a people and an age.
(Rev. 14:6; Matt. 10:6; 15:24. El Morya, *The Chela and the Path,* pp. 115–22. Jesus and Kuthumi, *Prayer and Meditation,* pp. 246–53. Elizabeth Clare Prophet, *The Astrology of the Four Horsemen,* pp. 52–53, 58–61.)

Michael, Archangel. *Archangel* of the First *Ray,* Prince of the Archangels, the first among equals unto whom all other Archangels and their legions defer. Known as the Defender of the Faith, Champion of the Woman and Her Seed, and Leader in the Battle of Armageddon who stands as the defender of the *Christ consciousness* in all children of God. His name means "who is as God." His intercession on behalf of God's people in this age is prophesied in Daniel 12:1: "And at that time shall Michael stand up, the great prince which standeth for the children of thy people: and there shall be a time of trouble, such as never was since there was a nation even to that same time: and at that time thy people shall be delivered, every one that shall be found written in the book."

Archangel Michael is the *Angel of the LORD* who comes to quicken the elect of God with the lost teachings of *Jesus* Christ and to deliver the true and righteous judgments of God upon the seed of the

Wicked One. This deliverer sent to us by the LORD has figured as the greatest and most revered of *angels* in Jewish, Christian, and Islamic scripture and tradition. In the Old Testament he appears as the guardian of Israel and is identified in Jewish mystical literature as the angel who wrestled with Jacob, guided Israel through the wilderness, destroyed the army of Sennacherib, and saved the three Hebrew boys from Nebuchadnezzar's fiery furnace. Standing mighty in the LORD's presence, sword drawn, Archangel Michael appeared to Joshua as he prepared to lead the Israelites into battle at Jericho, revealing himself as Captain of the Host of the LORD—impartial defender of all who espouse Truth and Righteousness. (Josh. 5:13–15.)

It is recorded in Jewish legend that "the fire that Moses saw in the bush was the appearance of Michael, who had descended as the forerunner of the Shekhinah." Indeed, wherever the term "Angel of the LORD" is given in scripture it is a reference to this messenger of God—the divine figure of His appearing. The Book of Enoch describes Archangel Michael as "the merciful, the patient," "one of the holy angels, who, presiding over human virtue, commands the nations." In *The War of the Sons of Light and the Sons of Darkness,* one of the Dead Sea Scrolls, Michael is the "mighty, ministering angel" through whom God promises to "send perpetual help" to the sons of *Light.* Called Mika'il in Muslim lore, he is the angel of nature, providing both food and knowledge to *man*.

Saint Michael, venerated by Catholics as patron and protector of the Church, was also the heavenly physician revered in the early Christian community for the miraculous cures wrought by his intercession. Moreover, the beloved Archangel was among the three heavenly visitors who revealed to the young peasant girl Joan of Arc her mission to deliver France. Revelation 12 tells of Archangel Michael's key role as the defender of the Woman clothed with the Sun as he casts the adversary of her *Manchild* out of the courts of heaven: "And there was war in heaven: Michael and his angels fought against the dragon, and the dragon fought and his angels, and prevailed not; neither was their place found any more in heaven." In Revelation 16:1, he is the first of the seven angels to "pour out the vials of the wrath of God upon the earth"—marking the descending woes of mankind's *karma* returning to their doorstep their misuses of God's Light.

As the Archangel of the First Ray, Archangel Michael embodies God's consciousness of faith, protection, perfection, and the will of God. From his retreat on the *etheric* plane at Banff in Alberta, Canada, he goes forth into all the world with his legions of blue-lightning angels to protect the children of the Light and preserve freedom on earth. With his hosts he descends into the pits of Death and Hell to bind the adversaries of the Christ consciousness, remanding them to the Court of the *Sacred Fire* for their final judgment. He sweeps through the *astral* plane, binding demons and discarnates that prey upon unsuspecting *souls,* rendering incomparable assistance to those beset by the dark forces. His keynote is "The Navy Hymn," "Eternal Father, Strong to Save." The keynote of his retreat is "The Soldiers' Chorus" from *Faust,* by Charles Gounod. The name of his feminine complement is Faith.

At this end of the Piscean age, with two thousand years and more of unbalanced karma falling due paralleled by a period of accelerated initiation—when the Lightbearers are facing greater challenges on the path of personal Christhood in order to enter the Aquarian age—the Father has accorded the Lightbearers unprecedented opportunity to invoke the comforting presence and intercession of this Angel of the LORD. As they offer prayers, invocations, hymns and dynamic *decrees* in the science of the *spoken Word*—such as those included in *Archangel Michael's Rosary for Armageddon* released through the *Messenger* Elizabeth Clare Prophet—the armor and shield of Archangel Michael is immediately theirs. Responding to the needs of mankind, they give the impelling call for the saving of the nations in this cycle marking the return of personal and planetary karma delivered by the Four Horsemen. Surely, in the midst of this time of troubles the Lightbearers are daily proving the law: "The Call compels the answer." If you are in trouble, shout unto the Angel of the LORD this dynamic decree until he responds: "Lord Michael before! Lord Michael behind! Lord Michael to the right! Lord Michael to the left! Lord Michael above! Lord Michael below! Lord Michael, Lord Michael wherever I go! I AM his Love protecting here! I AM his Love protecting here! I AM his Love protecting here!" *See also* Archangel.

(See Elizabeth Clare Prophet, "Archangel Michael's Rosary for Armageddon," in *Pearls of Wisdom,* 1985, vol. 28, Book I, no. 19; *Archangel Michael's Rosary for Armageddon,* audiocassette and booklet; "Putting on the Armour and Shield of Archangel Michael," audiocassette. *Devotions, Decrees and Spirited Songs to Archangel Michael,* beginning pace, audiocassette. *Decrees and Songs to Archangel Michael,* medium pace, audiocassette. *Hail Light Victorious! A Salute to Archangel Michael, Captain of the LORD's Host,* songs on CD and audiocassette.)

Microcosm. (From the Gk., meaning "small world.") (1) The world of the individual, his *four lower bodies,* his *aura,* and the forcefield of his *karma.* (2) The planet. *See also* Macrocosm.

Misqualification (of energy). The "mist" qualification of fallen man and woman; the spawning of *evil,* or the energy *veil,* through the misuse of *free will* by *souls* evolving in time and space. The misapplication of God's energy. The negative qualification of God's consciousness and life-force to multiply darkness, doubt, disease, degeneracy, and death instead of

Light, Love, Divine Wholeness, Peace, and Freedom. The **misqualified energies** that burden the *aura* and electronic belt of the people and their planet are the direct result of this perversion of alchemy, the all-chemistry of God, the science of creation that the Father and Son invite us to "TRY" as co-creators with the Great Alchemist himself.

Monad. *See* Divine Monad, Human monad.

Morya. *See* El Morya.

Mother. "Divine Mother," "Universal Mother," and "Cosmic Virgin" are alternate terms for the feminine polarity of the Godhead, the manifestation of God as Mother. *Matter* is the feminine polarity of *Spirit,* and the term is used interchangeably with *Mater* (Lat. meaning "mother"). In this context, the entire material *cosmos* becomes the womb of creation into which Spirit projects the energies of Life. Matter, then, is the womb of the Cosmic Virgin, who, as the other half of the Divine Whole, also exists in Spirit as the spiritual polarity of God.

Jesus himself recognized *Alpha and Omega* as the highest representatives of the Father-Mother God and often referred to Alpha as Father and to Omega as Mother. Those who assume the feminine polarity of consciousness after the *ascension* are known as *Ascended* Lady *Masters.* Together with all feminine (femininely polarized) beings in the octaves of *light,* they focus the flame of the Divine Mother on behalf of the evolutions of mankind evolving in many systems of worlds. However, being androgynous, all of the heavenly host focus any of the masculine or feminine attributes of the Godhead at will, for they have entered the spheres of the Divine Wholeness. (See the following by Elizabeth Clare Prophet: "The Path of the Divine Mother East and West," 3 audiocassettes, A88055. "The Path of the Divine Mother," 3 videocassettes, GP92043; 3 audiocassettes, A91116. "The Worship of the Goddess—the Path of the Divine Mother," two 1-hr. TV shows on video; 3 audiocassettes.)

Mother Mary. *Archeia* of the Fifth *Ray,* divine complement of *Archangel* Raphael, Queen of *Angels,* and the Blessed Mother of *Jesus* Christ. Her name means Mother Ray (Ma ray). Called by the Father to embody on earth to give birth to the *Christ* who would save those *souls* that had been led astray by Luciferian rebels, Mary is one of the LORD's hosts who throughout her incarnations on earth has ardently exemplified the Motherhood of God. From the earliest days of Atlantis she prepared for her final embodiment, when she would nurture in the Bethlehem babe the 'son' (soul) of David, born again to be the Saviour (avatar) of the Piscean age. Mary served as a priestess on Atlantis in the Temple of Truth, teaching and studying the healing arts and directing, through her Immaculate Heart, the *light* of the ineffable *Word* to the teeming millions of that continent. She was also the mother of David, king of Israel. It was her masterful development on Atlantis of the science of the *immaculate concept,* which she had practiced in heaven, that enabled her to be the LORD's handmaid, preparing her *four lower bodies* for the incarnation of the Word in Christ Jesus, her son. At the conclusion of that blessed life, her divine plan fulfilled, Mary ascended to the heart of the Father. Today she serves humanity and the 'living Church' from inner levels, very close at hand with the hierarchies of angels and *Ascended Masters* who comprise the *Great White Brotherhood.* Mother Mary's intercession is immediate through the giving of her New Age Rosary, which she dictated to the *Messenger* in 1972.

(See Mark L. Prophet and Elizabeth Clare Prophet, *My Soul Doth Magnify the Lord! Mother Mary's New Age Teachings and Rosary with a Challenge to Christendom. Mary the Mother On the Temple of Understanding: A Challenge to the Christian World, Pearls of Wisdom,* 1972, vol. 15, nos. 29–41. The following lectures by Elizabeth Clare Prophet: "Prophecy: Fátima and Medjugorje," 1-hr. TV show on video. "The Path of the Divine Mother East and West: Mother Mary and Kuan Yin," 3 audiocassettes, A88059. "Mother Mary's Twentieth-Century Prophecies," 1 audiocassette. "The Divine Mother and World Karma: Mother Mary Intercedes for Mankind," 1 videocassette. *Mother Mary's Scriptural Rosary for the New Age,* 8 audiocassettes. *A Child's Rosary to Mother Mary,* 4 albums, 3 audiocassettes each. *Sanctissima: Music for World Peace,* on CD and audiocassette.)

Nada. *See* Chohan, Lords of Karma.

Path. The strait gate and narrow way that leadeth unto Life. The path of initiation whereby the disciple who

pursues the *Christ consciousness* overcomes step by step the limitations of selfhood in time and space and attains reunion with Reality through the ritual of the *ascension.*
(Matt. 7:14. See El Morya, *The Chela and the Path.*)

Paul the Venetian. *See* Chohan.

Physical body. The most dense of the four lower *bodies of man,* corresponding to the earth element and the fourth quadrant of *Matter;* the body that is the vehicle for the *soul's* sojourn on earth and the focus for the crystallization in form of the energies of the *etheric, mental,* and *emotional bodies.*

Power, Wisdom, and Love. The trinity of the *threefold flame*—Power representing the Father, Wisdom the Son, and Love the *Holy Spirit.* The balanced manifestation of these God-qualities in and as the flame within the heart is the prerequisite to personal Christhood. Attributes of the Hindu conception of the Trinity as (1) Brahma, the Creator, (2) Vishnu, the Preserver, and (3) Shiva, the Destroyer of *evil*/Deliverer of *souls.* According to the Eastern tradition, the Divine *Mother* is the universal force, Shakti, who releases the *light*/action, energy/consciousness of this threefold flame of *Spirit* into the *Matter cosmos* through the precious hearts of her children. *See also* Threefold flame.

Presence. *See* I AM Presence.

Psychic. (From Gk. *psyche* 'soul'.) One who has developed his *soul,* or solar, faculties for heightened
awareness of the physical, *astral,* mental, and sometimes the *etheric* belts of earth and her evolutions. A
psychic, or one who is psychic, has, in this or previous embodiments, developed faculties of sensitivity
or extrasensory perception not generally accessed by
mankind. This may include altered states above or
below the normal threshold of awareness and the
tapping of the computer of the subconscious or the
superconscious mind. Although some use these faculties constructively with a respectable degree of accuracy, in many cases the information as well as the
discrimination thereof is unreliable.

The term "psychic" has come to be used synonymously with the term "astral" in its negative context
and pertains to the penetration and manipulation of
energy at the level of the astral plane. According to
the *Ascended Masters,* one who has involved his energies in the psychic, psychicism, or psychic phenomena is functioning on the lower astral plane. Thus, by
the strong ties established with entities of the lower
octaves, he postpones the day of his true spiritual development and oneness with the penetrability of the
Godhead. Conversely, through oneness with God and
direct apprehension of the higher octaves, he may de-
rive spiritual benefit for his soul in the etheric plane
(heaven world), journeying in his etheric sheath to
the retreats of the Ascended Masters of the *Great*

White Brotherhood and the cities and temples of *light* located in that plane. True spiritual God-mastery is not measured by clairvoyance or psychic phenomena but by the God-control of the *sacred fires* of the heart and adeptship on the path of Love.

Raphael. *See* Archangel.

Rays. Beams of light or other radiant energy. The *light* emanations of the Godhead which, when invoked in the name of God or in the name of the *Christ,* burst forth as a flame in the world of the individual. Rays may be projected by the *God consciousness* of *ascended* or *unascended beings* through the third eye and other *chakras* as a concentration of energy taking on numerous God-qualities, such as love, truth, wisdom, healing, etc. Through the misuse of God's energy, practitioners of black magic project rays having negative qualities, such as death rays, sleep rays, hypnotic rays, disease rays, psychotronic rays, the evil eye, etc. *See also* Seven rays.
(See Mark L. Prophet and Elizabeth Clare Prophet, *Lords of the Seven Rays.*)

Readings. Probings of the records and *soul* memory of past, present, and future and of planes of consciousness beyond the physical. If readings are done by a *psychic* or through regression by hypnosis, they may be a probe of or an accessing of the *astral body* and *astral* belt of the earth, hence the *human consciousness* in all its personal and planetary astrological aspects. Since this takes into account experiences of the *lower self* without benefit of the soul's ongoing integration with the *Higher Self* and its point of perspective—looking down upon herself from the plane of causation to the plane of effect—such a reading is at best one dimensional. It may be a rerun that evokes deep emotions, but it will fail to re-create the rapture of the soul's self-transcendence in Higher Consciousness—the victorious denouement of her passage through the dark night.

Readings by an *Ascended Master* on behalf of a *chela* are given in order that lessons may be learned, goals set, and right choices made based on the totality of the life picture, involving the *karma* of the scene, the priorities of self-mastery, service with one's *twin flame,* and a vision of future freedom. The realization of this freedom may depend on a commitment to sacrifice in the present—to willingly embrace obligations and debts in a one-pointed striving for the mark. When the Ascended Masters give a reading, they give it for the disciple who wants to know not for curiosity or self-importance but that he may pay the price for the soul's separation from the Law of the One, balance karma, get off the treadmill of reembodiment, serve the I AM Race and their endeavors on behalf of humanity, reunite with his twin flame, and ascend to God. The Ascended Masters present an accurate assessment of the soul's integration with the *Christ Self* in the four planes of *Matter.*

They quicken the memory of the divine plan for this life and tell their students what is their progress on the *Path*. On the basis of the evaluation of the *Lords of Karma,* the Masters reveal what is most essential to the soul's salvation, drawing from the Book of Life and the hall of records maintained by the Keeper of the Scrolls.

Since a reading taken from the subconscious opens the records that have been sealed in wisdom's name by the Christ Self for this lifetime, the Ascended Masters recommend that instead of a reading the *violet flame* be invoked to "clear," i.e., transmute, these records without prior probe in order that the soul may daily ascend to God, transcending the past, living in the Eternal Now, strengthened by Higher Consciousness. The violet flame itself may reveal to soul and mind flashes of the past as these pass into the flame for transmutation. Transmutation by the violet flame frees us to be who we really are by our victories in God, unencumbered by the mésalliances of our yesterdays.

Real Self. The *Christ Self;* the *I AM Presence;* immortal *Spirit* that is the animating principle of all manifestation. *See also* Chart of Your Divine Self.

Recording angel. The *angel* assigned to the *soul* to record all her actions, words, deeds, feelings, thoughts —in short, her comings and goings in the planes of *Mater.* The recording angel records each day's events and turns them over to the Keeper of the Scrolls, who is the head of the band of angels known as the angels of record and of all recording angels assigned to the lifewaves evolving in time and space.

Sacred fire. The Kundalini fire that lies as the coiled serpent in the base-of-the-spine *chakra* (the Muladhara) and rises through spiritual purity and self-mastery to the crown chakra, quickening the spiritual centers on the way. God, *light,* life, energy, the I AM THAT I AM. "Our God is a consuming fire." The sacred fire is the precipitation of the Holy Ghost for the baptism of *souls,* for purification, for alchemy and transmutation, and for the realization of the *ascension,* the sacred ritual of the return to the One. (Heb. 12:29.)

Saint Germain. The *Ascended Master. Chohan* (Lord) of the Seventh *Ray* of Freedom, Hierarch of the Aquarian Age, sponsor of the United States of America; initiator of *souls* in the science and ritual of alchemy and transmutation through the *violet flame* by the power of the *spoken Word,* meditation, and visualization. His retreat in North America is the Cave of Symbols at Table Mountain, Wyoming. He also uses the Royal Teton Retreat at the Grand Teton, Jackson Hole, Wyoming; the retreat of his Guru, the Great Divine Director, the Cave of Light in India; and the Rakoczy Mansion, his focus in Transylvania The keynotes of the Rakoczy Mansion are "Tales from the Vienna Woods" and "Rakoczy March." Following are his soul's incarnations as revealed in various dispensations/activities:

Ruler of a golden-age civilization in the area of the Sahara Desert 50,000 years ago.

High priest on Atlantis 13,000 years ago. Served in the Violet Flame Temple and was schooled at the retreat of *Archangel* Zadkiel.

The Prophet Samuel, eleventh century B.C., Israel. Great religious leader who figured as prophet, priest, and last of the Hebrew judges.

Saint Joseph, first century A.D., Nazareth. Protector of *Jesus* and *Mary*.

Saint Alban, late third or early fourth century, town of Verulamium, renamed St. Albans, Hertfordshire, England. First British martyr. Sheltered a fugitive priest, became a devout convert, and was put to death for disguising himself as the priest so he could die in his place.

Teacher of Proclus. The last major Greek Neoplatonic philosopher, Proclus (c. 410–485, Athens) headed the Platonic Academy and wrote extensively on philosophy, astronomy, mathematics, and grammar.

Merlin, c. fifth or sixth century, Britain. Magician, seer, and counsellor at King Arthur's court who inspired the founding of the Order of the Knights of the Round Table.

Roger Bacon, c. 1220–1292, England. Philosopher, educational reformer, and experimental scientist; forerunner of modern science renowned for his exhaustive investigations into alchemy, optics, mathematics, and languages.

Christopher Columbus, 1451–1506, probably born in Genoa, Italy, settled in Portugal. Discovered America in 1492 during first of four voyages to the New World sponsored by King Ferdinand and Queen Isabella of Spain.

Francis Bacon, 1561–1626, England. Philosopher, statesman, essayist and literary master, author of the Shakespearean plays, father of inductive science and herald of the scientific revolution. Took the initiation of the *ascension* May 1, 1684, then reappeared as:

Le Comte de Saint Germain, the "Wonderman of Europe," eighteenth and nineteenth centuries. According to Prince Karl of Hesse, the Count revealed himself as the son of Prince Ferenc Rakoczy II of Transylvania; others have speculated he was a Portuguese Jew or son of the king of Portugal. Outstanding alchemist, scholar, linguist, musician, artist and diplomat; worked behind the scenes to bring about a United States of Europe and to forestall the bloodshed of violent revolution. His powers included bilocation, appearing at court and then dissolving his form at will, removing flaws from diamonds and other precious stones, and precipitating an elixir that prevented aging. He was also ambidextrous and could compose simultaneously a letter with one hand and poetry with the other, or two identical pieces of writing with each hand. He visited Marie Antoinette and her intimate friend, Madame d'Adhémar, who later wrote the story of his adeptship and warning of the coming debacle and death of the king and queen. (See Madame d'Adhémar, *Souvenirs de Marie Antoinette,* excerpted in Isabel Cooper-Oakley, *The Count of Saint-Germain* [Blauvelt, N.Y.: Rudolph Steiner Publications, 1970]. "Saint Germain on Freedom," in *Pearls of Wisdom,* 1977, vol. 20, nos. 31–52, 1978, vol. 21. nos, 1–7; *Saint Germain On Alchemy; Saint Germain On Prophecy.* Mark L. Prophet and Elizabeth Clare Prophet, *Lords of the Seven Rays,* Book One, chap. 7; Book Two, chap. 7. *Saint Germain: Chohan of the Seventh Ray of Freedom,* 2-audiocassette album. Lectures by Elizabeth Clare Prophet: *The Golden Age Prince: A Lecture on Francis Bacon,* 2-audiocassette album. "Saint Germain: 'The Man Who Never Dies and Who Knows Everything,'" 1-hr. TV show on video. *Saint Germain On Alchemy,* 2-videocassette album; 3 audiocassettes. "Christopher Columbus: The Man and the Myth," three 1-hr. TV shows on video; 2 audiocassettes.)

Satan. (From Gk., Heb. 'adversary'.) A lieutenant of the fallen *Archangel* Lucifer and ranking member of his false *hierarchy,* mistakenly thought to be the arch-deceiver himself. However, before his fall Satan had never attained to the rank of Archangel. Thus in the hierarchy of fallen *angels,* neither he nor any other ever exceeded Lucifer. The "Devil" was Lucifer and the surviving fallen angels that were under him are all called devils, Lucifer's seed still outranking the seed of the lesser powers and principalities of Darkness. Even so, in their personification of *Evil,* or the *Energy Veil,* those who deified and were the embodiment of Absolute Evil were referred to by the generic term "devil." Both Lucifer and Satan and their various lieutenants have been referred to in scripture as the adversary, the accuser of the brethren, the tempter, the *Antichrist,* the personification of the *carnal mind* of mankind, i.e., the planetary dweller-on-the-threshold, Serpent, the beast, the dragon, etc. On January 27, 1982, Satan was remanded to the Court of the *Sacred Fire,* resulting in his final judgment and second death.

(See Jesus Christ, "The Final Judgment of Satan," in *Pearls of Wisdom,* 1982, vol. 25, Book I, no. 16.)

Science of the spoken Word. *See* Spoken Word.

Seraphim. Also known as the seraphic hosts. The order of *angels* dedicated to the focusing of the flame of purity and the consciousness of purity before the throne of God, in the electronic fire rings of the Great *Central Sun,* and throughout the *cosmos* in the planes of *Spirit* and *Matter.* Justinius is the Captain of Seraphic Bands. Under his direction they serve at the altar of God in the Great Central Sun and at the *ascension* flame and the Ascension Temple at Luxor. Serapis Bey, the Hierarch of the Ascension Temple and *Chohan* of the Fourth *Ray,* was originally of the order of the seraphim. Isaiah saw "seraphims" (Heb. 'burners', 'burning ones') standing above the LORD's throne, each one having six wings: "With twain he covered his face (before the LORD's glory), and with twain he covered his feet (in reverence before the holiness of the LORD), and with twain he did fly (accelerate his vibration to the planes of the Great

Central Sun, decelerate to the planes of physicality and form)." The seraphim are initiators of the LORD's servants on earth, purging and purifying the ones chosen to be his ministering servants—priests, prophets, *messengers*, etc. Isaiah himself received the seraphic initiation, which he vividly describes: "Then flew one of the seraphims unto me, having a live coal in his hand, which he had taken with the tongs from off the altar: and he laid it upon my mouth, and said, Lo, this hath touched thy lips; and thine iniquity is taken away, and thy *sin* purged."

Serapis Bey describes his vision of the seraphim in his *Dossier on the Ascension:* "The seraphim came and they were as flaming streaks of fire passing through the atmosphere, and I knew that they possessed the quality of cosmic penetrability. Like cosmic rays they could pass through the flesh form of *man*, through his thoughts and feelings. When penetration occurred and the seraphim flew through *human consciousness,* what residue was left behind or what absorption was accomplished?

"I saw clearly that absorption was accomplished and that residue was left behind—absorption by reason of instantaneous transmutation of all substance that came nigh unto their trajectory. I noted also that the residue left behind was of intense white-fire devotion, charged with a yearning for purity. I perceived that this quality lingered within the consciousness of many; and yet, unless it was fed or accepted by them, its decay rate in their consciousness would be of relatively short term, for a disassociation of these ideas would cause the lingering sparks of the seraphim to pursue the parent body and leave their temporarily unwelcome home. Affinitizing with the consciousness of the seraphim is tantamount to retaining the benefits of the seraphic hosts.

"I know of no power more valiantly capable of assisting anyone into his own ascension in the *light* than the transmutative efforts toward Cosmic *Christ* purity that are emitted by the seraphic hosts. In our retreat at Luxor, the meditations upon the seraphim are a very important part of our spiritual instruction. *Jesus* himself spent a great deal of time in communion with the seraphic hosts. This developed in him the superior power whereby he could cast out demons and take dominion over the outer world of form." The *mantra* of the seraphim that they chant without ceasing before the throne of the LORD is: "Holy, holy, holy is the LORD of hosts: the whole earth is full of his glory."
(Isa. 6:2, 3, 6, 7. See Serapis Bey, *Dossier on the Ascension,* pp. 115–40.)

Serapis Bey. *See* Chohan.

Seven rays. The *light* emanations of the Godhead, e.g., the seven rays of the white light, which emerge through the prism of the *Christ consciousness*. The seven rays are (1) blue, (2) yellow, (3) pink, (4) white, (5) green, (6) purple and gold, and (7) violet.

There are also five "secret *rays*," which originate in the white fire core of being, and numerous cosmic rays personally qualified by the heavenly hosts that radiate through the sacred hearts of the Father's emissaries to lesser evolved *lifestreams*.

Seventh root race. An evolution of *souls* sponsored by the Great Divine Director and destined to embody on the continent of South America under the seventh dispensation, the Aquarian age, and the Seventh *Ray*.

Shigatse. A city of Tibet. On the *etheric* plane over Shigatse, *Kuthumi* maintains a retreat for disciples of *Christ* and *Brothers and Sisters of the Golden Robe*, devotees of the flame of wisdom.

Sin. Broadly, any departure from *cosmic law* that is the result of the exercise of *free will*.

Sons and daughters of God. (1) Those who come forth as the fruit of the divine union of the spirals of *Alpha and Omega;* those who have the *Christ* with them as the Immanuel. The creation of the Father-*Mother* God *(Elohim)* made in the image and likeness of the Divine Us, identified by the *threefold flame* of Life anchored within the heart. (2) On the *Path*, the term "sons and daughters of God" denotes a level of initiation and a rank in *hierarchy* that is above those who are called the children of God—children in the sense that they have not passed the initiations of the *sacred* *fire* that would warrant their being called joint-heirs with Christ, hence sons and daughters of God.

Soul. God is a *Spirit* and the soul is the living potential of God. The soul's demand for *free will* and her separation from God resulted in the descent of this potential into the lowly estate of the flesh. Sown in dishonor, the soul is destined to be raised in honor to the fullness of that God-estate which is the one Spirit of all Life. The soul can be lost; Spirit can never die.

The soul remains a fallen potential that must be imbued with the reality of Spirit, purified through prayer and supplication, and returned to the glory from which it descended and to the unity of the Whole. This rejoining of soul to Spirit is the alchemical marriage that determines the destiny of the self and makes it one with immortal Truth. When this ritual is fulfilled, the highest Self is enthroned as the Lord of Life and the potential of God, realized in *man,* is found to be the All-in-all.

(See Mark L. Prophet and Elizabeth Clare Prophet, *Climb the Highest Mountain,* 2d ed., pp. 8–13.)

Spirit. The masculine polarity of the Godhead; the coordinate of *Matter;* God as Father, who of necessity includes within the polarity of himself God as *Mother* and hence is known as the Father-Mother God. The plane of the *I AM Presence,* of perfection; the dwelling place of the *Ascended Masters* in the kingdom of God. (When lowercased, as in "spirits," the term is synonymous with discarnates, or *astral* entities;

"spirit," singular and lowercased, is used interchangeably with *soul.*)

Spoken Word. The Word of the LORD God released in the original fiats of creation. The release of the energies of the *Word,* or the Logos, through the throat *chakra* by the Sons of God in confirmation of that lost Word. It is written, "By thy words thou shalt be justified, and by thy words thou shalt be condemned." When man and woman reconsecrate the throat chakra in the affirmation of the Word of God, they become the instruments of God's own commandments that fulfill the law of their re-creation after the image of the Son.

Invocations offered by priests and priestesses of the *sacred fire* on Lemuria in this power of the spoken Word were originally given according to the science of the Logos. The perversion of this science in the practice of black magic occurred later, in the last days of Lemuria, bringing about the destruction of the temples of the Cosmic Virgin and the cataclysm that sank the continent. The Easter Island images are the remains, marking the site of the wars of the gods that shook the earth in those terrible days. By contrast, this science of the spoken Word was used in its pure form by the Israelites to fell the walls of Jericho. Today disciples use the power of the Word in *decrees,* affirmations, prayers, and *mantras* to draw the essence of the sacred fire from the *I AM Presence,* the *Christ Self,* and Cosmic Beings to channel God's *light* into matrices of transmutation and transformation for constructive change in the planes of *Matter*.

The science of the spoken Word (together with that of the *immaculate concept*) is the essential and key ingredient in all alchemy. Without the Word spoken, there is no alchemy, no creation, no change or interchange in any part of Life. It is the alchemist's white stone which, when successfully applied by the secrets of the heart flame, reveals the "new name written, which no man knoweth saving he that receiveth it." Blessed is he that overcometh the *carnal mind's* opposition to the exercise—the practice that makes perfect—of the science of the spoken Word in the offering of daily dynamic decrees unto the LORD, for unto him shall the *Holy Spirit* "give to eat of the hidden manna."

The Master of the Aquarian age, *Saint Germain*, teaches his disciples to invoke by the power of the spoken Word the *violet flame* for forgiveness of *sins* and for the baptism of the sacred fire in preparation for transition into the Higher Consciousness of God. *See also* Decree, Mantra.

(Matt. 12:37; Rev. 2:17. See Mark L. Prophet and Elizabeth Clare Prophet, *The Science of the Spoken Word.* Jesus and Kuthumi, *Prayer and Meditation. Prayers, Meditations, and Dynamic Decrees for the Coming Revolution in Higher Consciousness,* Sections I and II. Mark L. Prophet and Elizabeth Clare Prophet, *The Science of the Spoken Word: Why and How to Decree Effectively,* 4-audiocassette album. Elizabeth Clare Prophet, *"I'm Stumping for the Coming Revolution in Higher*

Consciousness!" 3-audiocassette album; *The Liberating Power of the Word,* album 1, 6 audiocassettes. Call or write for information on audiocassettes of decrees, songs, mantras and rosaries, including decrees to Archangel Michael, El Morya, and Lord Lanto and healing, love and violet-flame decrees.)

The Summit Lighthouse. An outer organization of the *Great White Brotherhood* founded by Mark L. Prophet in 1958 in Washington, D.C., under the direction of the *Ascended Master El Morya,* Chief of the *Darjeeling Council,* for the purpose of publishing and disseminating the Teachings of the Ascended Masters.

Threefold flame. The "divine spark"; also called the *Christ* flame and the liberty flame. The threefold flame is literally a spark of *sacred fire* from God's own heart. It is your *soul's* point of contact with the Supreme Source of all life. The threefold flame is anchored in the hidden, or secret, chamber of the heart (Skt. *Ānanda-Kanda* 'the root of joy'). It has three "plumes" that embody the three primary attributes of God and that correspond to the Trinity. The blue plume (on your left) embodies God's Power and corresponds to the Father. The yellow plume (in the center) embodies God's Wisdom and corresponds to the Son. The pink plume (on your right) embodies God's Love and corresponds to the *Holy Spirit.* By accessing the *Power, Wisdom and Love* of the Godhead anchored in your threefold flame, you can fulfill your reason for being. *See also* Chart of Your Divine Self. (See "A Trilogy On the Threefold Flame of Life," in *Saint*

Germain On Alchemy, pp. 265–352. Mark L. Prophet and Elizabeth Clare Prophet, *The Science of the Spoken Word,* pp. 126–31, 134, 138, includes color illustrations for visualization. Elizabeth Clare Prophet, *Saint Germain's Heart Meditation I,* audiocassette.)

Transfiguration. An initiation on the path of the *ascension* that takes place when the initiate has attained a certain balance and expansion of the *threefold flame.* (Matt. 17:1–8. See Jesus and Kuthumi, *Corona Class Lessons,* chaps. 13–18.)

Tree of Life. The Tree of Life is symbolical of the *I AM Presence* and *Causal Body* of each individual and of the connection, depicted in the *Chart of Your Divine Self,* of *Light's* children with their immortal Source. It is referred to in Genesis and Revelation: "Out of the ground made the LORD God to grow every tree that is pleasant to the sight and good for food; the Tree of Life also in the midst of the garden, and the tree of knowledge of good and *evil.*" "In the midst of the street of it and on either side of the river was there the Tree of Life, which bare twelve manner of fruits and yielded her fruit every month: and the leaves of the tree were for the healing of the nations." The twelve manner of fruits thereof are the twelve qualities of the *God consciousness* that man and woman are intended to realize as they follow the initiations on the path of the *ascension.* These are God-power, God-love, and God-mastery, God-control, God-obedience, and God-wisdom, God-harmony, God-gratitude, and God-justice, God-reality, God-vision, and God-victory.

The Tree of Life also refers to the diagram used in the Jewish mystical tradition known as Kabbalah to depict the *sefirot*—the ten aspects, or emanations, of God. In Kabbalah, the Tree of Life is a pattern for divine and human action and interaction. It is a blueprint for the inner workings of God and the inner workings of our own bodies and *souls*.

(Gen. 2:9; Rev. 22:2. See Elizabeth Clare Prophet, *Kabbalah: Key to Your Hidden Power*, published in *Pearls of Wisdom*, 1992, vol. 35, Book I, pp. 33–34, 43–86; "The Creation of the Tree of Life," 1-hr. TV show on video, part 2 of "Keys from Judaism: The Kabbalah and the Temple of Man," also on audio.)

Tube of light. The white *light* that descends from the heart of the *I AM Presence* in answer to the call of *man* as a shield of protection for his *four lower bodies* and his *soul* evolution. *See also* Chart of Your Divine Self.

Twin flame. The *spirit's* masculine or feminine counterpart conceived out of the same white fire body, the fiery ovoid of the *I AM Presence*.

(See "Twin Flames in Love," in *Pearls of Wisdom*, 1978, vol. 21, nos. 34–47; 8-audiocassette album. *The Ascended Masters On Soul Mates and Twin Flames, Pearls of Wisdom*, 1985, vol. 28, Books I and II. *The Coming Revolution: The Magazine for Higher Consciousness*, Summer 1986. Elizabeth Clare Prophet, *Twin Flames in Love II*, 3-audiocassette album; condensed in 1-audiocassette album *Twin Flames and Soul Mates: A New Look at Love, Karma and Relationships*.)

Unascended being. One who has not passed through the ritual of the *ascension:* (1) One abiding in time and space who has not yet overcome the limitations of the planes of *Mater* (as opposed to an *ascended being,* who has ascended into the *Presence* of God). (2) One who has overcome all limitations of Matter yet chooses to remain in time and space to focus the consciousness of God for lesser evolutions.

Uriel. *See* Archangel.

Violet flame. Seventh *Ray* aspect of the *Holy Spirit.* The *sacred fire* that transmutes the cause, effect, record and memory of *sin* and the *karma* that is the record of and the penalty for that sin. Also called the flame of transmutation, freedom, and forgiveness. The violet flame is the gift of the Holy Spirit that comes to us under the sponsorship of *Saint Germain,* Lord of the Seventh Ray and Hierarch of the Age of Aquarius. The violet flame works in microcosmic and macrocosmic worlds and is the key to individual and world transmutation. The violet flame can alter, mitigate or entirely turn back prophecy. When you invoke the violet flame in the name of your Mighty *I AM Presence* and Holy *Christ Self* through the heart of *Jesus* Christ and Saint Germain, *angels* of the seventh ray direct it into density, discord and the accumulation of negative karma. *See also* Chart of Your Divine Self, Decree.

(See Mark L. Prophet and Elizabeth Clare Prophet, *Climb the Highest Mountain,* 2d ed., pp. 359–62; *The Lost Teachings of Jesus II,* softbound, chap. 13, or pocketbook, Book Four, chap. 13; *The Science of the Spoken Word.* Elizabeth Clare Prophet, *The Astrology of the Four Horsemen,* chaps.

39, 40; "Saint Germain and Violet Flame Decrees," 1 video-cassette; "On the Violet Flame and the Chakras," 1 video-cassette. *Save the World with Violet Flame! by Saint Germain 1–4,* audiocassettes of decrees and songs. *Violet Flame for Elemental Life—Fire, Air, Water and Earth 1* and *2,* audiocassettes of decrees and songs. *Saint Germain's Violet Flame for the Age of Aquarius: Meditations for the Purification of the Seat-of-the-Soul Chakra,* audiocassette of songs; *Hail, Freedom Flame! For the Liberation of the Oppressed Peoples of the World,* audiocassette of songs.)

Word. The Word is the Logos; it is the power of God and the realization of that power incarnate in and as the *Christ.* The energies of the Word are released by devotees of the Logos in the ritual of the science of the *spoken Word.* It is through the Word that the Father-*Mother* God communicates with mankind. The Christ is the personification of the Word. *See also* Christ, Decree.

World Teacher. Office in *hierarchy* held by those *ascended beings* whose attainment qualifies them to represent the universal and personal *Christ* to unascended mankind. The office of World Teacher, formerly held by *Maitreya,* was passed to *Jesus* and his disciple Saint Francis (*Kuthumi*) on January 1, 1956, when the mantle of Lord of the World was transferred from Sanat Kumara to Gautama *Buddha* and the office of Cosmic Christ and Planetary Buddha (formerly held by Gautama) was simultaneously filled by Lord Maitreya. Serving under Lord Maitreya, Jesus and Kuthumi are responsible for setting forth the Teachings in this two-thousand-year cycle leading to individual self-mastery and the *Christ consciousness.* They sponsor all *souls* seeking union with God, tutoring them in the fundamental laws governing the cause/effect sequences of their own *karma* and teaching them how to come to grips with the day-to-day challenges of their individual dharma, one's duty to fulfill the Christ potential through the sacred labor.

The World Teachers have sponsored the education of souls in the Christ *light* at every level, from preschool through primary and secondary education to college and university levels. In every nation on earth, they have inspired teachers, philosophers, scientists, artists, professional and nonprofessional people with the wisdom of the ages as it applies to each particular culture, even as the many cultures of the world serve to bring forth the many facets of the Christ consciousness.

The term "world teacher," lowercased, refers to the embodied disciple who dedicates himself to the lifetime calling of planetary enlightenment under the Universal Christ. This appellation is descriptive of the disciple's chosen sacred labor and dedication to it. It is not an indication of his attainment or that he has necessarily qualified himself to share the office or mantle of Jesus and Kuthumi.

Zadkiel. *See* Archangel.

Spiritual Techniques to Heal Body, Mind and Soul

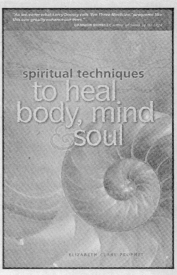

"As we enter what Larry Dossey calls 'Era Three medicine,' programs like this one greatly enhance our lives. ...Allows a deeper connectiveness and understanding of how, in a fast-paced world, we can maintain spiritual cohesiveness. I recommend this tape for the novice, avid seeker and advanced student."

—DANNION BRINKLEY, author of *Saved by the Light*

90-min. audiocassette
ISBN: 0-922729-59-X

Elizabeth Clare Prophet, best-selling author and pioneer in practical spirituality, explores dynamic techniques for using the creative power of sound to transform our personal lives and bring spiritual solutions to today's global challenges.

Learn how to combine visualization, affirmation and meditation to fulfill greater levels of your own inner potential. Shows how to access a high-frequency spiritual energy to improve relationships, increase mental clarity and energize the body's seven energy centers. Includes research from well-known experts on the science of mantra.

SUMMIT UNIVERSITY PRESS®
To order call 1-800-245-5445

THERE'S MORE TO YOU THAN MEETS THE EYE...

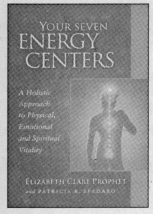

pocket guide 4 x 6 (100/150mm)
234 pages $6.95
ISBN 0-922729-56-5

"What is so beautiful about this book is that it can speak to everyone about revitalization and inner peace."

—MAGICAL BLEND MAGAZINE

Your Seven Energy Centers contains powerful insights and tools for wholeness based on the science of the body's subtle energy system and its seven energy centers (or "chakras"). Drawing from the wisdom of the world's spiritual traditions, it shows how you can nurture your soul through the seven stages of personal growth that correspond to these centers.

Includes an overview of holistic techniques that help restore the body's energetic balance—from homeopathy, vitamins and spa therapies to meditation, affirmation and visualization.

"Marries ancient healing wisdom with practical spiritual insights to help you create your own dynamic and uniquely personal healing journey. Your 21st-century guide to integrating and healing body, mind and soul."

—ANN LOUISE GITTLEMAN,
author of *The Living Beauty Detox Program*

"This is a small book with a big message.... This handy little guide is packed with useful insights.... Even experienced body workers who deal with the chakras on a daily basis can glean new perspectives to enhance their work.... This is one pocket guide both professionals and novices alike may find inspirational."

—WHOLE LIFE TIMES

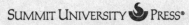

SUMMIT UNIVERSITY PRESS®

To order call 1-800-245-5445

WHAT CAN WE EXPECT THROUGH 2025?

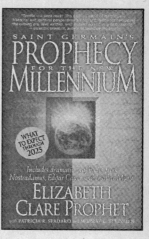

pocketbook 394 pages $7.99
ISBN 0-922729-45-X

Saint Germain's Prophecy for the New Millennium

explores the most compelling prophecies for our time, including new interpretations of the celebrated quatrains of Nostradamus and prophecies from Edgar Cayce, Mother Mary and Saint Germain. It reveals that prophecy is not set in stone— and it introduces us to a high-frequency spiritual energy that can help us create the future we want.

SUMMIT UNIVERSITY PRESS®

To order call 1-800-245-5445

ABOUT THE AUTHORS

Kuthumi and Djwal Kul are Eastern adepts who have devoted their lives to awakening humanity to their spiritual potential. The little that we know of their lives can be pieced together from the work of their students.

Kuthumi, also known as Koot Hoomi and K.H., was a Punjabi whose family had lived for years in Kashmir. He is believed to have traveled widely, attended Oxford University in 1850 and studied at Leipzig University in Germany in the 1870s. While at Leipzig, Kuthumi became acquainted with Dr. Gustav Theodor Fechner, philosopher and founder of modern psychological research.

In later years Kuthumi led a secluded life in Shigatse, Tibet. With El Morya, he founded the Theosophical Society in 1875 through Helena P. Blavatsky. Through their teachings given to Blavatsky, El Morya, Kuthumi and other adepts revealed the ancient truths that underlie both Eastern and Western religions. They also sought to acquaint mankind with the spiritual brotherhood that works behind the scenes to help mankind grow spiritually. Under the tutelage of these adepts, Blavatsky wrote *The Secret Doctrine, Isis Unveiled* and other works that were instrumental in introducing Eastern teachings to the West.

El Morya's and Kuthumi's letters to their students in the Theosophical movement are published in *The Mahatma Letters* and other works. Some of these letters are in the manuscript collection of the British Museum.

Djwal Kul, known as D.K. and "the Tibetan," was

the foremost disciple of Kuthumi and is said to have lived near his teacher in Tibet. He assisted El Morya and Kuthumi in their work with the Theosophical Society.

In the late nineteenth century, both Kuthumi and Djwal Kul reached higher levels of spiritual advancement and became "ascended masters," enlightened spiritual beings who have become one with God. In the 1950s, they began working with Mark L. Prophet and later Elizabeth Clare Prophet to publish their instruction through The Summit Lighthouse.

The Human Aura was originally dictated to the Prophets as a series of letters from Kuthumi and Djwal Kul to their students. Their instruction on many subjects, from the human aura to techniques for self-mastery, has been a source of inspiration to spiritual seekers throughout the world.

―――――――――――

Mark L. Prophet and Elizabeth Clare Prophet are pioneers of modern spirituality and internationally renowned authors. Among their best-selling titles are *The Lost Years of Jesus, The Lost Teachings of Jesus, The Human Aura, Saint Germain On Alchemy, Fallen Angels and the Origins of Evil* and the Pocket Guides to Practical Spirituality series, which includes *Your Seven Energy Centers, Soul Mates and Twin Flames* and *Alchemy of the Heart*. Their books are now translated into 20 languages.